Vast Contrast

An American's New Start in Shanghai, China

VOLUME
I

by Petie DiFlip

About Me

I'm Petie DiFlip. In **Vast Contrast**, I mainly write in short article form. I started this blog to keep in touch with my friends and family back home and it tracks the first 30 days I moved to Shanghai, China and then spreads into certain highlights of my continuing stay. There's a lot that I am not at liberty to share about myself and this nation, but you will find that some of my stories share very personal information and thoughts. I never intended to write more than a couple of blog posts when I arrived and I sure didn't expect anyone to read them. Thanks for checking it out and coming along with me on some of the most interesting experiences of my life.

Contents

Quick Lesson
about Toronto

Most of Canada lives in Toronto. It's cold more often than not. After English, most Torontonians speak Chinese. There are more Chinese in Toronto than Latin Canadians and African Canadians combined, yet Toronto has the largest population of Blacks in Canada. There are signs that say, "street hockey is prohibited" in neighborhoods. Gas costs over $4.25 per gallon. Third generation Canadians remind me of Will Ferrel. I lost twenty bucks buying Canadian currency. The customs checkpoint guy was an asshole. French is written everywhere, but more than a dozen languages exceed it in popularity and less than 2% of the population consider French as their primary language. Canadian citizenship costs about $10,000 for a Chinese. Your local Political Representative represents your national vote for Prime Minister.

Few Days in Toronto

So, it's ironic, or at least strange that there was a championship boxing match in DC, WWE Slammys in Fairfax, and a UFC title match in Toronto these last few days I have been here. I am staying with my good buddy Mike P. and his soon-to-be wife Jodie. We went to Montana's Restaurant Friday night. Saturday, I got to run around outside and do some kungfu in the park. Saturday night we went to a house party followed by a pub and participated in Karaoke for Mike's birthday. I was terrified to sing, but I picked some songs I have sung before and it actually felt pretty good to sing them. I got props by Mike's friends here and I also got my buddy Mike pretty drunk for his birthday. Sunday we went downtown into the city and started to journey around from Union Station, went into the underground mall (the largest in the world), and then drove through China Town and some rich neighborhoods – including some giant castle. Monday, I helped Mike walk dogs as his day job, and drove around different areas of Toronto. It seems every house has a guitar in it. It's also neat seeing so many Chinese, but not in a crowded city in China. Monday night we had a big feast at Mike's mother-in-law's penthouse. One of her son's there is the Executive Director of Canada's version of BBC news for the weekend broadcast. It was cool learning about Canada's history and a bit about how National News works here.

Last night I showed Mike how I meet some people in China online. I think he found it very interesting. I decided, today, to book a room in Shanghai. I leave tomorrow and I haven't made firm plans to stay anywhere until now. I am excited to get to use Chinese. I told my Mom that before I got on the plane to China last time and she is still laughing at me for it. For some reason, she doesn't understand why it is an awesome feeling to step into an environment where a language you have been practicing is used. I guess, sometime yesterday, I got this website setup. I am writing here because otherwise I would be sending one email to one person one day, and another email to another person another day, and at least more than one person would like to hear from me. I want to share and keep in touch, so I think this the best way to include people that want to know what I am doing and if I am doing OK. I don't think anyone really wants to write about their day on a public website, and it's especially nerve-racking writing from a place that isn't keen on free journalism. These days, with GPS tracking, it's not necessarily in my best interest to be "reporting" from China. All in all, I think my friends and family back home will appreciate this, at least for the time being. It would be more mysterious to stay incognito and only share certain highlights.

I can say that I have not been nervous about moving to China. I was much more nervous about going back to the US on my last vacation to China. There is something about heading in the direction that you want to go that gives you hope and confidence. That is why I bought a return ticket to China upon my first pay check after my vacation. If you are resourceful and ambitious, Shanghai is a gold mine. I don't aspire for fame and fortune. I just want to elevate and grow in the direction that feels natural. My parents are sad about it. I wish they would see the huge good instead of the tiny bit of bad. I have a lot of people to effect positively that are waiting for me. It's going to come back to you and yours.

First Day Back

Preflight

I didn't get to say how grateful I am for my friends to help me set off for China. When I visited China a few months ago, I almost stayed. I decided, with great difficulty, to return home. Mainly, I decided this because all of my belongings would have been abandoned in the place that I was living in Virginia and my roommate/landlord would have been left to sort it all out or get rid of it. I also would have been abandoning my coworkers at my job that would have to cover the projects that I was responsible for at working and particularly leaving them to learn a product that I was responsible for without any guidance. Yes, I had some financial concerns as well, but they were the least of my concerns because I was offered a good job here in Shanghai. Coming back home was very difficult to do after years of hoping and dreaming to get back to Shanghai. I hated my job, my work commute, and being bound to my hometown due to lack of sufficient funds. Being in China is exhilarating. Anyone can tell you that I have been a Sinophile for the last twelve years with half of those years having a particular focus on Shanghai. When searching for jobs in my hometown, I would always calculate the salary in terms of how soon I could move to China.

Returning home was the right choice. I remember how immediately I felt that my Director at work did not appreciate my return by his continuous lack of respect. I remember mentally tying myself to my chair while my colleagues were quitting, so I could make it long enough to have enough money to get back to Shanghai. On my last trip, I went to visit a place known for being environmentally clean. I had to spend time in Shanghai because the lady I was traveling with had to return to move apartments. My love for Shanghai was rekindled and I decided that I was never going to be able to search China, while living in America, for some special clean city. Shanghai could be my landing pad, my hub, and my home base for future explorations.

When I moved in with Randy T. almost three years ago, he told me, "You can stay at my place until you move to China." At that time, I didn't have a job or any money, and he took me in with good faith. I stayed with Randy without financial contribution for almost two years. He allowed me to maintain a level of focus, whether on my inventions or passion for China. I was able to keep certain standards that I would have otherwise lost. I would be insincere if I said that my parents did not allow me the same while I was living with them. I am grateful to my parents and Randy. I am also grateful for Micah F. and Greg G. for helping me finish taking care of business during my final days preparing to move. This was defiantly the way to leave;

hiking Shenandoah Valley and staying the night on top of a Virginian Mountain, having a big Chinese feast with a big group of my hometown friends, and having a home-cooked Italian dinner with my family and roommates at my parents' house. In the end, I was able to train my colleagues on my product and sell all of my belongings. Randy would have had to quit his job to have the time to do that.

Most friends and family know that I committed my early twenties to developing a guitar product and business. When someone new learns about my patent, they will ask, "So why aren't you doing something with it? It sounds like a great idea." Besides that I did so much with it before losing most of my belongings, money, health, dreams, and etcetera on the invention, I was more focused on its success then my own wellbeing. Seven plus years were focused shifting between my kungfu dedication and invention/business success. Eventually the business took over my focus. When the bills became too much to handle, I had to cancel the entity and try to find myself again. I spent an infinite amount of stressful time trying to solve enormous problems with all odds against me. I spent my money responsibly, almost always investing in the business and rarely purchasing anything unrelated to the success of the business. One day, while researching ways to manufacture the difficult product, I found a manufacturing trade show would be held in Shanghai in less than a month. I called a close friend and soon-to-be investor and said, "I think I need to go to this event." His reply was literally, "Let's go, but I'm not staying for less than two weeks." We really wung it. He followed my lead and we took a bus to New York City to try and catch a direct flight to Beijingfrom there. We bought the tickets at the airport. From Beijing, we took a train to Shanghai, having almost no idea the distance or length of the trip. We were only at the trade show for a few hours and it wasn't very prosperous, but we spent two weeks in China with the majority of time being in Shanghai. I like to think of that expense, out of the $100k I spent on my development, the most personally rewarding money spent.

My First Night Back

Mike P. dropped me off at the Airport on his birthday. We bonded during my stay and I really love his fiancé and I am so happy that they are getting married this New Year's Eve. Even though I will not be attending their wedding, I got to participate in some of the planning, meet the extended family, and spend some quality time with them. We make each other laugh and that allowed me to stay worry-free before leaving North America. We also had a final supper consisting of authentic Chinese food. The night before the flight, I was desperately trying to get ahold of a mutual friend I met online that lives in Shanghai. He is a fellow American and recently offered to let me stay in his apartment while he visited his hometown in the USA. I was unsuccessful. I changed my first few nights booking from staying with a stranger I met through a language exchange website to a familiar hostel. And I contacted Heena, who is rarely available to speak with ever.

The fellow-American wrote me an email the next

morning that he was visiting Thailand and to give him a call when I am in Shanghai. That was more comforting, but not a lot because I had never got an answer when I called him a dozen times before and most emails went without reply. In any case, I set off for my 16 hour flight. I prepared a lot for my last flight for China, being highly concerned about what I was bringing on my carryon and doing extensive exercises before the flight. This time, I didn't prepare very much. Somehow, the flight was no big deal and went by pretty fast. Air Canada's jumbo jet was better than Continental Airways and that was better than Air China. Someone should do a write-up about all of the airlines' jumbo jets because what they offer in-flight makes a giant difference when you are stuck in the air for that long. A girl sitting in my row told me this was her third flight on her journey back to her hometown to visit her Grandmother, and more than a three hour car ride awaited her from the airport. I spoke to her at length standing up in the back of the plane.

I want to say that I learned more in 30 minutes talking to her than I learned in a week at home. First, my $10,000 Canadian citizenship purchase may be off. I heard that number from my Chinese teacher that moved from Henan to Montreal during her time teaching me. According to the girl in my row, Sabrina, it cost her family much more than that and she heard it has since doubled. Sabrina had a fear of America because the news coming from America is always about guns and violence. Sabrina is a college student and loves living in a small island outside of Nova Scotia. She said, "There are less people living on my island than there are people shopping in a mall in my hometown." She is from Nanjing and says she never gets sick living in Canada, but she is sick the whole time she is home in Nanjing. I got her contact information and I will keep in touch with her.

After the weird, backwards, eating of dinner, lunch, to breakfast and the strange light-time patterns in the airplane, we landed in Shanghai at about 4pm. I passed the first tests of getting my bags through security and baggage size and weight requirements. Now was time for customs. I had little concern for this before, aside from an incident at the visa office for applying for a second visa so soon after returning. However, the Canadian customs officer gave me such a hard time and Mike P. told me he was even called in to speak with the next level of Immigration officers at the airport in Canada, so he kept telling me that because I do not have a return flight and because I don't have clear plans, they might detain me. He was half joking, but it was a concern of mine. As I suspected, the customs officer stamped my passport without question. None of my bags were investigated at any time throughout my journey, which is kind of strange because my carryon bag is full of electronics. Did I mention that I have an electric guitar with me? After your passport is stamped, you are home free – just walk straight out into the arrival area.

The arrival area is usually a rock concert crowd at most international airports that I have been to. I only saw Heena once before, and that is just not enough when there is a crowd. I met Heena on a Personals website for Shanghai. That is a little misleading. So, I signed up for a Personals website for Shanghai after the lady that I traveled with last suddenly decided that she didn't want to talk to me anymore. I discovered after talking to a woman from the website, that it also shares a website address for an entirely different website about meeting people from around the world. So, in reality, I signed up for a personals website for expats visiting Shanghai, while innocent singles signed up to meet people from abroad. I contacted Heena because her profile was humble and her picture was obscure and mostly out of frame. You see, Chinese are enamored by glamour photographs, so there are limitless photographs of smoking hot Chinese girls with airbrushed faces and crystal sharp focus on eyes and so on. I didn't want to meet someone purely because they looked attractive in their photograph. After all, anyone can look attractive and desirable with some good photography.

I called Heena, as I have called some other people I have met from other means that live in China. You might think that, for whatever reason, calling a foreigner is always similar and the conversations must be similar and personalities must come off as similar. That is not the case at all. People are all the same in that it would not be very different to call a stranger in your home country to have a conversation. Yes, the level of English that can be spoken can vary, but beginning conversations are always more about character than they are about third-level descriptive words. One thing I have learned while learning Chinese is that people don't say very much. You use the same words constantly and say the same things all of the time. We simply repeat a lot of the phrases that we hear and conversation becomes a medium for connecting to people and sharing emotion. That was deep. Anyway, Heena was great to talk to and I could tell that she was more friendly than actually being interested in romance. She had a great sense of humor and was very easy to share an understanding with.

I found that Heena speaks four languages, Chinese being her third most proficient, and is heavily involved with her career. We only spoke two or three times in addition to one visual webcam conversation because she is constantly traveling. She assured me that she would be back in Shanghai for long enough to meet me at the airport and take me to my destination. That was true, she was back in time to meet me, but she had to hurry back to the airport to catch a flight on another business trip. Can you imagine that someone that I knew so little would meet me at the airport, take a bus with me all the way back to the other side of town, hail a taxi cab for us, help me check in, only to turn around and go all the way back to the airport during rush hour? If that isn't amazing enough by itself, she also refused to let me pay. Believe me, I tried, but after being denied three times, I thought it may be a cultural thing and I didn't want to get angry and insult her. She also paid for the cab and told me, "I have too much money."

I was hoping to spend a lot more time with Heena, but she told me a few days ago that she will probably return to Japan next month for work. She is so kind that she offered to introduce me to her roommate. I didn't know that level of compassion existed in the world. The lesson I am learning is that the only way to show gratitude for that, is by doing that for someone who needs it. I learned that in more detail last night, but I will get to that in a minute. That money comment she made, it would not surprise me. Of course, no one has too much money, but some of this current Shanghai culture reminds me of growing up in America in the 80's. Do you remember how it was cool to be futuristic? The punk culture going mainstream to some degree? Businesses making money in ways that never existed before? Foreign trade prospering between Japan and America? The end of the Cold War and a time of prosperity? That is a little bit what it feels like here to be young. I can see it in the youth and in their fashion. And for abundance, if you walk inside a newly developed plaza shopping mall here, next door to another one being constructed, you can find up to five coffee shops in a row, all mainly empty during the day. They cannot build fast enough. I think the government may have the right understanding of national economics, but for private businessmen, it is inevitable that some relish in a bubble economy and figure the supply cannot keep up with the demand. It might be like a 60 mile an hour car crash for some of those investors, but no-one can see the future.

My First Day Back

The room is freezing. In Toronto, Mike had the temperature set at 75 degrees Fahrenheit in the house and told me to open the window if I got hot. Sabrina, on the plane told me, "The weather might be the same in your hometown as in Shanghai, but in China, people do not usually have furnaces."

That's a nice little midflight surprise. I layered up and slept like a cocoon. This morning, I decided I better go for a walk after all of yesterdays' traveling and sitting. I bundled up and set off. In 2006, I came here with a $600 handheld translation computer. It was intended for Chinese to use to translate to English, so it was difficult to use, but it was the only Chinese/English translation device at the time. Can you believe that? There wasn't even a manufacturer in America that produced it. Midway through that trip, I lost it or it was stolen. Now, with the iPhone, I have some incredible Chinese applications. It is fantastic. I am loaded with tools and have a lot of background in the long and short history of China and Shanghai. I know more words than I know how to use and I am completely comfortable with Chinese people. On the whole trip, I never had any real emotion – no anxiety, no excitement, no regret, and almost no concerns at all. I have just been, "going through the changes". Taking my walk on my first day back, just for a moment, I had some feeling of, "finally". I am exuberating confidence like when I was 20 years old calling and meeting with executives in New York City, or 21 years old wheeling and dealing at trade shows in Miami and Las Vegas. I might call it, unprepared and overconfident. This time, in China, on my first day of many new days to come, I am paying attention to the street signs. Previously, I thought there was no way I was going to be able to remember which is which or where is what, but I walked around for 3 hours without any fear of getting lost. Since landing, it has felt like I hit the ground running and haven't missed a beat. I didn't expect that whatsoever. I am still fully aware that it is only a matter of time until some feeling of loneliness, solitude, helplessness, or homesickness overtakes me. There is no way of telling when that will happen. It could be tomorrow, in a few weeks, or in a few months, but it will come.

I am eager to improve my Chinese. I can't tell you what a relief it is to be in a place that I have to use some Chinese to communicate. I am going to have to use Chinese over and over again and that is exactly what I want. There are lots of other things that make me smile about being here. The food is always organic (maybe not). They don't have to label food as organic here, it would be more rare to find ingredients that are processed. Exercising in different ways is totally acceptable – I saw five advertisements of people standing in Bruce Lee's famous ready-position fighting pose for fitness centers today. Speaking of that, I think most people have no idea how Bruce Lee single-handedly changed the world and influenced east and west relationships. Bruce Lee is probably the most popular hero in the world, and for all of the right reasons. I downloaded Shanghai Daily newspaper on my Kindle and love the content, data, and stories written in it.

I made myself eat breakfast, even though my body wasn't hungry and probably wanted to sleep. I went to a McDonalds that I remembered inside one of the subways stations. It wasn't good food, but I knew I would be avoiding the drinking water. The drinking water here will make you sick. I bought some bottled water that I have been drinking. Of course, by noon, I abandoned my staying clear of Chinese drinking water and went up to a street-side vendor to order Pork Noodle soup. They were fascinated that I wanted to eat their food and kept coming over to watch me. It was probably the last thing that I should have ate; the pork was cold and the soup water came from the tap, and I am not sure how clean those chopsticks were. Yet, I felt like a kid getting cotton candy at the carnival. I didn't finish off the soup liquid, to avoid too much Chinese water, and left the bowl unfinished. From that point on, my stomach was inflamed.

I came back to my room and took a long nap, from 2 to 5:30. That morning, I finally talked to Jay who told me to call him after 6. He wanted to make sure that I was ok and I have a lot of gratitude for that. Meantime, I also checked in with some of the Chinese people that I chat with regularly. One, now local, friend said that she was available for dinner tonight. I wanted to make sure it was ok with Jay if I met with her and met Jay the next day. I got it sorted out and she met me at my subway station. She offered to treat me to a meal so we went to a popular mall and she chose a restaurant. The food was fascinatingly exceptional. We had; "Wood Ears" which is the fungus that grows on trees, marinated in a sharp vinegar mixed with cilantro and red pepper flakes, a steel bowl full of cauliflower and some slices of bacon fat above blue hot alcohol flame in cooking oil, crab-filled steamed wanton dumplings, and beef short-ribs cooked in peppered sauce and onions. It made American food look like a joke. I was thinking, it's hilarious that people are spending tens of thousands of dollars to go to French culinary school in America and learning how to cook unhealthy crap bound by the laws of butter, sugar, oil, and dairy. Don't get me wrong, French culinary and restauranturship is top of the trade, but it does not surpass other culinary and is not a complete mastery of chef education by any means. During our meal, I asked Shauna why she is being so kind to me with such short notice. She replied, "I want you to feel warm. One day I want to visit abroad and I want someone to do this for me." That is big. That is bigger than school, bigger than work, and bigger than any selfish or greedy ambition imaginable. That's when it clicked. That is the lesson.

Afterwards, I bought us some ice cream and she took me to buy an electric heating pad for my bed. She is very sharp witted and has no trouble telling you what she thinks. My street-side lunch finally caught up to me. We had to find a toilet, which required walking a tremendous amount and much exploration. I made it just in time and it is miraculous that I happen to take some toilet paper with me in case I had to blow my nose, because the stalls did not have any. I think that is a habit that I will continue to practice. My train was arriving when we got to the platform, so I hurried to catch it and did not get the chance to thank her again. I will talk to her again soon and I have to treat her to dinner next time. I got back to my bed and passed out. The thing about world class jetlag is that, a hint of tiredness is lethal when you decide to give in and have a rest. It is equivalent to a black out. You cannot get up from it and your brain shuts down. I fought to get up after a few hours and plug in my new heat blanket. It's awesome!

I don't know how much time I will have to write these in the future. Even though this is long, I don't know how many or how frequent they will be. It's also very difficult deciding what to write about when everything is new and interesting. Not to mention, some of the new and interesting things maybe too personal for a blog. That's coming from me, and I share more than most. I hope to meet with Heena tomorrow and finally meet Jay at his apartment. I also want to do a little bit of shopping for winter vest and a few other items. I am investing my time where I have been wanting to for so long and it feels good the same way a weekend feels good to the working man. Be kind.

Second Day

I went over to meet Jay for the first time. His subway stop wasn't too far. We met at the station because I still don't have a cell phone. He is quiet with a quiet sense of humor. I talk fast and Jay eases into his sentences, so I have to let him finish. After all, he is my implied mentor here and I want to know what he has to say about everything Shanghai.

I met Jay through an awesome website, airbnb. com. I was searching this website to find a place in Shanghai that I could rent for a month while I explored employment opportunities. Once, when I was loging in, the loading screen got stuck looping. I didn't like to login on other websites via their Facebook login because I didn't want Facebook to keep track of my life. However, to get passed the broken load screen, I went ahead and clicked to login via Facebook. Well, all of the apartments for rent in Shanghai are listed by their popularity ranking or their price value, and which ever sort order it was, Jay's apartment was at the top. It was actually a listing to crash on his couch. Next to Jay's avatar image on the listing of apartments, there was a little icon stating that we shared a mutual friend on Facebook. I thought, that can't be, I don't have that many friends on Facebook and even less friends that live in China.

Jay and I's mutual friend on Facebook was my good friend's cousin Nicole. Nicole came down from San Francisco to help me exhibit my Guitar Jacket invention at a music product trade show in Anaheim, California back in January of 2006. I checked with Nicole and she said Jay is a great guy, so I introduced myself to Jay and told him my plan of moving to Shanghai. We went back and forth a few times about the dates I am arriving versus the dates his place might be available. He told me that he would likely be traveling at the end of December. The dates didn't become firm until about two weeks before I arrived.

Jay walked me around the neighborhood towards his apartment. I had never seen this part of Shanghai. It must be the heart of the French Concession because it doesn't look or feel like the part of Shanghai that I have been staying in or the other areas that I have visited. It is kind of a piece of Europe. It is calm here with big thick trees and fancy sidewalks with fashioned buildings. We walked by a number of busy fresh produce markets and small stores spilling onto the sidewalks. There were flowers and plants for sale on the sidewalks and numerous boutiques. Where I have been staying, everything is very raw. People are cooking in the streets, sleeping in huts, and there are only hole-in-the-wall stores and offices where there is really no way of knowing what is sold inside of them.

We walked up to his fourth floor apartment and he showed me around. There is a good-sized kitchen, a commendable bathroom area, a big bedroom with a wardrobe and two desks, and a big living room. The rooms have some really nice dark shiny wood floors and there are big windows that open to a courtyard area with some giant trees and birds singing. Jay said, "I love this apartment. It's in the heart of the city, but it's silent." There is a washing machine, which is a huge relief, a couch, a TV, refrigerator, WIFI, and two heaters – one in each room. He told me the code to the front door, showed me the neighboring streets, and gave me the keys to both of the two front doors. He invited me to walk over to his previous boss's yard sale.

A few blocks down, we walked into a definitely European built building with an old fashioned gaudy entrance. I was thinking, what the fuck is this, this isn't China at all. We got off the elevator and a dude, probably a few years older than me, opened the door to his nice apartment. All of these other Americans were in there going through his and his girlfriend's belongings. It was way too soon for me to be surrounded by Americans and I was kind of sour about it. At the same time, I was wondering if I would be able to achieve a place of that caliber in Shanghai. When we were at Jay's apartment earlier, he asked about my work background.

I told Jay that after my invention, I did a lot of things, but my last job was consulting Associations to fit their business into my company's management software and before that I was doing different things in multimedia. Jay said, "You are going to kill it here." I told Jay that I was more interested in teaching English than going back into the office or living on the computer. He told me that there are a lot of yuppies that come here straight after university, but they have no experience working so they are not very desirable. I can understand that this is the case, after all, not many 30 year old men or women that are successful in their field stay single or want to take a chance in a foreign country. Jay came to Shanghai because he wanted to work in Advertising and said that it's impossible to change feilds in America, but here you can do something different and it's okay.

Jay's x-boss was preparing to move back to the US after many years of living and working in Shanghai. I learned that his previous job was running some kind of multimedia network in Bagdad's Green Zone in Iraq. Somehow, he started a company in Shanghai and was very successful. I don't know much more than that about him, except that he was kind of geeky, but I liked him and imagined that he would be fun to talk about some geeky multimedia stuff with. His girlfriend appeared to be Chinese, but spoke English as a typical American. I understood that owning a company in China required that at least 50% of company ownership would have to be Chinese, so I would like to know how he was able to have his own company here.

I saw he had a computer monitor for sale at about $50 and I thought to myself, I was selling my computer monitor on craigslist in northern Virginia for the same price and no-one inquired about it, so he will never sell it for that price. As soon as I thought that, a guy walks over and says, "I'll take the monitor for 50." I don't know what's going on here, but money is moving. I was thinking of Heena the whole time because she was waiting for me at the shopping mall to help me shop for some clothes. I told her I needed to get some things. I borrowed Jay's phone to call her and she told me that she was at a coffee shop on the second floor of this mall. I said I would leave right away and be there in twenty minutes.

Jay and I walked out together and I ran for the subway. My legs felt so good running because I like to run for exercise, but since my flight I had only been walking. I got to the mall and the crowds were like the front row for some touring band's final concert. I took a few videos on my phone that I will try to post. The mall is enormous, to say the least. I got to the second floor and circled around it five times at full pace. There is no coffee shop on the second floor, so I thought maybe she mispronounced and met the 7th floor, so I made my way up there and circled around it five times. I was getting angry at that point because I wanted to find it so badly and I was feeling exhausted and knew that I would have to give up soon. After about 45 minutes since I had spoken to her, I went inside a restaurant and spoke to the Manager asking where a coffee shop might be. She wasn't sure what I meant, but she gave me the password to her WIFI. I called Heena from my Skype account and was so frustrated at this point that I wasn't even really listening to her. All of the background noise didn't help either. In fact, I didn't even say anything when I couldn't understand her, I was just feeling defeated. I gave the phone to the Manager and they spoke for 5 minutes. Heena was actually on the first floor and she came up with her roommate to meet me.

Heena wasn't at the mall to do any shopping for herself. Her and her roommate went to the mall that morning and waited for me until the afternoon. Even after leaving to meet her and taking so much time to find her, she was waiting in that coffee shop with her roommate. When they met me, they weren't the least bit aggravated that it had taken me so long. We decided to try and get me a mobile phone and I told her that Jay's boss told me there is a way to unlock my American iPhone so that he can use a Chinese SMS card.

Heena and her roommate took me to a big electronics store, but they were not able to help. Her and her roommate spoke Korean together. Her roommate is genuinely sweet and they both enjoyed speaking and learning English from me. Unlike how an average American will ask how to say something in a foreign language and give it half a shot and forget about it, they analyze it, search it in their dictionaries, ask for examples of ways to use it, and then they freeking remember it and use it again later. Heena called her boss and asked him in Japanese where he unlocked his phone. Off we went to another shopping mall. Actually, it was another two shopping malls if you count the underground booth when they talked a guy there about unlocking my phone.

I think that I walked about 30 miles, without

exaggeration. My legs were starting to fail on me. We did find a guy that could unlock my phone eventually, but he said I would lose all of my applications, so I had to refuse. My phone is full of Chinese applications that I must have. I thought Heena and her roommate Linda were going to be upset that we went through so much work and achieved nothing. They should feel that way, they spent all morning waiting for me, we went to a number of places far away from each other, had to transfer trains, talked in length with different clerks about my phone, and they only expected me to buy a few clothes in the mall. Frankly, it is astonishing to me that they were completely fine and didn't show the smallest sign of aggravation. I don't know if this is culture shock or what but I have a hard time processing that in my head.

It was dinner time and they wanted to have Korean food with me in Korean Town. I owed Heena a dinner and we had spoken about eating Korean food before. We took the subway a good distance and then took a taxi from that station to a place she knows. She ordered spicy octopus and it was killed and cooked in front of us at our table. There was an assortment of foods to eat from and I didn't hold back. We feasted with the addition of hot Korean tea and Chinese beer. I caught Linda staring at me while I was eating. I don't think she expected me to eat Korean food or know how to use chopsticks. Our waitress was beautiful, but I don't think she knew it, as is probably often the case in foreign countries. When it was time for the bill, Heena refused to let me pay. Her roommate defended Heena paying. I fought it and was beginning to feel pathetic, but she said it is customary for a visitor and I can treat her after I find a job.

I was fighting jet lag all evening amongst normal exhaustion, but I know my time with Heena is limited. She is out of town all of the time and will leave Shanghai permanently next year. When she replies "yes" she has a strong affirmation and a deep nod of her head. How can I not love this woman? I deeply regret that she is gone so much and will be moving away. I am starting to like her so much that it hurts. That's kind of cool. I haven't had that horrible feeling since I was a teenager. There are a million women here and plenty of babes, but you know how it is when you really like someone.

So from here out, I think my Shanghai journey will be normal living like yours. It won't be very interesting, so instead of a daily account, I will just share highlights. I don't know how long the honeymoon will last, but I have to get on with normal living like everyone else now. That and some new stuff. Chinese is tight.

Sunday

↔

the Amazing Hot Pot

I slept about 11 hours Saturday night. I think I fell asleep before 8 PM and woke up around 7am. I did wake up twice in the night and played a round of golf on my iPhone. It's funny that the English commentary in the game is kind of comforting. I decided that today I would go over to the plaza across the street and see if I could find a place that serves coffee and a sandwich. I learned a lot of Chinese words over the last seven years, but I don't have a running account of them – they just pop into my head at the right time. I remember, in 2006, screaming at a lady in Shanghai "Bu yao! Bu yao!" after she took my 10 RMB for a 1 RMB trinket and started to walk away without giving me my change back. I don't remember learning to say that and I didn't even know its meaning, but I was properly shouting that I don't want it and by grabbing her shirt and hanging on to her, she gave me my change back. I walked into the plaza saying, "san ming zhi" to myself – the Chinese word for sandwich.

Right through the opening of the plaza there is a Dunkin Donuts across from a Starbucks. It's a ghost town. 80% of the mall is vacant and still being renovated for the new tenants moving in. I walked down the hall to take the elevator to the second floor, but the elevator was not even running. I had to walk up a turned-off escalator where another coffee shop was, UBC Coffee. They invited me in, sat me down, and then tried to explain to me that they were not serving breakfast yet. It was a legit restaurant, with a menu, so I thought I should wait a little bit because there was nothing else around. I used my phone to look up some Chinese phrases and asked when they would serve because I was on a schedule to check-out of the hostel today and get over to Jay's before he left for the airport. It's really fun to try and speak Chinese and if a place isn't busy, the younger people like to try and understand what I am saying and use their English to verify my meaning. I ordered an egg & ham sandwich with a strong cappuccino and a small Italian pizza to go. An hour after getting there, my food came. My metabolism is still backwards here, so I was starving and it felt so good to eat. Western food here is like a premium, so all of that cost me about $20.

Back at the hostel, I asked the lady at the front desk if I could check out later than noon. I talked to them often and one of them was there a few months ago when I stayed there, so we developed a bit of a friendship. I gave them some slices of pizza and we had some conversations about Chinese history. I am carrying around an old Shanghai five dollar bill from 1930 that I bought in 2006 in Beijing. They were impressed with it and one of them told me, "There was no China at that time". That's true, there was a People's Revolution followed by a civil war for the Cultural Revolution and during the World Wars. Therefore, this bill was only used in Shanghai at that time and has an American bank note on it with a picture of Sun Yat-Sen, one of the fathers of the Chinese Revolution. I got the hostel's email address and told them I wanted to stay in touch because that hostel is my only conception of home in Shanghai. I would like to visit them sometimes and maybe have some language exchange, but I don't know what my schedule will be like in the future.

Back at my room, I packed up my belongings. I use these air sealant bags, called space bags, to compress my wardrobe into about six bags in one big suitcase. I called Jay about five times and as usual his phone was turned off and there is never a messaging service for Chinese phones, so I was getting ready to play a game of memory, looking at a map and hoping I could tell a taxi where to take me. I have about 80 lbs. of luggage with me; a carryon, my computer (article), a maximum size suitcase, and my heavy electric guitar. If I didn't get the drop-off location correct, I would be stranded with my luggage somewhere without being able to move. I can tie it all together and roll it, but only on big smooth surfaces – not Chinese sidewalks. Before I was about to try my luck, Jay finally answered and helped me pinpoint the location. I showed one of the ladies at the front desk where I want to go on the map and she wrote the address in Chinese and drew a map of the surrounding streets. That is the best way to ensure getting to your location. As Jay told me, "There is a rule in Shanghai. If you ever want to get anywhere in a cab, it's all about the cross streets." I wrote about a taxi ride in Shanghai on my Myspace page back in 2006. They are exciting.

When I got to the door of the building through the back alleyway, I pulled all of my luggage inside and was preparing to carry it up with a few different trips to the fourth floor. An old man came around the first flight of steps and ran down to grab some of my luggage. He was easily in his 50's and I told him in every way that I could that he doesn't need to help, I can carry it, it's nothing, there is no need, and I can do it, but he refused and carried half of my luggage to the fourth floor with me. I asked him his name and he just answered in Chinese, "No need. I live on the Second Floor." I asked him again, thinking he didn't hear me, and he said again, "No need, no need, I live on the Second Floor." As he went downstairs, the lady from across the hall opened the door and give me a bright warm smile and I gave her one back with a, "ni hao". As I was carrying my stuff into the apartment, I couldn't help but think how awful it is that Americans only talk about communism, lead poisoning, and eating dogs when the subject of China is brought up. Without exaggeration, that is the consistent and continuous commentary that I have received throughout the last decade. While China is blasting into the future with more growth in the shortest amount of time in human history, Americans can't get over some dirt-corner chum-rotten facts about China.

I laid on Jay's couch until he got back. I was still exhausted from the previous day and my body and brain felt shot. I thought I would sleep a bit and maybe do some yoga later. Jay came back to the house and we went over a few important things, like how to use the DVD player and control the heat. Then he had to leave for the airport in a mad dash. I gave him some American money and some Chinese money because I thought he might need it and it's the least I could do for him. I laid on the couch some more and couldn't really function. My traveling partner from my last visit messaged me a few times on some messaging applications, asking if I want to meet for coffee. We used to talk all of the time, but she changed after I went back to the US. For whatever reason, she likes me but she hates me. I like her, but of course it is disappointing that she is being this way and I just try not to be too concerned with it. I asked if we could meet later instead and she didn't reply, but continued to message me at random times asking where I was. I wasn't hungry, but I have been getting really hungry in the middle of the night and I don't know this neighborhood, so I asked one of my online Shanghai contacts if they wanted to meet for dinner. Surprisingly, Emma was finishing some overtime work nearby and said she could be here in 15 minutes.

Emma met me right away and appeared to be very fashionable, wearing a velvety red hat with a black bow. She dresses very pretty and wears some pretty makeup with some light jewelry. She only recently came to Shanghai from a nearby city. She helped me bring Jay's trash out and found a place to dump it, then she tried to point out some landmarks so I could find my way back in the future. She chose a small Chongqing restaurant with a screaming child, a googley-eyed mother, and an out-of-it father/chef. I have no idea how people chose restaurants here. They are like mechanic shops to me. How can you tell if the guy knows what he is doing, the food is sanitized, and the service will be any good? There is no music and no decoration, just some chairs and in this case, electric stoves in the middle of the table. The chopsticks and plates are wrapped in plastic film because the washing is done by another company that exchanges cleaned eatery with dirty. The guy that seemed pretty out-of-it dropped off a menu that was a list of Chinese characters with check boxes next to them. It looked like the bubble answer sheet for the SATS. Nope, there wasn't a chance that I could have eaten there by myself.

I have always heard about Hot Pot, it is Chongqing's famous style of cooking. Emma took the wheel and ordered everything. The out-of-it chef was eating dinner with his screaming child and googley-eyed wife and would periodically go into the back into the kitchen. When he came out with a bubbling pot of red water, the magic began!

The Amazing Hot Pot

This iron pot had a rolling boil and steam pouring out with the distinct fragrance of Chinese spices. The chef guy turned on the electric stove and sat the iron pot on it. Then he put an array of separated vegetables and things on a shelf beneath the table and sat back down to eat with his family. Emma said she was not very hungry and told me that I need to eat all of the meat so that we can drink the soup afterwards.

In the red peppery liquid were slices of red onion and red chili peppers with bits of coriander, Chinese pepper flakes, and other spices. The meat consisted of a heavily marinated chicken wing and chicken foot, along with chopped up bull frog. The pot continues to boil while you fish around for meat and vegetables. I had overcooked pan-fried frog legs before back in northern Virginia, but this was entirely different. I absolutely loved how soft the meat was and sucking it right off the bone with so many delicious flavors of spices, onions, and fat rendered from the chicken.

The liquid in the pot stays boiling with a constant heavy steam that causes the liquid to reduce. After most of the meat has been eaten, in our case we left the chicken foot in, Emma took out two small piles of vegetables from the shelf under the table and droped them in. These ingredients were slices of Chinese squash and kelp seaweed tied in knots. The flavor of the Hot Pot intensifies as the new ingredients cook. Five to eight minutes later, we started to fish for the ones boiling at the top and set them on our plate for a moment for them to cool down. The kelp has the consistency of a fruit rollup and tastes like the soup, but with a musty taste of algae. The slices of squash become soft and was similar to eating zucchini. Midway through picking them out and finishing those ingredients, she calls the chef guy over and he pours hot water into the pot, filling it up again. The kelp is from the ocean, so after all of the liquid reduction, the food became extremely salty. After filling the pot with water and doubling the amount of liquid, the overwhelming salty taste subsided and everything tasted perfect again.

As the liquid began to boil again, Emma took out more ingredients to add. We must have been eating for 30 minutes already. This time the ingredients were noodle-like slices of firm spiced tofu, and mung bean flat noodles. We waited about three to five minutes and started to pull them out of the boiling soup. They were probably the most flavorful noodles I ever had in my life. I was beside myself. 45 minutes into the meal I was beginning to wonder when it would ever end. Emma called the chef guy over again to add more water. She finally took out the chicken foot and ate it while I took my last few bites and asked if I could take the rest home. I was wondering how I would be able to take something home that is currently boiling. The chef guy, still out of it, poured it into a Styrofoam bowl with a plastic shopping-bag-like bag inside of it, pulled up the edges, tied it closed, and tied another shopping bag around the bowl holding the soup bag. I guess that kind of plastic doesn't melt easily. Again, I was astonished. That meal cost about $13 and there is no tipping in China.

We walked back to Jay's place, passing by numerous people cooking on the street at midnight. It gives you the feeling of camping, grilling, and butchering all at once. There was a dead pig lying on someone's doorstep, while cats are scowling around, and butchering is taking place on the sidewalk of meats of all sizes. I told Emma, "In my hometown, there is nothing like this. I come from one of the wealthiest counties in America and it is not very interesting. People make a lot of money, but they just work. At night, there is nothing happening. How can I go back to America after this?" I know that is the wide-eyed

China newbie me talking, but of course that is how I feel at the moment and especially that particular moment. I offered to walk Emma home, but we both knew there was a good chance that I would not be able to find my way back. Tomorrow I start to adjust to a new neighborhood, or try to.

Greatness & Depression

Yesterday: I woke up and tried to fix my iPhone for something like six hours. After that extravaganza Saturday trying to find a way to use my iPhone and turning down purchasing a new one, I have to make it work. It doesn't help that if I found results from a web search and then click the link, that website is blocked in china. There are useful YouTube videos to help guide me fix my iPhone, but I couldn't watch them.

My iPhone is jail broken, so I have many Chinese applications that I did not pay for that I will lose when I unlock my phone. I know this is some boring stuff here, but it's a bigger challenge than adapting to living in China to make sure I can get these programs again and use my iPhone in China. Very few people ever try to solve their own technical problems when they become exceedingly difficult, so just know it's a horrible experience, extremely time consuming, and has very little reward. That's a whole story in itself and it is pending completion.

I talked to Emma who told me I could exercise in one of two parks. I had to look them up on a map. The maps on the internet here display all of the street names in Chinese characters, so I can't read a lot of the streets and the satellite images don't match the maps in China due to national security concerns. I rerouted my proxy to an American server so that I could view google maps in English, but after five minutes, the connection would get interrupted and I would lose my visual map. Then I remember from my past there are 3D maps of many major cities in China online, so I found a 3D map of Shanghai and found my location in relation to the nearest park that way. I was able to focus on skyscrapers as landmarks and it worked out very well. I got to the park.

This particular park is wonderful. The view of the neighboring skyscrapers is aweing. I realized at that point that there is a ton of Shanghai that I have never seen and that every so many blocks, a whole other city is hiding. It truly is an urban jungle here. In New York, most of the boroughs are not sky scrapers and Manhattan is a perfect grid, so it's not really a jungle. Here, it seems that there is more and more monstrosities and interesting places around every corner. I suppose the strange thing is that just about everyone is Chinese. In a city environment like this, you would expect a melting pot of ethnicities. It wasn't hard for me to imagine Shanghai long ago, before the skyscrapers, full of ethnicities and nationalities like mine. Now, this is a western city inhabited by Chinese and therefore the Chinese are not normal Chinese here. Don't expect to see much kungfu or haggling for prices.

I got to the park easy enough, but I was feeling

extremely weak and I'm not exactly sure why. I stopped in a bar that wasn't serving food for another two hours and had a beer. I chatted with the bar tender in broken Chinese pointing out that none of the bars appeared open and it was 5:30 at night. I went out this time with only some bills in my pocket and my door key. No iPhone with maps and translators, no passport, no card to give a taxi driver, no phone numbers. I got lost walking home, but I didn't get too concerned about it, I just asked someone in Chinese where my street was and they responded in English. It's that kind of a place. As eager as I am to use Chinese, the Chinese are eager to use their English. I realize that English is the king language of the Caucasian, because no one hesitates to speak English to me. I know in my hometown, I would ask an Asian person if they are Chinese before trying to speak to them in Chinese, but then again, other Asian peoples don't learn Mandarin like Europeans learn English.

I went to a little market and bought a few items. It's funny that I was thinking I am sick of Chinese characters and where the hell is the cereal. It is funny because I came here to adapt to the circumstances and learn a different way, so even though I was complaining to myself, I was secretly glad. I went to sleep early and was up by 2 in the morning. At that time, I searched the internet and purchased a VPN provider. VPN is a way to access the internet from another country, similar to proxy, but more secure. Success, for the annual cost of $55, I can access sites like Facebook, Hulu, YouTube, and my favorite… all of the sites that link from Google and Bing. I went back to sleep and woke up at 5:30.

This time I started to exercise for real. Jay has some speakers here that I hooked up to my laptop in the living room, and thanks to my new VPN, accessed Pandora to get some good exercise music happening. I moved some of the furniture out of the way, wiped down the floor, opened the window, and started doing stretches and qigong. Then I went into chain punching and into the old school chair-lifting exercises. After doing some more martial art stuff, my body started to feel more human again. I hadn't exercised in a week and I was literally feeling like the Fred Flintstone cartoon with a belly and feet that walked two-times too fast. All of the stress in my body was compressing in my lower back and that is not cool for someone that religiously kicks, jumps, and runs. After an hour of that, I wanted to go out and grab a coffee.

As soon as I got outside, I wanted to run. I didn't plan on that or I wouldn't have brought my iPhone and so many coins, but I just started running. When I got to the alleyway, I jumped around for a second, then turned and ran back. I kept doing that for at least a half hour. Back and forth, back and forth. Yes, there were people walking down the alleyway and some scooters, and at one point a car that left no room to even get out of the way, but my legs were feeling so good. Nourishment was pushing through my legs in places that had all but died. I got my coffee and came back to the apartment.

Here's the thing, it feels completely normal in the apartment. I'm streaming music from my favorite jazz station in Newark, New Jersey, doing kungfu, and chatting with Chinese online. I was listening to the same Jazz station on the radio when I was staying in Washington Square in New York, doing the same exercises on a similar wood floor with a similar view out my window. It is a solid reassurance that you can count on yourself being yourself.

By noon, I was tired. I'm getting sick of the jet lag. I started to work on my resume, and then felt exhausted and my brain got warm. I laid down, and was kind of dreaming, but not falling asleep. I decided to check what jobs are posted on Craigslist here. I had that depressing job searching feeling come over me. I shouldn't have done that, but I thought maybe there would be some kind of post like, "yes, we are looking for Pete DiFlip to come here and sing, dance, and play music while learning Chinese and teaching English." Ya, instead you get the white collar, dry, too-high standard, "we need you to be Ivy League and work all of the hours where your friends are free." That probably started my slump. I was getting hungry and even more depressed because I still don't know how to eat here. I just want to get some sliced meats in the grocery store so I can make lunch when I am hungry, but there are no sliced meats. There are no proteins that I know how to manage or anything other than Ramen noodles for me to have for lunch. I had to go on a really long hike and I passed up some places that were clearly expensive. I didn't even see many restaurants.

It is lightly raining and cold. I am tired and hungry and depressed that I am going to have to lock myself into an annual contract and I don't know where I will be teaching, how little I will get paid, or if I will have a schedule where I will ever be able to spend time with anyone. I finally saw a place called The Food Central. I had to pay top price for a turkey sandwich, fried onion rings, a house salad, and some Coronas. The beer was to numb my sadness, keep me awake, and it was happy hour, so I got one free. They wouldn't let my first beer count as happy hour because it was 2 minutes before happy hour. Yet, the place was totally empty. I stayed there for over an hour, messaging people on my iPhone via their WIFI. Some people can be comforting when you are feeling down. Anyway, it's about time I felt down with all of this up I have been experiencing.

I left the restaurant and just a few buildings down was a yoga studio. I walked up to the third floor and bought a yoga mat. I had been thinking that I really need one because this floor is hard and so many of the exercises I do are on the floor or barefoot. I was not in the mood to be picky about the price, but I felt like I was punched in the stomach for paying what I paid. I sold my belongings at such a low price in Fairfax, and everything I have had to pay here is at a premium price. I also treated Mike and Jodie well when I stayed with them due to their hospitality and it being his birthday and wedding. I was feeling sour, but also glad I finally got the mat because there are a few items here that I wake up in the morning telling myself I better hurry up and get; like some walking boots, a down hooded vest jacket, a ball cap, and some thin gloves, but I won't let myself spend the money until I find work. That's part of the bitterness I feel when I have to pay so much for gourmet shit when I would be happy throwing two slices of bread around a slice of ham for lunch.

That's how it is though. When you start a new lifestyle, you don't start off optimal. It's impossible to do that. In my experiences, you start off way off, taking the long way, over-doing things, missing the details, and getting lost. It usually doesn't start off as smooth as my first few days did in this case for something open to so much possibility of hardship, so in reality I am doing fine and growing. I will watch one of Jay's movies tonight and wake up in the morning to do some exercises on my new mat. Adjusting better to the time, maybe sleeping more steadily through the night, and staying in control of my health. I am determined to find a way to make my own lunch here. See how I deal with that next.

Grocery Shopping
⊹ Glum Weather

Sleeping: Slept on the couch last night. I keep waking up with a sore throat here. I'm sensitive to dust, so I know these heating all-in-one units have some dust in them that is probably a decade old. It's not my place, so I can't break them down and scrub them. I would if it was straight forward, but I don't want to break anything. This place has a bedroom and a living room, so there are two different all-in-one units. I think the one in the living room is a little cleaner, so I decided to sleep in here last night. It didn't work very well. I used my heating blanket as my blanket and was still getting a stuffy nose, so I turned off the unit altogether. I was cold, wearing my jacket as well, even though there is a big heavy cover in the other room. I don't know what is making me sick, so I was trying this. There are two small floor heaters here, so I plugged in the space heater and it put it next to me. I couldn't get it to stop rotating, so one moment I was warm, the next I was cold. Meanwhile, outside there are some cats roaring loud crying out for sex. I thought if they don't shut up, I would have to go out there and fuck them myself. Another unsuccessful night of sleep, but maybe with a little improvement.

Breakfast: I poured some milk in a pot until it simmered and added a few slices of butter, a cube of sugar, and a chopped-up banana. I blended the banana and liquid together and then put some oatmeal flaks in it that I bought the day before. Then I added a little salt and brown sugar. It would have been easier to eat a banana with a glass of milk and a bowl of oatmeal, but then again, we could have corn on the cob instead of corn flakes. No coffee this morning. I didn't want to pay the price for a cappuccino and didn't want to hassle with the marketplace to find some kind of coffee teabag in the morning.

Work: Yesterday I went through my emails looking for a résumé of mine that was mostly accurate. I only found uneditable format files, so I knew I would have to go through my suitcase to find my extra hard drive that has a number of old résumés in it, including one I did in Chinese language and Chinese format. I also did some research and found a way to link my Flickr account with my blog so that I could share some photographs and videos. If you look below, I have linked you to the videos and photographs I have already uploaded. I also sorted my blog post links, the "Random Posts" isn't very useful for something being written in chronological order. This morning I finished creating that link, edited some videos, and uploaded them to Flickr. Then I went out to buy things to make a lunch.

Lunch: Today I was ok with having noodles for lunch. I

didn't want to sit in a restaurant to order them either, I wanted to buy one of the ten kinds they have in the store that just need hot water added. I went through the store yesterday, but this time I spent more time looking at everything. I got some of what we would call Canadian ham, different kinds of Chinese chili sauce, a bottle of Chinese cooking wine, a sample coffee mix, nail clippers, American almonds, and two kinds of noodles. There was a British lady shopping in there with her child and if you think I have an obsession with China, the kid's name was China Hen Mei. "Hěn měi" means "very beautiful" in Chinese. Every time the little girl was trying to open something or wondering off, she would shout, "China Hen Mei, don't open that. It's not yours," or something like that. They were both 100% Caucasian. I wanted to get some beef to make dinner later.

One block up the street is a butcher shop. Ordering meat from a butcher shop hasn't happened in my family since probably 1956. I thought I was going to have to try and tell the guy in Chinese that I want cow meat, and then direct him on where to cut the meat, how much, and then sort out the pricing. Instead, he already air sealed stacks of different cuts of meat. I still couldn't tell what was what. He kind of directed me towards a particular slice of meat, although I looked at some others, I resorted to buying what he recommended. It kind of sucks going shopping alone for that kind of thing because I have no idea what fresh meat costs on a street in the middle of Shanghai. I don't imagine there are many cows nearby and there are 28 million people that eat meat here including every other restaurant serving beef. He showed me the weight, but I wasn't paying any attention at all. The price was 138 RMB, with my quick math it was about $20 for something that would cost about $15 in Fairfax. Then I went over to a, I don't know what to call them yet... place that bakes things kind of like pastries. They make little circle biscuits, called moon cakes in English, that I don't think are made with any butter. I got two of them for like half of a dollar. Then I stopped in an open-side fresh produce store. It was full of white people, "lao wei", and they sounded like some Australians and, oh god, China Hen Mei's mum was there as well. I just got some Shanghai (baby) bok choi. I had to cross the street for the third time for a few more things.

Crossing the street is like a cultural test. I just wanted to get a few coca-colas from a tiny hole-in-the-wall vendor. If you wait for an opening to cross, you'll never get across. You have to walk with confidence, stay going in one direction, and don't veer off course. The bicycles, scooters, cars, taxi drivers, and other pedestrians instinctually calculate your projection speed and distance and will swerve to miss you at the last minute. Keep faith, don't hesitate unless you see the face of someone coming at you actually acknowledge your presence. If you are acknowledged, that means they aren't able to make a calculation fast enough and you might have to jump. I got my cokes and crossed the street back. I am always proud if I cross the street before a local Chinese gets across.

One last stop, the bakery. It has to be the French influence, but there are world class bakeries scattered throughout this side of the river. This place makes a mean ham sandwich, so I bought half a sandwich and half a loaf of raisin bread. The guys behind the counter there like to make jokes and laugh. It made me want to work there. If the prices weren't comparable to my hometown, I would probably buy everything in there.

The weather is glum: dark and wet. I didn't go out much today. I don't know if I will eat dinner tonight, again. At least this time I have some food if I get hungry. My only mission tonight is to stay up until 9 PM. It's 5:45 PM now. I will make a coffee. I am worried that a lot of days are like this in Shanghai. I accidently read something about that from a past article. I don't know if it's still accurate. I know a lot of change has been made here in terms of environmental cleanup. I guess I will find the answer out one way or another. Tomorrow morning I will use this yoga mat some more. I wish I could find another place to run other than this alleyway. I bet by the time I find a better place here, I will be relocating to another place and have to start everything over again. I heard a lot of English jobs pop up at the end of January due to expired contracts, but the beginning of January is the best time to find a place to live, due to Chinese New Year and the best time for people to relocate. That's backwards for my needs, but maybe it's the right way to go. I will find a place to stay in January, no matter what job I take.

Departing Words, Pharmacy, and more Chinese

Hanging out in the room all day, my body finally gave in and I got a full-on cold. Last night my nose was dripping. I had a more normal night of sleep, meaning that I laid on my stomach which I haven't done in a week and its how I would normally sleep. I stayed mostly warm, but it was hard work. I slept in the bed. I am going to have to replace Jay's Hello Kitty tissues. I wrote Jay an email.

Before Jay hurriedly took off to catch his flight to America, he told me a few things like:

- if someone knocks on the door demanding payment, pay him

- if a pipe bursts like one did last week, call a person he will give me the number to later

- if the electricity goes out, flick the breaker in one of two places

- if the landlord comes by, tell him you are just

checking on the place

- there's a washer if you want to change the sheets

- the electronics are ghostly, if the TV goes off, change the channel

- play with the heater until it works, but don't leave it on when I go out, it runs the bill

I had to figure where the garbage goes, with some assistance. The light above the sink won't turn on. There is a strategy needed to get accommodated. I have a deep gratitude for Jay. He gave me the keys, some words of wisdom, and left me to get started. My door will forever be open to him. I have been taking baby steps here and it didn't have to cost me a fortune.

Yesterday I tuned up my guitar. Jay has some computer speakers here with a subwoofer. I have a special little device that works with my iPhone and simulates the sound of guitar amplifiers. It's not as soul-grabbing as a real amp, but god it's an amazing thing. I plugged in and was able to play guitar. You have to be a guitarist to know that playing an electric guitar without an amplifier is like dancing in a swimming pool, you can't do much. I tried to record it using Mike P's older brother's website, Gigstarz. He has been developing it with some friends for the last three years and has been asking me to record some content there. Unfortunately, the quality leaves much to be desired or I would share the recording with you.

This morning I had a bowl of noodles and worked on my computer to see if I could get it to connect automatically to my VPN without manually having to connect. I watched an episode of Comedy Central's Daily Show with John Stewart. It really makes you wonder. What will become of the American political system? I ran out of food and thought I better go out and have a walk. First, I webcamed with my good friend Micah F. and got to share some stories. His internet connection went out and a girl from a northern province called me on webcam that I never met before. We talked for 40 minutes without a word of English. Then I left the house. Holy shit it was cold.

My first sensation of super cold from the other side of the world. When the clouds covered the sun, it felt like the end of the world. I walked all the way over to Jiao Tong University because I wanted to check out the running track there. When I got there, there were guards in front of all of the entry gates, and I didn't feel like trying to explain to them what I mean when I say "running track" or ask if I have to be a student to use it. Anyway, it was so deathly cold that I wanted to get indoors quickly. I went into a 7-11 to look for some nasal medicine, but I couldn't find any. I took the subway back to my area, instead of walking, and went into a larger corner store. Same trouble, no nasal medicine on the shelves, so I asked the clerk lady. Sometimes you get people that don't want to spend any effort dealing with a foreigner. Of course, those people don't speak any English, so they aren't able to try out their fancy shmancy white-people talk. She more or less told me to fuck off, and then the other clerk came over and understood I wanted medicine for my nose, but just said they don't have any. I was trying to ask where a pharmacy is. I don't know why the hell that phrase isn't in my software, but that's an important one.

I walked back to the busy street next to the place I am staying and eventually found a store that looked like it had drugs. The doctor didn't take any leap of faith to guess when I showed her that I was blowing my nose and wanted drugs for a running nose. I had to look up the word for snot before she wrote me a prescription for Tylenol Cold pills. Then I went and bought some eggs, slippers, oranges, coffee, and bread. I asked a vendor where I could buy rice. He walked me to another vendor selling noodles, so I used another word and he got it. He pointed down the street and told me to look for a red sign. He was really nice, but I never found anyone that sold rice. It is a relief being able to understand Chinese because I spent so long learning it and never using it. I haven't studied Chinese in over a year and I have been able to converse and read it pretty well. Every day it's more clear to me, but I am still shy to say a lot of things and I am not usually sure if I am saying what I mean to be saying.

There was a white lady on the street that I asked about where to buy rice. She told me to go to chinaharvest.cn or harvestchina.cn and they will bring it to my door. She told me the price and we talked for a minute. I thought she had an ugly face until we talked, then she seemed quite beautiful. That's the magic of friendliness. That was a cool experience too because English wasn't her first language, but it's mine. Around here, it's pretty badass to be able to speak English as a native. Now I notice how lazy I can speak English. It takes me no effort. That's different. In English, I can say the same word 30 different ways. In Chinese, I can hardly say one word correctly in one way. In general, I hear accents more, perhaps because of my ear for music. When I hear an American speak Chinese, I get a little irritated when they sound like they are speaking Chinese in English. Just make a little effort to speak it as its own language.

Well that was strange. I was typing that last sentence when the doorbell rang. A little Chinese man came in with four other people and another one waiting at the door. I tried to ask if he knew Jay, but he didn't understand me and walked right by me with them and started showing him the apartment. It's kind of messy at the moment and I told him that I am sorry, but I am sick. I was able to say that in Chinese and welcome them in, otherwise that would have been even more awkward and confusing for both of us. Of course he showed the bedroom with my underwear laying out on the bed. At least there was no trouble. Jay told me that he rents from a British guy that rents from a Chinese guy, and then there's me, so I guess he just wants to get paid. I'm glad I wasn't in the middle of doing kungfu, making dinner, showering, or with anyone.

I started to search and contact places for renting a room today. I am aiming for a modern apartment, smaller space, but maybe more consistency in room temperature and hot water. I'm also looking for a location I am somewhat familiar with and with some conveniences. My price range is about

$600 including utilities and a three month lease. I have been searching for room rentals in Shanghai for months and I never saw so many before. I am glad I am here now. Taking about two weeks to adjust to the time change, while adapting to the lifestyle change and get acquainted with the map. Might as well get sick now and get over the cold before starting work. There's a ton of places to live. I haven't had a stomach ache since I been here, aside from that street food, and that's excellent. Jay said his stomach was sick for 8 months when he got here. I'm going to wipe my visitors' foot prints off of my yoga mat now and get back to work. Maybe tomorrow I will get an email from Jay – I'm pretty paranoid about some catastrophe happening. One more day closer to normal time living.

Locals, Foreigners, and Getting Home

Friday night I met with a local Shanghainese friend to view an apartment north of Jing An. There was an advertisement on Craigslist to call the lady if you speak Chinese, or to email "Jane" otherwise. So, I emailed Jane at about 5:30 in the morning. There was an instant replay back with her address and that she might have guests for a few days, so she asked when I would I like to stay there. We went back and forth over email about a time I can come and some directions to get there. I was taken back by how so many street names were English and recognizable. I was especially surprised to hear that I have to take a right onto "Country Club Lane". My local friend agreed to come with me and we were all set, but I decided I should try to find on the map before completely relying on my friend to find the place. Of course, I couldn't find any of the streets in the directions, until I decided to search the globe. Sure enough, these were directions to a house in San Jose, California. That explained the early email reply and the strange context of her emails. She was subletting her house while at the same time, her Mother in Shanghai was subletting an extra room.

We worked it out and got there a bit late. Some of the subway transfers require walking a few blocks down the street and some flyer-promoter-guy bullshitted me that I should walk for another ten minutes before finding the subway. I'm sure that's because I took no interest in his flyer. The subway station was right behind him and I didn't notice until half a block when I realized that this guy would have gotten some joy out of misleading me. I walked back and went into the station. Most of these subway stations are very clean and modern. There are full-time street cleaners all over the place, and it's still grimy. I got off the train and Ginger walked right up to me and poked me, "You're late." I followed behind her, we didn't even get a good look at each other and I was trying to keep up. If you don't walk close enough, people will begin to fill the gap – similar to following a car on the highway. I'm glad I was with her because she walked up to a number of people to ask for clearer directions.

Ginger was born and raised in Shanghai, so she speaks Shanghainese in addition to Mandarin. Almost everyone she spoke to, on our way to finding the apartment, was in Shanghainese. She said she can just tell when someone is Shanghainese, but she can't explain it and I will never understand it. She is mostly right, but I have an idea that it is in a certain swagger and characteristic of a local person. When we came into the apartment, it was cold, mostly empty except for some antique carved wood furniture seats with no cushions. There was a piano covered in a blanket, a TV with a towel on it, and some fancy carved seats on a wood floor.

That's it. The room was small and clean, but right up against her bedroom wall. Considering that I will be home most of January researching and applying for work, I didn't see how this would work out. She did not speak any English and I did not speak enough Chinese. Ginger and her spoke in Shanghainese for five minutes, then I thanked her and we left.

Shanghainese doesn't sound like Mandarin whatsoever. I asked Ginger later, "Are there any words in Shanghainese that are the same as Mandarin?" She thought for a few minutes and then said, "Subway". That doesn't really count. Shanghainese doesn't sound like something I ever heard before. You could say it sounds like a Middle Eastern dialect with some south Asian dialect and French phonetics. We had the rest of the night and the weather was getting more and more like winter, so I asked if we could shop for a coat for me. There were some small shops on the street there, so we walked into one of them. I was afraid to go in because I had so many harsh bargaining experiences in 2006 when I went shopping. I was really surprised and relieved to find that the owners did not come up to me and demand I buy something. They just let me browse – a small miracle.

Since before I came to Shanghai, I knew I needed a winter coat. It can get so cold here that I was running out of time. The coat fashion here is dominated by a particular plastic down-coat. I think we call them puffy jackets. Some of them are normal polyester material and some of them are treated with extra water resistance, which gives them a sheen and glossy appearance. I remember having dinner with 11 Hong-Kongnese guys in Boston's China Town when I was in college. There was only one Chinese that was not Hong-Kongnese. He was from Shanghai and could not understand the dialect that the others were speaking in, so him and I had our own conversation. That was probably the first time I ever learned anything about Shanghai. He told me, "If you think New York is crazy... I have been to New York and seen it all. It's nothing. You come to Shanghai. I'll show you around." I remember, that guy was wearing one of these coats that everyone wears here. You're first inclination when you come here needing a coat is that it's gotta be one of these fashionable puffy jackets that everyone wears, but I was debating if it is acceptable for wearing to work or not.

We took the subway to another location, West Nanjing Road, and there we went in 5 giant clothing department stores. Most of the stores had this kind of coat, all similar in price, anywhere from $50 to $100 USD. I have my brown leather jacket with me, so I really wanted something that was waterproof, with a hood, and that I could wear over my leather jacket if I wanted to. I almost gave up on finding something until we went into American Eagle. I find it very fitting that the jacket that worked best for me was there. In one of the department stores, that song, "Drift Away" by the Doobie Brothers was playing. I'm a real sucker for music. I light up and get goose bumps very often because of music and you might find my eyes watering and me dancing on occasion. I started singing it and dancing around and it felt so good. In America, I didn't particularly care for this song, but that is some good sweet American heart music that really strummed me the right way and lifted me way up. Ginger said, "You are not like the other expats that I have known."

I think the younger expats here are on their parents' dime and take some Chinese and business courses in the day time and go out to clubs at night time. I saw some of their room rental advertisements and you can tell pretty quickly that they are full of themselves and how cool they are. A lot of expats here don't have to have much interest in China itself. They might have some interest in Shanghai and modern/future China; the fashion, the style, and the sprawl, but they act like they are above it all. I can see how that could happen because the foundation of the city is Western, so you could potentially come here and think that Chinese are following us and therefore Westerners are of a higher class. Like other Asian countries, it's also a place where a Westerner can come and have a girlfriend much younger than himself, even if he is married with children in his home country. So there are some of those walking around as well as loads of Westerners here exploring their business options with a little side-kick Chinese woman to show them around at all times. It's so far from where I want to be that when I see any of that, I just get distaste. I think there are plenty of second-generation Americans that feel this way when a foreigner shows up in America that just wants to profit by changing a business with no understanding of American tradition. Chinese culture is rich, so it's a real shame that the only motivation for some visitors here is money and sex.

Ginger and I ate in a Southern Chinese Food restaurant. Many restaurants in China are cold and people keep their coats, scarves, and hats on when they eat. I had stewed beef in soy sauce with kiwi juice to drink. They didn't bring us any rice. Ginger had some kind of yogurt fruit desert because she already ate earlier. Southern food, from Guangdong, is characterized a number of ways. There is a saying that Guangdong people eat anything and everything. However, this was just one restaurant, so they served a more particular style of food and in this case, small platters. They often slow cook their food from a few hours to a few days. The beef wasn't spicy and there were only a few slices of ginger, peppers, and onions. When Ginger and I took the train home, we had to separate and I had to switch trains.

The thing about China worth fearing is when things don't work out. Maybe ordinary Chinese can be helpful, but often the employed, or official, Chinese doing a job are not helpful at all. It feels acceptable that they could just suddenly say, "You have to go to jail now" and take you away. I think that's a common Chinese fear. No one wants to have to deal with Official Chinese, because they are not independent people and they are making decisions in a way they can account for and as they are trained to. In America, people can separate their job's duty from their own personality and take exceptions into consideration. When I went to transfer onto Line 10, there was a rope and one of the subways guards said, "Line 10 closed". That's when you get the feeling of trouble. I know I wasn't going to get an explanation, but I asked "what time?" in Chinese. I guess I just missed it. I had to wait on the side of the road in the cold for a long time before a cab would drive by that was not carrying people. I never have trouble getting cabs in America, except when it's raining in New York. Here, you might find yourself waiting for a cab for an indefinite amount of time and never get one. That's when you have to resort to riding on the back of some guy's motorcycle. I eventually got a cab and I was glad I had my new coat on because it was deathly ill outside.

The cab ride took a long time, much longer than the subway. He had to drive on the highway and it seems like we went for miles and miles. On the subway, it doesn't seem this way at all. I only had to go 4 or 5 stops. When we got to my corner, I thought I would try to get him to drive me up the block to drop me off, so I showed him the pictogram that the hostel clerk drew of my location from before. He said OK, but took a left instead of a right. I turned around in the cab and said, "It's that way" and the cab driver basically said, "Ya I know, I am just turning around." So, we hit some late night traffic and circled the long way around the block and eventually got me home. That long ride was only about $8 USD. I finally got my winter coat and Ginger proved to be a good and helpful new friend.

All I Want for Christmas is a Penthouse

It was Christmas Eve in Shanghai, but you wouldn't know it. There's plenty of Christmas decorations around town and you can hear some Christmas music coming out of the entrance of some stores, but it's not all-encompassing like it is in America. Christmas here is kind of like Easter. There are some store specials, some restaurants offering special meals with reservations, and there are some decorations. I thought there was the possibility of suddenly getting a feeling of missing out by late in the evening, so I researched a place to go ice skating.

There was one outdoor pool conversion venture that seemed abandoned. There were two department store ice arenas, ultra-small, and finally there was a big arena in the basement of a Mercedes Benz Arena. They even decorated it like a winter wonderland. When asking around online, I found that no one knew how to ice skate. It was one of those many things you kind of realize afterwards about being in China, that of course average people don't know how to ice skate. That's not really a Chinese past-time and this place itself is a big concrete jungle.

I thought I convinced one of my friends to go, but her phone number didn't work when I tried to call her earlier in the day. I was going to lay it on thick how much I am looking forward to going and how happy I was that she was going. I knew, otherwise, she would get cold feet. I got the email by early evening that she really can't ice skate and didn't want to go. I probably would have been really disappointed, but something else happened that made my day.

I was spending half of my day researching and contacting people about room rentals. Out of close to 30 emails, I had a personal top three that I really wanted. One place was ultra-modern and ultra-luxurious. Listen to this: it had an indoor basketball court, an outdoor tennis court, a swimming pool, and an aerobic area. The apartment itself had central air (one out of a million), a large modern equipped kitchen, a big open living area, and a sizable clean bedroom (bed included). It was near a subway station in a great area and it came to about $550 a month. Some problems with the place is that there were two advertisements for two separate rooms in the apartment for the same price and one room was much bigger than the other. Suspicious. The advertisement was pulled soon after I contacted the person about it. The person would ask one question in a series of emails to me and wasn't sure which advertisement I was calling about. The lease was only until March, which was fine with me, but also means I would have to go through all this again while having a job and in a time with less places to choose from. I had to ask who was living there now to find out 4 people were already living in a 4 bedroom apartment. And finally, for three days in a row they weren't able to schedule a time for me to come see the place.

Another apartment that I really liked was similar, minus the wicked indoor basketball court and other amenities. That lady responded and wanted me to send her an essay about myself. I sent it and after two days from not hearing back from her, I figured I'm not the one for her. Not having a job isn't a great asset. That place was about $500 monthly. I was looking at places from $300 to $600, with an emphasis on lower pricing, open space, clean, and in an area I was somewhat familiar with on this side of the river. That includes being in the vicinity of a subway station. There were good bedrooms at good prices in good areas, but the pictures of the living room were really important. Since paying for the use of the living room is included in the rent, I didn't want a place that was opposite of how I would be comfortable. If the couches looked like you couldn't sit upright in them, or they were jam packed with furniture and stuff, it was just going to be a room I couldn't use or have any space to move around. Sometimes after a rough week, I am in serious need of stretching and dancing around. If the opportunity is open to use the living room, I wanted the space to do that. Then there was a real winner that I thought I could only be so lucky to even talk to the guy that placed this advertisement. It was a place I knew I could thrive in, or at least not blame a bad experience living in Shanghai on the housing's living conditions. The ad was titled "Great Penthouse" and read:

Easygoing, tidy, considerate, roommate wanted for at least a six month stay from January 2nd 2012, in a great room in a huge 32nd/33rd floor, 300sqm duplex penthouse. Space! The apartment has four bedrooms so you'd be living with 3 guys: an Australian, a Taiwanese, and a Frenchman. The room has a double bed, a small shelf, a desk, a closet, black-out curtains, and a window bed with a fantastic view of a park and the Suzhou Creek. There are two large balconies with fantastic views. There's also a giant accessible roof area. Very big living room with window bed, sofas, flat-screen tv, and plants. We have a cleaning lady that comes 3 times a week. Walking distance to subway lines 7, 3 and 4. Please tell us a little about yourself in your email.

I can't remember how soon the Australian, Ken, responded, but it was at least 24 hours after I emailed about it. I was thinking that someone must have moved out of their place and moved into this one as soon as the ad was posted. In my experience, good things on craigslist go extremely quick. I called him via Skype and got the most detailed directions that I could from him, which still weren't great because I didn't really know the names of the streets to tell the taxi driver, I just kind of knew how Ken pronounced them. I asked him a lot of questions about the directions and didn't want to sound like I was bothering him too much, since I know him liking me is the most important thing. I showered, put on some clothes, and went to catch the subway.

Ken told me the easiest thing to do would be to take the closest subway train from me to a stop closest to him, without having to transfer trains, and telling the cab driver, "Aomen and Changhua". Of course, I don't know if I am hearing him clearly or not when I write this down and I'm nervous as hell that the cab driver was going to yell at me that he doesn't understand me. Then I was to look for a residential building on one of the corners, walk towards the taller buildings, and look for a triangle sculpture, and his building was behind that. I told him that I didn't have a phone, but he said getting in the building wouldn't be a problem. That was another concern of mine, that I wouldn't be able to get in anyway. When I got off the train and came up to the street, I found a heavily crowded and busy sidewalk with music blasting and waves of people going every direction. There are signs and enormous TVs on the sides of buildings like New York's Time Square. I had to walk up and down the sidewalk for 30 minutes trying to hail a cab that wasn't already occupied. Finally, one screeched and I dove in. Success! The cab driver seemed to understand me and we were off.

As I continue to mention how taxi rides in Shanghai are more thrilling than rollercoasters, this guy's ride was so insane that I literally thought I was going to puke. Of course, I had no choice, except to stay in the cab and hold tight. I can't tell the guy, "take it easy!" or "hey, next time you stop, I'll just get out then". I think there was some built up aggression in the guy and he wanted someone to hit us. I am really at a loss for words when trying to explain what it's like to zig and zag at top speeds between vehicles in the mists of changing lanes; trucks, cars, other taxis, scooters, and bicycles, and for every opening it was his cue to slam on the gas. There is massive honking, hitting the breaks, and up to three cars trying to fit into the same lane at the same time with all of the drivers unconcerned about crashing or anything else for that matter. He let me off at the intersection.

I looked around and, not too surprisingly, I didn't see any clear residential building. I thought, "Well, it could be that general area... or that one... and that area looks like it could be it too. Let's see, tall buildings, yep, there are some over there... and some over that way... and so on." I knew it was on the waterfront of a river, so I thought I should ask someone where the river is. My translator applications said there were a few ways to say river, so I tried them at a produce stand. The lady didn't understand any of them, even when I showed her the Chinese characters on my phone. Her assistant didn't either, until I remembered the word for swimming and just said, "Water, swimming", and he smiled and pointed in a direction. I still wasn't sure if he knew what I meant. I ended up having to walk to the river and back and around the side of the complex to get in. The neighborhood, if you can call it that, was just a farm of high-rises. It was kind of dumpy, but still above standard for China. I walked over, found the pyramid, and the building's front door was open. Didn't anyone know it was winter? There wasn't much of a lobby, and I found the elevator around the corner. There were only two elevators and when I got inside of mine, it was dirty, small, and smelly. Great, no express elevator for the upper floors and a 13 person weight limit. Up to the top floors, 32, with possibly 12 stops before mine. I was alone this time, but I was dreading the inevitable future of an additional 30 minute commute home in a stinky box.

Ken answered the door with a Band-Aid on his nose and quick explanation that he owns a bar and got punched in the face last night. There was only one bathroom for four guys (as far as I could tell), and a really small kitchen. The kind that like only one person at a time can stand in. However, the living room was just as the pictures showed, large, open, and clean. In addition, there was a sunroom balcony on the first level, and bigger sunroom on the second level. In shanghai, pretty much everyone that has a sunshine area dedicates the room for drying their laundry. This was true in this case also. One thing that was not pictured in the advertisement was the view from the bedroom. It would be a tourist attraction in most cities in America. How can you be so high and see so far from your bedroom? I'm scared of heights and have a fear of earth quakes, but it's funny how that takes backseat to a big living room with English-speaking roommates. I found that there was no-one sleeping above me, below me, or on any side of the room. Ken showed me that we have an express entrance to the house from the 33rd floor, which is great if I want to avoid having to go through the living room. He asked if I wanted to see the roof that no-one is ever on. Of course I did!

The roof is just cement. There weren't any radiators,

satellites, or anything else up there. It was a private place that I could do my kungfu exercises, outdoors, without having to take the elevator or having a crowd watch me. Not only that, but I guess all of the surrounding buildings are also 33 floors tall, and you could see much farther from the roof and in all directions. It was quiet up there and the air seemed a little bit better. Not only did I have my own personal outdoor kungfu area, but it seemed like I also had my own personal place outside of, or at least above, Shanghai. From the roof, Ken pointed to me the surrounding grocery stores and the closest subway stop, across the bridge on the other side of the river. The place was certainly nice, but it was still going to be a challenge to adjust to. The place I am currently staying is only about 50 meters from a busy street full of groceries. If I got this new place, I would have to carry my groceries a half kilometer to a full kilometer, and up the long and terrible elevator ride. Not to mention, what if I have to pee on the way?!

Ken told me more about the utilities and how the maid does the dishes and laundry as well. The rent came to about $500 a month and before I could say anything he asked, "So do you want to move in?" I said "Ya," without thinking about it. We walked over to an ATM so I could give him some money to hold the room for me. We got to talk about this and that on the walk. Ken is almost 40 years old and owns a bar, next to where I am currently staying, called "The Otter". It is a western bar that serves hamburgers and fish & chips. I thought that's great, when I get a craving, I can probably order at cost there and maybe if I am lucky, Ken would bring home some food every once in a while. He has been in Shanghai 8 years, his Chinese is really good, his English is native, and he has lived in the penthouse for four years. Since he works at night, I don't know about the other guys there, but I think there will be periods of the day when no one is home and the living room is open for dancing around or just a feeling of being in a house in my hometown.

When I got home, I checked the map. There is a big outdoor park right next to the water that I didn't notice. Years ago when I was first wanting to move to Shanghai, I told myself that I wanted to be near a park and a western restaurant. This time, when I moved to Shanghai, I didn't have any standards or expectations. In fact, I expected the absolute worst. So far, it has worked out as good as it could work out. The next big item will be acquiring the working life; from reaching out, to winning the position, and navigating the commute with the tricks required to making it work best. That will be the month of January, since everything closes down for the spring festival. I can make a lot of connections beforehand and start a position when people return back to work. I am looking for small exchanges or gigs in the meantime. So, I kind of forgot it was Christmas Eve and about ice skating. I just got the gift I really wanted, a good place to live in Shanghai.

Dimensions of China

It was Sunday morning and the sun was already up, so I knew my time was limited. I called everyone in my family the morning before for their Christmas Eve – only I had sides of the world mixed up. After more than six years of communicating with people in China from America, I was used to their being a half day time difference; I just am NOT used to it being the other way around. If time is as many people say it is, cyclical, then EST America could be considered 13 hours ahead. Time is now for both of us in any case. That's a physics problem. Anyway, I needed to have breakfast before Skyping with my family. I didn't actually get ahold of anyone the day before because they were all out at a Christmas party. We were able to see each other with our webcams and I got to tell them about the new place I secured and about the area I am living in now. When I told my Dad, "Everything here is like the epitome of everything you hate," he had a good laugh. My Dad kind of cracks when people are shouting inside, or when they are rude, or when people drive bad, or when a place is overly crowded, or when you have to cross streets quickly and at the right time. I am sure there are other things that go against his grain here, but those are the ones I think about a lot because I feel similar to some of those, especially shouting inside, which is really common here.

There are some gifts that I would have liked to given each of them and it feels weird not exchanging at least one present. On the other hand, it's good that we got to see each other and talk to each other without having to buy or receive a gift. We ended the call before noon China time, and managed not talking about anything negative. Mom later wrote me that it helped her feel like Christmas was complete by being able to see me. The only other Christmas plan I had was to meet with Heena at some point in the evening, but she didn't respond to my previous email from two days ago. After Mandy bailed on me the night before, I was already starting to feel like this wasn't going to happen either. Looking for her email response, I saw that Jay still had not replied to my email I sent days ago as well.

Shauna was online and I knew she was supposed to be playing badminton this morning. Apparently all of the players overslept, so she was free to join me to run some errands. I say join me, but when I leave the front door, I am not much of a leader. I can tell that ladies in general want to see a man that can lead and be strong and I sometimes wonder if that's why Mozzy broke up with me. I am not the same Pete DiFlip to people here as I can be in my country, because of the simple fact that I can't speak Chinese fluently. I'm so shy with my Chinese that even if I can say a sentence perfectly well, I will ask a Chinese friend to tell or ask someone something. It makes me a bit helpless in a lot of situations that I would otherwise be in control of. Shauna was on her way over and I hopped in the shower.

When I got out of the shower and was drying off, someone was banging loudly on the door. "Bang, bang, bang!", "Ding-dong, ding-dong, ding-dong." Over and over, fast and loud like someone needed save their grandmother from a burning building and I was stopping them. It didn't seem that I could throw on clothes fast enough. I thought if I didn't hurry, someone was going to die. I just didn't want to go outside naked and wet because I would have caught an pneumonia. I say, outside, because there are two doors to get in here and one of them is on the entrance balcony. When I opened the door, it was Emma.

"Did you eat? Do you want grab lunch?"

"Jesus, I thought you were the landlord or there was some kind of emergency."

"Sorry, maybe that is rude of me. I thought you were sleeping."

"No, no. I can't, someone is on their way over and I just had breakfast."

"Oh, okay, I didn't have time to login to MSN and I was walking by. I don't have time to meet later today and just wanted to see if you could join me."

"Sorry, if I would have known. I knew you were talking about having lunch today, but I didn't know. We can do it another time."

"Okay, see you later."

"Bye, thank you."

I feel like an asshole. I'm brand new in town and she took the few minutes she had available to take me to lunch and I have other plans. Why am I so busy? And who the hell do I know that is coming over? I figure those are questions running through her head. I was a little relieved that Shauna wasn't arriving while Emma was here because it would have made me look like someone that I'm not. I wouldn't be scheduling dates back to back and I certainly don't have a following of women banging on my door, although that analogy doesn't work so well in this case. When Shauna arrived, she said that she was impressed by the size of the place that I am staying in. Then we headed out.

I had an address and subway station written down for an iPhone specialist shop that was one of only two places in the world that I knew of offering a special service I needed. Apple's latest iPhone operating system has a number of safeguards against hacking that cannot be undone. One of these safeguards has to do with a baseline modem that cannot be overridden to allow international phone services. In older, previous versions of the software, it was possible to downgrade and change the boot up file to allow for this service. Now, you actually have to have an older computer chip replace the computer chip where this information is stored, in order to "unlock" the phone for international service. For being only one of the two places I found online that offer this service, it's pretty miraculous that it was only 4 subways stops from me and the other store, in Beijing, was closed until January 3rd. Again, this is the world, not just China.

Shauna came with me, but it quickly turned into me coming with her. She has a knack for direction here and we had to walk a few blocks before coming to a condominium complex. It didn't seem like the place for a business, but there were businesses and residences, comingled. She had to eventually ask someone where the building number was and we walked up to a small shop on the third floor. The guy I had emailed about the service was not there and, again, Shauna had to talk in Chinese with the clerks. They called their Manager and I spoke to him in English on the phone. The service would cost 600 RMB, plus 100 RMB service charge, and I could get the phone in a few days. I tried to give the guys there a sense that I'm a good guy and I expect my phone to be working when I return back. Shauna was begging to have lunch, even though our plan was to go jogging next, so we found a food court area across the street.

I recognized this food court. Like some other places I have been recently, I was here a few months ago with Mozzy. I remember it so well. This was where I learned that Chinese people don't tend to have a drink with their lunch because I couldn't find a place to order a soda and noticed that no-one had a drink in the dining area. We ate in a little Korean "fusion" restaurant. I can proudly say that the Korean restaurants in my hometown make better bulgolgi than this place did. After I finished my meal, I ordered a coffee. Shockingly, Shauna replied, "You really enjoy your life."

I was dumbfounded, "Why? Because I ordered a coffee?"

"No. I can tell. You just do."

I didn't know where that came from and just shook it off. When my coffee came, it was black. I asked for some cream and sugar, via Shauna. She talked to the waitress for two minutes about it. I was wondering what the big deal is. Then Shauna said, "Just try it, it's good."

I said, "I'm sure it's good, but I would like some cream and sugar."

She persisted, "Try it first."

My eyes were jumping around from her, to the waitress, to another waitress behind the counter, and back to Shauna. "If they have cream and sugar, I'd like to use it, do they have it or not?" They had another small discussion and the waitress went into the back room. I told Shauna, "My parents said when they ordered soda in restaurants in England, they never came with ice. And when they told the waiters they wanted ice, the waiters insisted that the drink was already cold." I was making a point that this felt like a similar scenario to me. When the waitress came back out, she said they didn't have any milk. I drank half of the cup, black.

Shauna called another friend of mine, Gong Fang Ping that told me to call at 2. I met GFP in a virtual online world, called Second Life, back in 2007. In Second Life, I would always go to a Chinese region of the simulation to meet and talk with Chinese people. China eventually banned it from its citizens, but I met more than 500 Chinese there, from nearly every province in China. In that environment, I could often disguise myself as a Chinese and watch how they type and speak with each other. I also carried around maps of China with me and ALWAYS asked someone new I met, to show me on the map where they live and talk about the geography. I learned a great deal about China this way. GFP was one of the nicer Chinese. I remember having a watermelon battle with him, a German lady that thought saying "damn" was inappropriate and said "fuck" constantly, and some other people, on a giant Chinese style boat using watermelon launchers. That's how cool Second Life is. I got his MSN name and talked to him sometimes on Messenger.

GFP lived in Beijingand had recently graduated college. We rarely spoke to each other, but I tried to help him get a job with some of my other contacts in Beijing. A few days ago he messaged me and I told him that I was in Shanghai. This was the day I was mapping out my walk to the park. It turns out that he is in Shanghai now and lives right next to the same park that I was headed to. Today, we planned to play basketball in the afternoon. Shauna said she would be happy to watch. GFP's English is subpar, so I'm glad Shauna spoke to him. He still hadn't found a basketball, so he would call back later.

Shauna and I decided to go forward with our plan to go jogging. I saw on a map that Jiao Tong University has a running track. We took the subway there and I helped navigate some of the way. Once we started walking around to find it, it proved to be very challenging. At some point we stopped to use the restrooms in Jiao Tong's cafeteria. In 2009, I was trying very hard to apply to attend Jiao Tong's Chinese studies programs. After seeing how crummy this cafeteria was, I felt good about the terms of my living in Shanghai now. We eventually found the track and started running around it.

Shauna was carrying a huge handbag and was wearing some kind of slipper boots that are in fashion now– definitely not running shoes. After a few laps, I asked if she would hang back and let me get some more running in. I was thinking to myself while running, "Another success. I am running today. I may never get to run so freely again. I better live this up. I am safe today, but who knows about tomorrow?" I was watching people on the center field play soccer and scattered people playing pieces of sports; like badminton, golf, and backwards walking. The golfer had the worst swing I had ever seen in my life. He was probably about 70 years old, and swinging the living shit out of his club, hitting these pieces of rolled up cardboard stockings from one end of a painted box to another. The only thing that represented golf was his club. I also saw the weirdest form of kungfu that I ever saw. I have seen some weird kungfu. Anything can be exercise in this part of Asia, but this was madness. A lady was walking backwards on the track, flicking under her chin, the same way a New Jersey Italian would gesture the, "Go-fuck-yourself" sign. One hand after the other, rolling – flick, flick, flick, flick. Her steps weren't even in sync with her flicks. She looked completely nuts. Maybe for two minutes, I could have let it slide, but I was running laps and passing her doing this each time. I am sympathetic to all things Chinese, but what the hell is that?!

It was too late in the day for basketball, so GFP and I called it off and Shauna and I headed back to my place to make dinner. I had some ingredients and we stopped to pick up a few more. I had a lot of experience cooking Chinese style food living with Randy, so I was confident I could make something. While the food was cooking, I was eager to show off my fancy new VPN to my unsuspecting guest. Check it out, BAM, YouTube. I started downloading South Park's episode, "The China Problem", which outlines some Chinese stereotypes, American fears, and how far you can push content in America. If you had seen this episode, you will recall how it graphically depicts Harrison Ford getting raped by the directors of the newest Indiana Jones film as a metaphor to show a classic film turned into crap at Harrison's expense. I was kind of proud to show Shauna what you can get away with in my country. While the episode was loading, a flash came to me.

"Hey! Do you know who Tank Man is?"

"Tank Man? What? Who's that?"

"Tank Man. He is banned in China, but he is a hero all over the world. Just watch"

I started to search for the video and I could see Shauna starting to get nervous. She was getting uncomfortable and defensive. "What is this about? Who is Tank Man? This is Tiananmen Square. A lot of people got hurt."

She was looking at me with sad eyes, like I was about to wrong her. "No, no, no. Don't worry. It's good. Just watch."

"This is really forbidden," she said.

I chose a clip that was only a minute and thirty seconds long. A line of tanks are coming down the street in Beijing, and a citizen walks right up to a tank moving directly at him. The tank stops at the last second, but it looks like it is going to run him over. Shauna grabbed my arm, jolted and gasped. She thought I was showing her how evil the government is and how this guy gets run over by a tank. She continued watching. The tank reverses a foot and moves forward turning, but Tank Man steps straight to his side, standing feet together. Shauna is still on edge. Then Tank Man climbs onto the tank and shouts down into the window hole. It is presumed that he is yelling at them to stop. Shauna is asking me, "What is he doing? That man is crazy." The clip ends. I told her there are hour long movies about this guy and he is a real hero because he put his life on the line to stand up to the army and tell them to stop the violence. She didn't have much of a reaction and I quickly switched back over to South Park. I think, in her case, that takes time to digest upon memory. I wasn't showing any kind of propaganda for or against China. I just wanted to show her a Chinese hero that the outside world admires and most Chinese are unaware of.

We finished our dinner and our beers and I played some guitar. She wasn't sure if I could play, so I played a bit and then pulled up some of my music recordings. Shauna said I could be famous in China if I wanted to. I said, "Ok with me." It was late, so I walked her to the subway station and said goodbye. There was never a word from Heena. It was Christmas day, but you could have fooled me.

A Starving Artist

Yesterday, I stayed in the apartment all day. I didn't have much here to eat, but I didn't want to go out and try to figure out lunch again. I still can't order a meal, or at least, I don't have a craving for Chinese food for lunch. Maybe for dinner, I can eat most anything on a menu, but lunch is still a mystery for me here. The other thing about staying inside all day is that I know I am going to spend zero dollars. I have been trying to figure out where I will stay for the three nights I will have to leave here and before I move into the new place. I don't mind going back to the same hostel, but it costs about $30 a night and I have been trying to think of a way to avoid having to pay that. In truth, that is the cost for a private room, which was necessary for me my first nights back here, because I was awake and asleep in really off times of the day and needed my own room. I could bunk up in one of the shared rooms for something like $9 a night. I'm not as worried about my belongings being stolen as I should be, but I can imagine that New Year's Eve would be a terrible time to share a room with 4 strangers. I might as well not have a bed because I'm sure there won't be a window of opportunity to sleep.

Heena asked me a few days ago if I wanted to go out with her and her roommate Lynda for New Year's Eve to go dancing. She told me that her cousin came into town for Christmas and she hadn't seen him in years, so she had to cancel meeting up with me. I don't think Heena has any particular place in mind and I would like to book a hostel near wherever we will be going that night. There's no sense in staying on the other side of town if I don't have to. I checked my old Facebook messages from Jay on December 5th. He said he would return December 30th and by that time I should have found a place, plus he is starting a new job. The same reason I wanted a private room when I got here, I'm sure he does too. I just want to leave the place like I found it and be gone by the time he arrives.

I was voice chatting with a new person I met on the other side of the river when we both found out that we have music recordings. It made me want to sing and a bunch of great songs came to mind. I was pulling up their lyrics and we were having a good time singing to each other. After the call ended, I took out my guitar. I thought, damn, I should learn some of these songs that I like singing so much, so I started to search the internet to find some music sheets of them. No surprise, they are all pulled from the internet due to copy write infringement.

You know, in my mind, an artist would prefer his work to be shared rather than coveted. It's all the businessmen involved that act as floodgates to the art community. I found some crappy, made-up, score sheets that weren't clever or in the right key. As what seems to be the reoccurring theme, I had to download a recording of the song and then try to figure the best way to play it on the guitar.

I had previously used my iPhone with my guitar to simulate the sound of a guitar amplifier, and then run that through Jay's computer speakers to get a louder and nicer sound. My iPhone is still in the shop. When I woke up this morning, I spent a good hour trying to figure a way to amplify my guitar sound. Nothing was working. I figured out a lot of the song I was trying to play, but I couldn't sing because it was too quiet. I get frustrated when I am sitting in a room with a guitar, a guitar cable, some cable adapters I brought, amplified speakers, and a computer and I can't figure out a way to amplify my guitar. Then, I saw an old CD player behind the dresser. I brought a special RCA to 1/8th jack cable with me, so I rigged it with the guitar. The volume knob was barely connecting, so the sound would go in and out. Eventually I got it to balance and stay on. Beautiful. I can play my guitar and sing.

I shaved, got my coat on, and was about to go out when I had a second thought of maybe laying down for a moment. I slept for two hours. I went to sleep at about 4 in the morning last night (bad English, but you get me) because I drank a lot of coffee and wanted to write another blog entry before too much time passed. When I woke up, I searched google maps for nearby places containing the word "sandwich" and "burger". I didn't actually want a burger, I just wanted to have lunch somewhere that understood lunch the same way that I did. I eventually decided on a place just a few blocks down in a direction I hadn't gone before. I put on my new winter coat, oversized jeans, tennis shoes, scarf, and wool beanie cap to head out.

I never know what to expect when I leave the door. The first feeling I get as I am walking out is that I should have practiced Chinese today. I feel really guilty about that. I mean, it's a major reason that I am here, and I'm not practicing. And now I don't have my iPhone with translating software with me either. The first few people that pass me are the ones that make me feel most self-conscious, then I'm back in the game. Crossing streets is becoming second nature and I almost find myself walking straight out into traffic because a crossable street and a non-crossable street here is a very gray area. What is much more rare is an obvious opening to cross, but they do happen. I crossed a major three lane intersection today when no one else was crossing. I totally rely on faith, persistence, and consistency of direction. Part of that philosophy is that if someone is going to hit me, they will at least know where my next steps are going to be so they can swerve accordingly. Old locals here just walk straight out into traffic without hardly looking and it's up to the car drivers to decide whether to hit them or not.

I made it to a corner with a number of western restaurants; Italian, Steakhouse, and a Latin Grill. I couldn't tell if they were open. It seems like places are open from 12 to 1, or from 5:30 until 2 in the morning, but Chinese almost never eat lunch after 2. I decided to walk farther down the block and passed the burger place I saw on the map, so I checked the entrance. No one was inside, so I kept walking. I was beginning to hit the point of walking where turning around seemed like a good idea before I got too far, when I saw a cool wooden deck and entrance into "Southern Belle". I couldn't resist this time, I walked in. There were two Chinese women sitting at a bar table and one of them said, "Yes?" I didn't want to even try to stumble with my Chinese and I figured it was an American restaurant, so let's just see if I can say, "Are you open?" The lady told me they were and I could sit anywhere.

This place was really cool. Everything was made with a really neat kind of wood. I have noticed in a number of places in Beijingand Shanghai, the decoration sometimes looks like it should be in a mansion. It's like they are going for some ultra-rare materials and taking no short cuts on cost when covering a place. The menu looked great! Everything was food I could have for lunch, but I decided to go with a kind of rice sausage gumbo. I miss how restaurants in America serve you water when you come in. They do that here, but only the Chinese restaurants. The western restaurants charge $5 for a glass of water. I was the only customer in the place, because of the time of course, and a friend of the staff stopped in with two little dogs fully decked out in clothes and boots. I thought, boy if my friends who joke about Chinese eating dogs only knew… Right next to my table was a small area for live performance.

This place was beautifully decorated and there were relics of southern USA signs, jerseys, and things like that. I was wondering what someone gets paid to play guitar here. There was even a guitar on the wall, so I was planning to ask about it. I found out that every Wednesday, and the first Tuesday of the month, a guy comes here and plays country music for three hours. I thought, goodness, I would consider myself loaded with material if I could play for one hour. Well, southern America and country music was close, in perspective, but it wasn't me. I asked the Manager about other venues where live guitar is played. She said the Cotton Club plays jazz, but they are very professional. A place called Oscar has rock musicians sometimes. I just have to search around and see if there is a venue that would be good for me. Either a place where people are expected to listen, or a place where they are expected not to listen. I just need a venue that seems to define that well, which has to do with the lighting, stage, acoustics, and other factors. Environment and audience is key. I don't mind being background music or foreground music, it's just the fading in and out of both is not my ideal.

It felt good to eat real food. Yesterday I pretty much had three courses of starch meals. Walking back I finally saw some synthetic leather gloves that I had been keeping an eye out to find. In Toronto, these were on sale for $25. I asked how much. I am finding that I have to quickly unlearn 30 years of politeness in order to get any service here. I am doing a bad job at it. They told me $5, or after conversion, but I just did a shitty job understanding them. It was perfectly clear Chinese and a number I learned 7 years ago, but I was nervous and panicked. They were nice guys, and I'm lucky they were. I gotta get better at this stuff. It's like I want to be taken advantage of. I don't, but the lack of confidence is going to get me into trouble soon if I don't shape up.

I stopped and got water and bread on the way home. Walking back down my alley way, two bicycles passed me with little white children sitting on the back. They were shouting, in a singsong way, various Chinese words,"Bao Zi, Bao Zi, Hui Jia, Hui Jia, Shui Guo, Shui Guo," (Dumpling, dumpling, coming home, coming home, fruit, fruit). It was awesome to see. The Chinese ladies picked them up off the back of the bike and they each held a child on one arm against their bodies. One of the ladies made eye contact with me and we both shared a smile knowing it was awesome that those kids were speaking mandarin. As I was putting the key in my door, I was thinking to myself, "You know what those kids are going to do when they grow up? Anything they want."

Becoming Chinese

As soon as I rolled out of bed this morning, I had the urge to get out of the house. My legs were itching to move, so I put on some clothes and left. I didn't brush my teeth or check myself in the mirror, I just wanted to get the hell out of here as soon as I could. I got outside, started to walk in one direction, and immediately turned around to go in another. I thought of a new street to go down so I could have a walk and discover something new. I figured I'd try to find an orange juice along the way and if I saw some kind of breakfast that struck me as yummy, I'd sit down and eat it. I got my OJ and crossed the street. There were guards standing in front of a big wall with pointed spikes at the top. A sign on the wall read, "US Consulate". The guards stood surrounding the fence, feet together and arms at their sides, standing on top of one-step metal boxes wearing their full uniform; a long woolen overcoat, a satchel, and a peaked cap. They look sharp left for five seconds, and then sharp right, back and forth. These guards surround most government complexes and they are there 24 hours a day. I had a good feeling, "Nice! Working together! Keep it up boys!" You think I'm kidding, but I really liked to see that.

There are video cameras everywhere. At the front of every gated community, there is a guard and a camera. There are so many gated communities here that I started to figure out why the blocks were so long and apart. I walk in a general direction and keep in mind that I can just circle back at the next block. The only problem is, the natural next block is closed off for that community, and so is the next one, and the next one, so that by the time I can finally take a right, I have actually gone four blocks and far out of my way. That doesn't help any time that you realize you are going in the wrong direction, but already half committed in length. The other thing that I'm starting to figure out gets me turned around here is that for a few blocks, there is mainly a grid of streets, and then this grid connects to another grid that is slanted, and that grid is surrounded by other grids that are slanted in their own directions, so even if you have a good sense of direction, before you know it, you are totally turned around. That's what happened to me today. My new and exciting direction ended me at completely opposite of the direction I thought I was headed. My nose was starting to run from the cold weather and I couldn't find a shop to buy some tissues in. I was walking right by the Shanghai Library, so I thought I would see if their bathrooms had toilet paper. Plus, Shauna and I walked by it the other day and she was excited to see it and said it is worth visiting.

I walked in the front and followed the signs towards the restrooms. It's like playing lotto to walk in a public restroom. You never know if they will have sit-down toilets, if it will smell like hell, if there will be mirrors, if it's maintained at all, and in my case, if there will be any form of toilet paper. Wow, great, this restroom met western standards and smelled clean. The toilet paper was square pieces of recycled cardboard paper. After I blew my nose, I thought, this bathroom is so clean that I better pee in it because you can't hit lotto twice in row. I came out of the restroom and tried to observe what everything is on the first floor. There was a reading room and some multimedia computers set up and normal library stuff. I started to go up the steps to the second floor when I turned to look over the edge and saw some kind of museum exhibit. It looked roped off, or I would have checked it out. The second floor was for library card holders only, so I started to make my way out of the building, when I came across their book store.

I looked all over the book store at what kind of books it offered. A part of me wanted to see what English language study books they had or English teaching books. There was a table full of children books that I was browsing through. I couldn't find any that would help me learn Chinese. Without pinyin (phonetic mandarin), I don't know how to read a new Chinese character. I finally came across some English school books, from levels 1 to 15. I picked up level 12 and flipped through the pages. It was completely full of sentences with missing words and 4 answers to choose from in multiple choice form. By the fourth sentence I read, I couldn't decide which answer was correct, it could have been either C or D. God, these people learn English well. I remember seeing some of the content Mozzy studied in University for English and there was a dialogue in her text book for a job interview that was crazy complex. Some of the earlier level books here had Chinese in them, but by level 6 or so, the books were all in English.

I noticed some books for studying abroad titled in Chinese, "I am in America!" Some of the books that I recognized were books about Steve Jobs, Bill Gates, Warren Buffett, and 911. I don't know why, but it was strange to see George Bush Jr.'s "Decision Points" in Chinese. I guess I felt like, if there was any real content in that book about American presidential decisions, they shouldn't be published and for sale in Chinese book stores. Then I saw a few books about America sucking, like conspiracy theories and a book titled in Chinese and English, "To Me, It's All Shit". Damn, where is that Chinese censorship I heard so much about? Speaking of that, someone should let the Communist Party know that this part of Shanghai is full of gated communities. I finally got up the nerve to ask the clerk a question.

My Chinese came out pretty well. He walked me over to the section I was looking for, Chinese language study for English speaking people. There were only two kinds of books to choose from, elementary level 1, or elementary level 2. Flipping through book 1, I felt I had that content pretty covered, and went to purchase level 2. Man, I spoke enough Chinese in that store that they might have thought I could have a conversation. At least I think I stopped my bad habit of repeating questions asked to me aloud. If someone asked me something and I didn't understand a word, I'd react immediately by repeating what I just heard them say. Turns out when you do that, they take that as your answer and will shuffle you through without having the chance to try and re-explain what you really want. I was really happy to finally get this book and it was only about $16. As I started to walk home, I felt my body jolting to want to do some intense Kungfu.

Shit. I need to do some pretty hard core kungfu as soon as possible and I don't have any idea where to do it. I can't just do it in front of the Library, can I? Ahh, aw man, I was feeling like a junky that was looking for a spot somewhere to get his fix. Man, what am I going to do? My philosophy is, if I am lucky enough to have the inspiration to do kungfu, then I should always do it. Otherwise you will slowly lose that inspiration and those abilities. Some kungfu is better to be done outside, northern kungfu, and other kungfu is better to be done inside. I wanted to some intense outdoor kungfu, not just a few movements either. As I walked on, I started to notice that I wasn't going a direct way home and my legs were getting more and more tired. I started to get sad and disappointed that I wasn't going to be able to do kungfu. I can't wait to have my own roof top.

When I got home, I learned that my iPhone was ready for pickup. I had them show me that it works and then headed to a China Mobile store. Finally, I was taking care of some business without help. When I was signing the papers for my own phone number, I felt like I was becoming a citizen of The People's Republic of China. As of now, that can never happen, but this might have been the next best thing. The service company next to my status bar is in Chinese characters. I feel more integrated. This is going to be crazy, an iPhone with Chinese service. I grabbed a beef kabob on the side of the road to hold me over until later tonight. Emma is taking me somewhere for dinner. Her, and many other Chinese I know, are going out of town for New Year's Eve. I will be moving into a hostel in two days, so this will be the last time it's so convenient for us to meet. I'm excited for whatever tonight's dish will be. One things for sure, it will be new to me.

Hard to Swallow

I just couldn't hold back this time. My jaw was open and my head was lowered in and cocked to the side for a closer look. Emma was taking the fish's eyeball out and bringing it towards her mouth. "Gulp", in an instant it was swallowed. I had pouched a fish before. There's more to it, but I pranked my roommate by boiling one of his pet fish and putting it back in the fish tank. So I knew that a fish's eye should turn white when it's fully cooked, and the eye that Emma just ate was crystal clear. She had come by my place to take me to a restaurant and we agreed to eat at a Hunan style restaurant together. Of course, I let Emma order the dishes.

I couldn't figure out why the food didn't look right when it came out, after all, what do I know about Hunan food? Then I realized why I felt this way. The food on the table was lacking the precision of the food pictured on the menu. I don't mean that the portion was smaller, like most restaurants do against their photographed food. I mean, the food pictured in the menu looked well defined, with sharper edges, and food on the table looked like slop. We had three dishes; some kind of potato slop, some kind of mushroom with ground beef slop, and then the king daddy, fish head soup.

Calling it soup makes it sound like someone put effort into stewing the right ingredients together for hours, but as far as I could tell, someone pulled this big fish out the tank, gutted it and chopped off its tail, and threw it into a boiling pot with lots of red pepper flakes. I mean, I think the thing must have been alive just a few minutes ago, because one side of its head appeared to still be raw. That didn't stop Emma from taking pieces of it and putting it on to my plate for me to eat. I had to try it. I don't know if its brain matter, although I suppose it would have to be, but there was whitish pinkish sludge on my plate that I had to try to chew and swallow. Some of the meat she put on my plate was white, somewhat normal, fish meat, but every time that sludge smooshed around my mouth, I had to spit it out. The fish was full of little bones that made eating it incredibly tedious and nerve racking. Emma asked me if I wanted to eat the eye.

"What? No way! You're going to eat that?! It's not even cooked! Oh my god. I want to see you eat that."

I was just wowed. This is something people would only do on a TV show for hundreds, if not, thousands of dollars in my country. When the other side of the fish head flipped around, it verified my conclusion. That fish eye was white– cooked. We were drinking a beer from north China, Harbin Beer, and I suddenly couldn't tell if I was drunk or sick, or both. I started to get dizzy and I was trying not to look at the food. My stomach started to hurt and swell. I tried to show that I was okay with everything going on, but I wasn't doing a very good job of it. I just kept shaking my head. Emma was a little bit insulted and said, "Why did you come to China again?" I was trying to convey the "newness" of the whole experience for me to her. I also tried to see if I could find out anything more about how they cook it, "So, in Hunan, I guess they live near a river and don't have much ingredients, huh? They just kind of throw a fish head in some hot water and cover it with spice?" I didn't make much headway. She just said, "I don't know, you can ask the chef."

My gut began to jerk around a bit. Damn it, I really did myself in this time. I started to think to myself. I saw a book in a doctor's office once, titled something like, "The China Way." I pulled it off the shelf and it was a big book full of world statistics with all measurable health problems that can be derived from food. China crushed the whole world with their level of health; cholesterol, life age expectancy, blood pressure, and all kinds of other things. China ranked so high in some instances that they surpassed the rest of the world two-fold, while the USA constantly ranked last. China's bar graphs towered over America's. I started to think, maybe by eating food like this, they build up an incredible immune system that can easily process nutrients and fight harmful bacteria. I was dreaming of getting something like ice-cream in my stomach and getting home to be nearby a toilet. Both of those dreams came true.

The next morning my stomach felt like I had been doing sit-ups all night. I couldn't help but think, this is one reason why Chinese are so healthy. It seems like everywhere you eat here, there is a lot of steam coming off the food and onto your clothes and hair. I'm figuring where that distinct smell, that so many Chinese have, comes from. That, and the drinking water. I think that I'm starting to get that smell too. A European lady passed me on the street the other day smelling like perfume. It was an incredible smell that I had forgotten. I wasn't in a rush to do anything this morning, just pat my stomach and work on getting my phone up to speed. I called the club that Heena wanted to go to for New Year's Eve to make a reservation. I gave the lady my full name and number and then she said, "That will be 3000 (RMB)". That was the cost of one month's rent for me. I told her that I would have to call her back.

I had to find a similar club to make reservations for. Unlike in the USA, you don't have to make reservations here weeks, or months in advance. NYE is only important to foreigners and the people attracted to foreigners. The best place I could find was a place called M1NT. Justin Timberlake's DJ will be playing there, so I figured he must be playing some good dance music. The entry fee was reasonable, 200 RMB per person. The catch was that the dress code is "black tie". I didn't bring any ties with me, or any black button-up shirts, or black pants, or black shoes. After making the reservation over the phone, I put on a windbreaker to walk over to a store I saw before that had ties and shirts. It wasn't that cold outside and I didn't think I would be out long.

I walked in the front door of the store and there was one elderly lady sitting behind the counter. Chinese language: Engage. I said I was looking for a black tie and she started talking to me. The problem with getting good at speed and pronunciation is that people think you must be able to have a conversation. I asked about a discount if I bought a shirt with the tie. There wasn't one that I could tell. I have the Calculator App on my iPhone on the main desktop now, and asked her to type the price for me. Here we go, I was going to try to bargain. She typed a number above 400 RMB, then I did the conversion math and typed 245 RMB to show her what I wanted. I knew what I wanted to pay, 33 USD, and her price started at over $60. She said something disgruntling, grabbed a different black shirt from the shelf that she didn't show me before, and then typed 300 RMB to show me the new price. I was so happy to finally be bargaining that I replied, "Hao", which means O.K.. Of course, that wasn't bargaining at all, she just got a cheaper shirt. My credit cards weren't working in her machine and when I took out all my cash from my wallet, it only came to about 270. I was hoping that she would just accept that, but she wasn't happy, so I told her I would go get more cash and come back. After I pulled more money from the ATM, I started to heavily doubt the value of the shirt and tie.

Every time I have bought a cheap button-up shirt in the past, they are never tailor-fit and they tuck in like a table cloth into pants. They bulk out and look so stupid, that I might as well have worn a t-shirt because if this was to improve my look, it fails every time. I paced around in front of the bank, weighing the overpriced shirt and tie, versus the 48 hours I had before the event. I finally decided to text Heena the price of the set and asked her if she thought it was fare. I also knew I was fooling myself because Heena can't see what kind of shirt and tie it is and I already know how I value apparel. She told me to go back to that enormous mall that everyone is always telling me to go to. She said there were some after-Christmas discounts. The steps to the subway station were literally 20 meters from where I was pacing, so I headed towards that god damned mall.

Here I was, circling the second floor of this fucking mall for the millionth time. Then the third floor. Sure, THEN I figure out that the first two floors are only women's clothing. Then I start browsing men's stores on the third floor and it seemed like no-one carried a black shirt or black tie. I was getting fed up. These "discounts" that were supposed to be so great, were still astronomical. A baseball cap was $30. This is fucking China, you are telling me that a factory within 6 miles of here isn't producing that baseball cap for less than $2? That just fueled my frustration. I finally just bought a black tie and crossed off buying any black clothes. I have some work slacks and gray button-up shirts that I brought. I will wear them with this stupid black tie and my white tennis shoes. You know what happens on NYE? You get drunk. You get drunk in a three or four hour time-frame, spill liquor all over yourself, possibly get thrown up on, peed on, and pass out half naked somewhere. I really don't need to invest in an outfit for that.

For my last New Year's Eve, I stayed home and did

kungfu all over the house to classical music. I had enough New Year's Eve parties. The year before that, I just remember holding a woman's hand to my heart when her boyfriend came over to me to give me the news. I can't even remember most of my NYEs except how quickly they come and go. I'm not going to make a big deal out of this one. I just want to have a few drinks and dance around with Heena before getting out of there.

I had just walked into my front door when I received a text message from Rachel. I met Rachel on the Shanghai personals website, but I didn't know her well. We had discussed her helping me study Chinese at some point and her text message was asking me if I was home. I called her, rather than texting her back, just to speak with her. Her voice was raspy, a little unsuspecting from the cute picture of her on the website. I tried not to judge her and told her that I could get together tonight or tomorrow night. We didn't live too close to each other, so I asked if she knew of a place that we could meet at in between our locations. She said, she will just come to my house if there is room here, so I told her it was messy, but that was okay with me. I walked over to meet her at the subway station, and waited, and waited. She took twice as long as she said she would. When I met her at the Subway exit, her eyes were focused very deeply and she was pretty. I couldn't help but wonder why she was single and so quick to come over.

When she came into the house, I had my books open and ready to go. We started right off and were making good progress. Every so often, she wouldn't know the English word to explain to me something, so I would use a dictionary along with a translating dictionary, and teach her the word. I spent a lot of time helping her pronunciation, and we covered three lessons in my book. It was challenging, but I thought we made a good language partnership. After almost two hours of that, I asked if she wanted to see a movie and pulled up Hulu on my laptop. She was sitting up against me and by the end of the film, we were cuddling. It was late and in this apartment, only one heater can run at a time, so this room was very warm and the other room was very cold. I was happy just to lay on the couch and sleep next to her. A few times she awoke and said that she had to go home, but she didn't stand up. Finally, once my arm was dead asleep, I said we should go into the next room because there's more room there. Again, she said she had to go home. I said it was late and she should stay and again, she said she had to go home. I wasn't going to argue about it, so I said, "OK". Then, I wasn't sure if I heard her correctly, because her English was very poor, but I thought she said, "OK, I need money for the taxi." I was kind of expecting and willing to pay for her taxi ride because the subway was closed and we didn't plan on her staying so late, so I got 40RMB out to give to her. That was enough to get clear across town and I knew which subway stop she lived near.

"40? No, no, no, no, no that's not enough. I need more money."

"Huh? More? 40's not enough? How much do you need?"

"No, no, no, no this is not enough. You give me more."

"How much do you need? You tell me."

"40's not enough."

"OK, duo shao?" I'm trying Chinese now, because I'm not getting an answer.

"You have more money? Give me more money."

Now I am going from confusion to weary, "I don't understand. 40 is enough to take you to the airport. You can get home."

"No, 40 is not enough for the airport. 40 is not enough for me to go home and come back."

"What do you mean, go home and come back? You just need to go home."

"No, I took the taxi here, and you aren't paying for it."

"What? I picked you up at the subway."

"No, I took taxi. You pay me now, and you can come over my place next time. You want?"

"How much do you want?"

"I want 200. Just give me 200. I need to buy some clothes. My clothes are no good. I need new clothes."

The whole time she is somewhat smiling and trying to act sweet, and loudly passing gas.

"I don't understand. Ting bu dong. Wo bu zhidao. Is this a Chinese thing? You just want me to give you money? I'm not giving you 200. Wo gei ni si-shi-quai."

"Come on. I teach you Chinese."

I am telling her that I don't understand her and that I am giving her 40 RMB. She starts getting loud and refusing to go. I put my jacket and hat on and I'm telling her in English and Chinese that she needs to come with me.

"No, you give me 200, I go. I don't need you to go with me. You give me 200, and I go."

I am not budging, but I'm getting worried. Twenty minutes has already passed. This reminds me of in 2006 when my friend and I went to a Karaoke bar here for his birthday and these girls came to sing with us. When the bill came, it was $600. I was arguing the bill when the cute, lusty-eyed girl that had been singing on my lap snapped at me that I ordered more than the one beer that I was proclaiming I ordered. This was a lot to handle. I wouldn't have gone out to get a prostitute and I sure as hell would have expected some form of sex before paying one. I was getting afraid that she might break something, like my computer that was right in front of her. I picked up her purse and handed it to her along with her jacket, "Come on, come on, come on, come on."

She reached in her giant handbag and I expected at any moment she was going to pull out a weapon. Nothing. I grabbed her and tried lifting her up. It was a title weight belt, "Spoiled American from Richtown, USA vs. Outdoor Clothes-Washer from Hillbilly province (with lots more experience in this situation than I have)." I was worried that she might also make enough noise shouting that the police would get involved. Foreigners have to inform the police of their residency within X amount of time here, so this could cause quite an issue. I gave her the 40, and walked down the stairs with her. We walked down the alleyway, not sharing any words. I was walking ten feet in front of her. It was 3 AM. I hailed a cab and as she passed by me to get into the cab, she said, "bye" and I said, "zaijian".

I immediately called my good friend Micah F. when I walked back into the house and told him the whole story and how crazy the whole thing was. I needed to see if Micah could figure out what just happened and why. I was so glad he answered and I could share with him right away. I needed to go to sleep because I had to start cleaning and packing in just a few more hours. I'll be heading to a new place tomorrow, and at just the right time.

A Lighter Shade of Smog

I cleaned up Jay's place pretty well and left his sheets, towels, and pillow cases hanging in the sun room to dry after washing them. I never did hear from him, but I assumed he would still be arriving later in the day. For all I know, he never left China. I packed up all of my stuff again, which is more of a chore now because I have some new things, and then I made a few trips carrying it all down four flights of steps. There was no friendly neighbor to help me this time. I have to roll a giant suitcase on two rollerblade-like wheels on its back edge, while carrying my laptop bag around my shoulder, my new yoga mat-bag around my other shoulder, and pushing my expanded carryon bag crooked on its two wheels with my long guitar case strapped on top of it, balancing. The alleyway street is textured in notches and it's horrible for my luggage wheels to roll over. I made it to the street, and there were too many scooters and bicycles parked on the sidewalk to use the sidewalk to get to the busier intersection, so I had to roll down the street this way, until I could hail a cab.

I made it over to this hostel, a sister hostel (same owner) of the other hostel I was staying in. It's back in another type of alleyway and this time the street is laid bricks. There was no other way to carry my stuff, other than to roll it, and eventually one of the wheels on my giant suitcase broke off. I checked in and was ultra-friendly to my new hosts, talking to them about the girl hosts in the other hostel and some of my stories from there. I asked where I could get a sandwich and after I dropped my luggage off in my room, I went out. This hostel used to be a towel factory and it's very large with a lot of open space and games. There's also a cool indoor/outdoor roof café. A lot of English speaking foreigners are coming and going here. I went out and started to follow my host's directions towards a busy restaurant area. Half a block down the street, there was a crispy fried chicken vendor and I bought a big drum stick for less than a dollar. It was so good that for the duration of my walk, I was in search of a KFC. I was thinking, it's too bad I am going to pay more for less, I should have just stayed at that vendor and bought 5 more drumsticks.

It was a long walk southward and I was, again, paying attention to all of the landmarks. I remembered visiting Mike in Queens, NY back when I was maybe 22 years old, and leaving his place early in the morning for a run. When I walked out the front door, I mentally noted there was a white building across the street and started jogging. The streets in Astoria, Queens are numbered and so are the avenues. Mike lived at approximately 33rd and 33rd, and it turned out that there were many other white buildings. After three hours of trying to find his building and trying to go inside wrong buildings, I used the five dollars I brought with me to take the subway back into Manhattan to my Aunt's store, looked up his phone number on the computer, and called him to get directions back. Since then, I am very observant of my surroundings. I am paying attention to every little thing I see.

The restaurant area my host suggested I visit was not much of a restaurant area at all. There were equally the same number of restaurants next to the hostel, including a SANDWICH restaurant on the corner. However, there was a large benefit to going this far out of my way, the sight of Jing An Temple. I haven't researched its history yet, but I at least heard of it and it's the name of one of the closest subway stops. I am in the Jing An district, but I don't know if it is named after the temple or vice versa. I saw the temple from a distance when the cab took me to the hostel, but it looked small from my view. Up close, I could see it's about 30 stories tall and elaborately decorated. It looked small before because it's neighboring enormous skyscrapers. It is very strange to see such a temple here. It raises a number of questions that need answering. I made it back to the crispy fried chicken vendor, brought 5 drumsticks back to the hostel, and took a long nap.

I woke up pretty late and had a number of thoughts during my walk earlier that day. I noticed how there was an extreme amount of effort to make Shanghai look appealing; lots of flowers, trees, decorative road blocks, continuous street cleaning. And I noticed how the best it does is make these streets seem decent. I started to think about the sun and how I haven't been able to see it since I got here. I was thinking about how most of the people in the world are outside somewhere and can see a blue sky and a bright sun with some puffy white clouds nearby. That hit me pretty hard and I had to kind of slap myself out of it. Shanghai feels like a party that never ends. A place you can check into and forget to check out of. I was thinking about the night before and was feeling sour about that too.

When I woke up from my nap, I browsed some books on my Kindle. I came across a book titled something like, "A Sex Guide for China". I downloaded an excerpt and decided this was mandatory reading after what happened to me the night before. Reading this guy's account for paying for, and not paying for, sex all over China repulsed me. It felt like I discovered my wife's (analogy, I'm single) secret stash of letters to and from her current sex partners. I hated reading it, but I couldn't stop. I started to feel so grateful for my experiences with Heena, Shauna, Ginger, and Emma here, because if I had only read this book, I wouldn't have seen any of them. Sure enough, under the Independent Prostitutes section of the book, I read the following:

"Play the Hero or Get Left with Zero: A very general rule in China is that good girls that are not prostitutes will not make the first move on a Westerner. The point is that only girls with schemes in mind will approach Western guys and ask to "practice English", or "show you my art", or even "go to a bar" – which may sound innocent, but is guaranteed to result in a large bill and a shocked look on your face long after the girls have ditched the scene in pursuit of another unsuspecting victim. If you didn't initiate the conversation, then beware- forward girls tend to be scammers with ulterior motives."[1]

That rang a bell, and I read that short-term prostitutes charge anywhere from 300 to 500 RMB. Rachel wanted 200, that's probably because we only studied together. I learned a couple of other important things to look out for. I am really glad that I learned many barbershops are brothels because I wanted to get my haircut the next day and knew what to look out for. The book kind of made me hate being here and I had the horrible thought that a fraction of my female English students would grow up to sell their bodies. I feel a lot more prepared now to stay on the defense and go by my guidelines when meeting someone new here. I woke up in the morning even feeling lower than the day before. That book was like the nail in the coffin. I hadn't had much exercise in days and I was beginning to feel

---

1   Parson, Robert. *China Sex Guide (An Adult Nightlife Guide)* 2011 [Kindle Edition]

like sludge. I had to do something about it, or I was going to be defeated by China, plus I was supposed to go clubbing that night with Henna for NYE.

I pulled myself together to look at the 3D map of Shanghai and started comparing it to a Bing map and the hostel's map to try and get my bearings. It's difficult, believe me. I searched for keywords like "gym", "martial art", "dance", "exercise", and "kungfu" and I wasn't finding anything in this general region of Shanghai. At least no results from searching in English. I looked for a park. Nothing anywhere. The closest park that I could see was far north, right next to the place I would be moving in to. That made me feel really lucky, but at the same time, just bewildered that there is no room in this city to do anything except walk and ride to places. Suddenly, I noticed a running track just a few blocks north of here and got dressed to go find it. I was ready to spend hours there and brought my tiny Shuffle iPod. Walking there, I thought to myself that Big Government should create parks so people can be healthy and have some hint of quality living here, but parks don't make any money, so instead you find the tearing down of small buildings to be replaced with high-rises. I read in the paper today that 24 billion dollars in foreigner investment came to Shanghai this year, a new record. There was a hole, an empty air space without tall buildings, and that's how I found the running track. Right when I was stepping onto the track, I heard, "Hey! Hey! Heyyyy!" As seemingly universal as "Hey" sounds, it's English, so I turned around to see who was shouting at me.

An angry guy walked up to me and asked me in Chinese if I was going to go running here. When I told him yes, he said no, I can't do that here. His face was bitter and he started to walk away, but I couldn't just let him kill my chance of happiness. This was the only place I could fight off my weaning delight for life. "Wei shenme?" I asked him why in Chinese, knowing full and well that I wasn't going to understand what he was going to tell me. He gave me an answer in two sentences, still looking ticked off, and then I asked him in Chinese, "Ok, then where can I run?" He said he didn't know, and when I thanked him in Chinese, he cracked a brief smile.

I couldn't just give up. I knew there was no real park in a 15 mile radius of where I was, so I was looking for some room on a sidewalk, or anywhere that I could hide away. It was impossible. There was nowhere to hide. I was about to start doing exercises on a wider sidewalk. Just like exercise in general, it's harder to exercise in front of people when you aren't in good shape than it is exercising in front of people when you are tuned up pretty well. I decided that I had to run first and made a little prayer for my iPod to keep me focused while running the sidewalks of Shanghai. Aside from the extreme difficulties and dangers of running through the streets here, you know how incredibly foolish you look to these people because their daily life is so brutally and physically demanding. There is not going to be the thought process of deciphering luxurious healthy running for enjoyment. I could only think, thank god that China hosted the last Olympics, because at least I know they have seen sport running before.

I didn't expect, or plan, to be jogging around the city like this and at least not so soon. It's weird for so many reasons. It's a harsh environment where you have to hulk loogies hourly just to breath. The whole time I was running, I was looking for somewhere to hide away to do kungfu. I found a boarded-up bank on a quiet road across the street from a construction site. It was the best place I could find, so I started doing some stretches, movements with a lowered center of gravity, and some kick stretches. It took me some time, but I noticed the building next to the construction site wasn't under construction. The giant 50 story residential building had burned – one of my biggest fears of living on the top floor of a high-rise. There were still people walking by and one guy was smoking a cigarette right in front of me. I was feeling a lot better because when I was first walking to the running track, I had felt a pinched nerve in my left upper left leg and I could now feel myself starting to repair.

I started running more around the city, turning the volume on my iPod as loud as it could go so I could focus. If there was ever a place *not* to go running, it's here. Then, on the corner of a street, I discovered another boarded up building, but this one had a stair entry with an overhead and some kind of columns in the front. I could almost hide there. Eureka. I stayed there for 40 minutes, first doing some light kungfu and then working my way up to some more intense kungfu. On the mega scale of irony, this weighed heavily with me. Millions of Chinese are walking around here that do zero kungfu, and here I am feeling like I am doing a series of completely foreign exercises, in front of these people, and these movements were invented by the Chinese. WTF? The truth is that, throughout China's history, kungfu became outlawed many times. From the earlier years where it threatened the military's defense against the emperor, to the later and most recent years of Mao's cultural revolution and his doing away with all things traditionally Chinese. Most educated kungfu masters relocated outside of China and today kungfu may consist of more elaborate systems outside of China's mainland.

After finishing my exercises, I went back to the hostel to ask where a barber shop is. I was really nervous about walking into the wrong kind of barber shop and asking for a "clean up" and being taken into a back room for a "rub down". I was so relieved to see young guys cutting women's hair when I walked into the door of the place I found. I used my translator and told them I wanted a trim. The experience was bar none. I am one of the few guys you will ever know that once paid $120 for a haircut, before going to Vegas for the first time to find a Guitar Jacket material manufacturer. My experience in this barbershop for $11, surpassed that $120 Vidal Sassoon experience, big time! I got a 20 minute massage and shampoo, followed by a 40 minute scissor-cut trim. I'm bald on top of my head and have very short hair on the sides. At some point, I realized that cutting my hair might be more tricky than cutting a woman's long hair. If you miss a single one of my hairs, it will be noticeable. I was so impressed during the whole haircut, I just wish I could have conveyed that to the guy. All I can really say is, "excellent" and "thank you".

Before heading back to the hostel, I wanted to have something to eat in that sandwich place I saw the day before. I walked in and there was a white guy in line ahead of me wearing snow pants, a snow jacket, a knit cap, and had his ear pierced. I just had a sweatshirt on. I could see he was agitated, and that he was French. I don't know another kind of Caucasian that will carry themselves the way some French men do – arrogantly. He was just acting like no one should mess with him. I started to order and he jumped in front of me and snapped at the young Chinese guy taking my order, "Hey, can I have my coffee please?" He looked at me and said, "Sorry, but I'm here waiting." He shook his head and walked out the door. I thought, "And that's why you lost your concession, dickhead." I was wondering how that guy was going to walk out the door and deal with Shanghai. We're guests here. I am unyieldingly nice to everyone I encounter here and can't believe that he would snap at someone in English about service. I wished all the worst for that guy and continued making my order and trying to use Chinese to do it.

I got back to my room and called Heena. She would be at my subway station in two hours and I had to iron my clothes. In the sister hostel I stayed at when I first arrived here, I asked about the iron I left there in 2006 and the lady told me their sister hostel (where I am now) has it. Well, in my hands again was the iron I bought back then. It barely fucking worked. My shirt was still full or wrinkles and none of my clothes fitted me right. It seems like the never-ending story, I think my clothes fit, then the next season I put them on and they are too big, or too long. There wasn't anything I could do about it now, and I still had to get my eye contact lenses in. I don't wear them often enough to be able to get them onto my eyes in any remotely normal amount of time. I headed out with just enough time to get to the station by the time Heena arrived.

Heena looked and smelled great. We never have much of a greeting, or a good-bye, when I see her. We just started walking to the hostel's bar to have some pre-party drinks. We stopped in a store to see if they had any black shoes that fit me, but they were too over-priced. I realized that I couldn't tell Heena exactly what I wanted to because her English wasn't completely fluent, and I thought that we would probably have some great conversations if we understood each other a little better. However, we did get to know each other more. I loaded up on some drinks at the hostel's bar while Heena sipped on her single rum & coke, which she didn't enjoy. Other Americans, Australians, Canadians, and Britts were at the bar sharing traveling stories. One scrawny, wraggely Australian guy had 4 hot Chinese girls come to meet him there and they all started to play cards with each other in the corner. I couldn't help but think that this guy's never going back to Australia.

Heena and I subwayed towards the closest stop to the club, and then had to take an unmarked car the rest of the way. It's never safe to do that, but it beats walking and if you work the price out first and you're with someone, it's not as dangerous. The club's bouncer was a white American guy, approximately my age. I thought, nice, I can handle this guy. Heena and I were both nervous about my white tennis shoes and shared that in Japan and the US, I could never get into a club wearing them. We passed the bouncer and walked into the front door where at least six Chinese security guards wearing suits were waiting for us. They directed us to a European lady with a list of names. She flirted with me about the name DiFlip being the same as a famous Dutch Boxer and so on. I was only thinking, be nice to this lady so we can get in. We checked our coats beside two Chinese girls wearing red dresses and rode the elevator up with them. I think I read about these ladies in my China Sex Guide.

The club was two stories tall and on the top floor of the building. Outside the window, there was a direct view of the Bund. The Bund is a German word for the waterfront here. Many of the famous landmark skyscrapers were towering outside across the river, lit up with dazzling lights. I ordered a red bull and vodka and Heena got a Japanese beer. The club was mostly tables and couches, so there wasn't a lot of floor space. It was 10:30 PM and it was still half empty. Along the wall of the hallway to the VIP rooms, there was one of the longest shark aquariums in China. Little dog-sized sharks swam alongside you as you walked down the hallway. The music was pumping hard and I was already ready to dance. I started to explain to Heena some of my club dancing strategies. I looked up the Chinese word for "defense" on my phone and showed it to her.

"You see this?" I pointed at the floor between her and I.

"That's space. I always try to cover as much space as I

116

can, and stay low to the ground."

I started demonstrating how I take dance steps to cover and fill as much area as I can between us and other people standing near us.

"If a big guy bumps into me, don't worry, he will never mess with me. I dance too hard. It's how I stay safe."

While I'm telling Heena my dance strategies, the white guy next to us is groping his Chinese girlfriend, squeezing both of her breasts. The party hasn't even really started yet and I think it's pretty inappropriate to do that right beside us. He was standing shoulder to shoulder with Heena and I was ready and waiting to punch him out cold if he touched Heena in any way. I thought to myself, 3 seconds, that's all it will take me. Every three minutes I tried to pull Heena onto the dance floor. The dance floor was really tiny and no one was dancing yet. I told her that I came to dance and exercise, otherwise why spend all that money. She agreed.

Finally, I got her to stand on the edge of the dance floor, leaning against a booth. I couldn't stop dancing and kept trying to get her to come onto the floor with me. I was trying to sell the benefits of dancing to her every way that I could and slowly, other girls started to come onto the dance floor. She kept saying that she would just watch me dance and I would then have to explain that we came together. I don't know if Heena had been to too many clubs, but when a male is dancing on the floor, other girls quickly come to dance with him. On the other hand, if a girl is standing on the edge of a dance floor watching, loads of guys will quickly try to buy her a drink. There was no way I was going to leave space between us and I eventually got her to at least stand next to me on the dance floor as more people begin to follow our lead and come onto the floor.

The dancing got more and more intense and I would shout to her, "Don't stop dancing! It's not safe. Never stop!" Unless you like being bounced around like a rag doll, you have to keep exhorting energy and moving your feet so you can stay stable. The more crowded it got, the closer I danced to Heena and eventually she stopped awkwardly swaying and started dancing. By midnight, I had a hand on her, really to protect her from the rowdy people banging around and people trying to push through the crowd. We were surrounded by white girls with lots of cleavage and I thought, this is these girls at their best, Heena crushes them on a daily basis. We had to leave by 12:30 because Heena has to catch a train latter in the day (traveling as usual). The party was really hopping now and there was a line to get in. I wasn't able to get a hostel near this club because I booked the one I am staying at when we planned to go to another club in a different location. I knew we weren't going to find an available cab and traffic was deadlock.

We had to walk more than three miles away from the Bund in pursuit of finding a free cab. The streets were totally crowded. I told Heena, "Watch this. When you see a foreigner, say Happy New Year." Every time a white guy passed, I'd say,

"Happy New Year!" and they would say, "Happy New Year!" back. There were huge crowds everywhere, actually a typical night on this part of town, except with the additional foreign crowd. It became hopeless to find a cab, so we stopped in a restaurant to eat. The chicken in China tastes like a different animal entirely. It's so flavorful and all of the bones are always included. When we finished, it was 2:30 in the morning and we were able to find a cab dropping someone off and quickly jumped in. I was dropped off at my hostel. Heena was in the front seat to help with navigation, so I rubbed her back and told her goodnight before she sped off in the Taxi. I thought, I must be one of the only guys going home alone from that place, but I don't care. I had a really good time with Heena and I know she had a good time too. She is lady that the author of my newest book would never get to know. Happy New Year.

Foreign Native 101

"I'd like to tell you what I mean, but I'm too fucking stupid." There you have it, through the eyes of a foreigner. At least twice today, probably more, I was caught staring blankly at a Chinese person like a deer in headlights when they asked me a question. I tell them that my Chinese is no good, but they act like it's a cue for them to ask me more questions. It's a crummy feeling and I try to tell everyone that I'm new here, but I have yet to have anyone understand me. Maybe "New" doesn't make sense in this context. I think that I have decided to stay in Shanghai until my level of Chinese is highly proficient, and then to move on. I imagine there are places where the air is opposite of here – cleansing instead of damaging. It's a fun place, with a lot going on, but life's too short and mother Earth does a lot better than this.

After a day of taking it easy, this morning I packed up my belongings and was dropped off at the wrong apartment complex I had to ask the security guard there if I could leave some of my luggage so I could take two trips to my new place in Shanghai. I felt abandoned because Ken wasn't answering his phone, but it turns out that it's not easy to get cell phone reception from the top floors. Ken quickly showed me a few things in the house, like how to wash my sheets because they weren't clean, and some other things around the house. Then he had to go to the bank and I had to pay him rent, so I came along with him.

Ken walked his mountain bicycle while I walked beside him and I started to ask him some of the million questions I had, like how he came to Shanghai, and, if he planned on marrying a Chinese. Ken is probably as close as you can come to being a Chinese citizen, without being married to one or having family here. He left Australia directly after graduating university to travel the world and ended up staying in Tokyo for two years. Then he heard of an opportunity to be Cruise Director of an American Cruise ship that sailed from Chongqing to Shanghai and back on the Yangtze River. He did that for two years and spent his winters staying in Shanghai, until some other opportunities came up for him to stay here. I don't know the details of how he came to own his bar yet, but I'm sure I will eventually find out.

I asked Ken about some of the horrible experiences he had being shiested by women here, or, tricked by some guys. I couldn't believe it, he couldn't think of one incident. Between my visiting Shanghai and being here for the last two weeks, I already have a number of stories. It was refreshing to hear that from him and gave me some hope that this can be a more normal environment to live in. Of course, when I walked in the door he told me, "Ya, we just got this new door. The other one broke when someone was trying to break in." Naturally, I responded, "What do you mean... someone was trying to break in?" And he just kind of shrugged it off. No element of security in this complex actually works. There are a number of things that look like they work, but none of them do.

I had to withdraw cash from the ATM four times before I had enough money to pay Ken for one month of rent plus one month security deposit. It felt like a lot of money to give someone, but that's because more than six one-hundred renminbi bills equals one one-hundred dollar bill. He came out of the bank exclaiming that they wrote his phone number down and would call him if they could give him change by breaking his larger bills into smaller bills. He told me that it's a huge hassle to find a bank that will give him change so he has smaller bills at the bar to run his business, so we walked over to another bank. After 10 years of living in China, Ken has no trouble with speaking Chinese and I swear that I can hear his Australian accent when he speaks it. This bank, Bank of China, would only give him about $80 worth of smaller bills. Every two weeks, Ken has to ride around on his bicycle with a backpack full of cash in pursuit of trading larger bills in for smaller bills. After he visits the banks, he visits another bar where they exchange the majority of his money because that owner's wife flirts with a banker. It's not over yet. Ken has to rely on his Chinese business partner for all legal ownership matters, including his domestic banking. For transferring money to Australia, he uses an international bank, and first meets with a Russian that converts his RMB money into USD. He told me it's very difficult to get renminbi out of the country.

I spent the next number of hours scrubbing everything in my new room. So far, I have used an entire paper towel roll and two rags, and I still have to wash the windows. This room was absolutely filthy, but it's starting to shine and I am looking forward to going to a department store tomorrow to buy some things to make it feel more like my room. The house looks like bachelors live in it and currently has the stench of stale wheat beer, hopefully just because of their New Year's Party. It appears that cleaning is completely reliant upon the maid, and it looks like she has a losing battle. I am trying to sanitize everything. I flipped my mattress, then sprayed it down, then ironed it. I am not using the blanket tonight. I need to find a way to wash it good before I start sleeping with it. It's too big for the washer, but I think I can use the shower and hang it in the sun room tomorrow.

I asked Ken if all the roommates were friends here and ever do things together. He said that Patrick works too much and the Frenchman is always at his girlfriend's. When I asked if he ever had trouble with any of his tenants, he told me that he had to ask someone to leave before. I was expecting to hear that the guy left his wet towels out or something like that. No. This guy would leave his used condoms on the floor, bring home hookers that would try to rob the house, and once left virgin blood stains on Ken's sheets when he was out of town. Wow. I'm a saint. Ken will be going to Australia tomorrow and that means I will be left to fend for myself here. Patrick is going to Taiwan and I don't know anything about the French guy, including his name or what he looks like. After hours of scrubbing, I was starving, but really didn't want to go out and struggle ordering some exotic food in some exotic new restaurant. I don't know this area yet.

Not eating isn't always the best alternative to having to deal with adversity, even though I have pretty much only been eating two meals a day to cut down on the challenge of knowing what to eat, where to get it, and how to order it. I went for a walk around the neighborhood to find a place that wasn't completely full of people and that had some pictures on the window of something I felt like I could eat. I walked in a place called 7 to 7 and looked at the buffet. I was hungry, but eating there wasn't a good enough excuse to play Russian roulette with my stomach. I continued on and just when I had completed a circle around the neighborhood, I found a Pizza Hut. It's actually right out front of my place and somehow I missed it before. The menu at Pizza Hut had a lot more than just pizza, but I ordered a pizza anyway. The restaurant didn't have anything to drink except Pepsi, so I told another customer that was waiting that I was going to go buy a bottle of water and come back. She knew my Chinese vocabulary wasn't very strong and decided to come with me to help me.

The pizza was delicious. It was no different than a Pizza made in America, except that it didn't have condiments to choose from like red pepper flakes or black pepper. I saw a shaker full of black pepper behind the desk and went to grab it, but it was glued down for direction only. When I came back, Patrick was here and we talked for a few minutes. He said he had to sleep for a few hours and then go to work at 1 in the morning. That sounds like a bit much and reminds me of that traditional Chinese work ethic. I'm in my bed now and can't sleep because the mattress is too hard and the room is too cold. The wall heater sucks and I don't have any blankets yet. I need to get a floor radiator, except I need these electrical outlets changed to three-prong for me to use it. That means I have to find an electrician, or handyman, as soon as possible. I hope he's able to make it work, cause I won't be able to power much with only two-prong outlets. I'll just wait for it to be morning and spend the day tired. Once I buy some blankets and a pillow, I'll come back here to finally get some sleep. It's kind of a good feeling to have my own place, and my own neighborhood. If you want to call it that.

ISDEP

Innovation, Sustainability, Diplomacy,

Economics, and Pizza

There's little and big lessons to be learned here. Not just for me, but as a nation. Little things like the lady in the subway station that has a number of contraptions in her vending space under a flight of stairs to be able to supply you with a drink, snack, or any little pick-me-up you need. I asked her for a cup of coffee. It appeared she only had a cold bottle of coffee and I was about to walk away when she told me to hold on and grabbed a cup out of the pantry. There were three jars and a big hot thermos of water and she took one scoop of each, put the cup in a contraption to seal a lid on it, asked if I wanted a straw, poked it through, and handed me a delicious hot cup of coffee – all in about 30 seconds or less. That's not the only good idea happening in the subway systems.

The subway stations have a couple different kinds of computer machines in them. You can search an interactive map of the subway station in 3D, or a map of the surrounding neighborhood. There's always at least one ATM machine and there's these other interactive touch-screens with restaurants on them, but I don't know how they are used yet. If you are purchasing a single-ride train ticket, you select the station you are going to on a touch-screen computer, in English or Chinese, and it calculates the amount for you. Dollar coins are everywhere and it makes a lot of snacks easy to purchase. A lot of the newer downtown subway stations have a glass wall that separates the underground track from the waiting platform, which keeps the station smelling fresh, climate controlled, and protects the tracks from accidents or homeless salvage. The trains come every few minutes and they are usually clean and warm. There is full mobile service underground and there are televisions onboard, and in the stations, to keep you entertained. The subway line is displayed, sometimes showing a light where you currently are, and the stops are announced in Chinese and English. Unlike every subway system I have ever been on in the US (Boston, LA, Chicago, DC, Miami, and NYC), the trains are full of totally unthreatening people (so far). There's nothing to worry about and no-one to avoid.

Steps usually lead you down into the subway station and escalators usually carry you out. The train rides are smooth, quick, and quiet. Somehow, the station floors are always polished, and often there are enormous LCD screens playing advertisements specifically designed for them. The exits leading out of the stations are always labeled by number, so you can give clear directions to people and establish meeting points. Sometimes, there are stores and shops inside, and outside of the gates. There is a manned ticket booth for placing more credit on your subway card, and there are security guards (usually in their early 20's) that determine whether or not they want to examine your bag in the X-ray machine. The subway lines are numbered, colored, and sprawl in every direction, including looping around the river. I have an application on my phone that calculates the best way to get to a destination, and there are interactive maps online as well.

One of the most un-American things about this place is the lack of energy consumption. Now, for me, hot water, warm restaurants, and bright lights are all things of the past. It's rare to come across all of these things except for in large public places. If you were to do the math on how much energy is saved by the people in Shanghai alone, you would most definitely reach a staggering number. I don't know how to comprehend wattage or voltage, or however you measure energy, but it would be financially accounted for in well past a billion dollars. The World Watch Institute, along with some other notable organizations, has estimated that Americans, on average, use ten times as much energy as Chinese. Shanghai might be an exception, but it's still not equal. In fact, if the people of China used as much energy as Americans, it would require more barrels of oil, per day, than the whole world can currently produce. The conservation of energy is one of the ONLY explanations I can come up with when imagining how this city can exist. Any rational person would tell you it's not inhabitably possible.

There are recycling, and non-recycling, waste bins

scattered throughout the city. No one pays any attention to which is which and they are filled with everything you can think of. The magic is that there are so many people going through trashcans here to sort out recyclables to turn in for cash, that all of the rubbish is sorted and recycled or disposed of correctly in the end. The street cleaning and garbage sorting is ongoing and continuous. For useful garbage, or to purchase second-hand items, there are thrifters on wheels. These guys exist in every city and all you need to get started in their industry is a tricycle with a bin on the back and a hand bell. These guys ride around on their bikes, all day long, ringing their bells. If you have anything you don't want any more, if it's too big to trash, or a hassle to move, these guys will take it off your hands or trade you something they have for it. By the end of the day, you can find these guys pulled over on the sidewalk with a heaping pile on the back of their bikes, or sorting their stuff out for sale. I don't know where they eventually leave the remainder of their findings, but some of them have a stack 10 feet high and 5 feet wide.

I will eventually share some common thought on communism and highlight some of the freedoms found here that are not found in America. In the grayer area, I have enjoyed the total ignorance of American media here. I couldn't tell you a thing about politics, celebrities, or sports since a few weeks ago. That's not entirely true, because I did watch a few programs on the internet after Kim Jong Ill died. After the second time that I heard the announcement, "Kim Jong Ill died, the brutal dictator of North Korea that starves his own people", I started take personal bets that the next person to make the announcement on the news about his death, will also add the tag line, "Brutal dictator that starves his own people". Some perspective on North Korea is that they are friends of China, in fact, the citizens of China have no real enemies. Kim Ill Sung and Mao Zedong appeared to be almost identical in vision and leadership qualities and Mao Zedong is considered a hero and the original Chairman of today's seated government.

Mao Zedong is like Abraham Lincoln here. Therefore, it is difficult to hold Kim Ill Sung in any kind of horrible light. The Korean society, under Kim Ill Sung's leadership, was modeled after China's PRC and bared the same symbols as the hammer and sickle to signify hard team work, but also added the paint brush to represent the importance of art and brainpower. There has to be some perspective that Kim Ill Sung saved the Korean people from becoming Japanese, Chinese, Russian, or American (like the South). For all of the horrendous stories about North Korea, China has its own in its recent history that are nearly the same as North Korea. The only difference is that America had no choice but to work with Mao Zedong in order to form a military alliance against Russia. It's an enormous tangled web and this is a different perspective. There is no comedy sketch or taglines about Kim Ill Jong's death here. Other than that bit of news, I haven't missed listening to Republicans and Democrats or the 24 hour news commentary and campaign polling. I am busy trying to become Chinese.

Today, I went shopping with Shauna to try and find

some larger items for my room, like a desk and a chair. We went outward from Shanghai, to a couple big outlet malls. I have never seen malls like these, corridors full of never-ending stores selling the same items. These were not bottom-pile crap items either. This was store after store of high quality furniture, beds, kitchen sets, doors, and so on. I started to realize that this is the zoo of Shanghai. If you want to be amazed, come look at the humans and the things they build and consume. Even with all of that selection, I couldn't find a corner desk. The journey goes from exciting, to mystifying, to trying to remember the hell we came there for, to, ok where the hell is what I am looking for. We spent the whole day walking isles to find some basic stuff and I ended up only buying a pillow. With all of the high-end, luxurious and useless items for sale in these mega malls, I was dying to know where all the people are that own stuff like this. I kept asking Shauna, "I'm hanging out with the wrong people. Where are all the Shanghai people that have homes like this?" In my mind, it is a hard fact that people living in McLean, Virginia are the ones that have all of the money in the world to spend, and they are spending it on furniture sets like these. But I would never expect to see someone's condo in Shanghai to have this kind of stuff. I took a few short videos on my iPhone and posted them on my YouTube account.

At the end of the day, Shauna and I came back to my place and she was so excited to be in a big house that she was jumping up and down. We continued looking for a desk and bed sheets online on Chinese websites and ordered a pizza for dinner. Shauna is beginning to grow on me and she was really adorable to watch after eating pizza. We were listening to old jazz music and she was dancing around the living room so happily. A few times in the day, and night, she had to take a call with her business partner in London, but it was a holiday in China, so we got to spend the day together. We never did get anything that I needed ordered, but it was another journey for the books.

Cat's Out of the Bag

I'm so pissed off. Whether it's justified or not, I have no idea. I woke up this morning and hurried to wash a quilt before meeting with Mozzy to shop for some boots. I had to wash the quilt in Ken's bathtub because it wouldn't fit in the washing machine, so I am glad he is out of town. I learned from Patrick that he went to Malaysia because he just bought a beach house there. The water in the tub was dark gray from the quilt I was left here. I heard my room has been a revolving door and, ironically, the last two guys that lived in it were from Virginia too. I was waiting for Mozzy in front of a McDonalds and on the phone with her to tell I was there and learned she was arriving on a bus. I stood waiting for her and as the minutes passed, the anticipation started to overwhelm me.

I met Mozzy over three years ago when she accidently friended me on American Myspace. Interestingly, I had already created a Myspace page on China Myspace and was friending people in Shanghai. She had just moved to Shanghai, leaving behind her small shack in the country side, two hours outside of Chongqing in west China. She was new to Shanghai and attending University at Jiao Tong, where I was dreaming of attending. I picked up the phone and called her and we became each other's friend in need. If you have ever visited a big city, you can imagine how difficult it can be when leaving behind a rural country side. I was a shoulder to lean on, as strange as that may sound. I finally got to meet Mozzy in person when I visited China for last August and we spent every day with each other traveling through three cities. I grew to have a real compassion for her and spending every day with her created a deeper love for her, but she is younger than me by about six years and less interested in me. In the beginning, I wasn't so interested in caring more than a friend.

I wasn't expecting to be so thrilled to see her, but I couldn't stop smiling and had an overwhelming urge to kiss and hug her. I refrained. I don't want to be selfish. We first ate because I was starving. I only had left over pizza for all of yesterday and I need some form of nutrients to go on. Together, we searched for some audio speakers. I may not buy them immediately, but I have to have music in my life and it needs to represent the real sound of the producer's intention. Walking around the other day, I had to sing aloud because it was such a deathly cold and gray day here that you would have thought this is what hell looks like. I noticed some other people were singing to themselves too and it was really the only way to have any spirit in the outer run-down looking part of the city. Cheap, crappy-sounding speakers here sell for about $100. You know those scam artists who say they were delivering speakers for a home theater and the customer canceled, so they have these great speakers that you can buy at a discount? They look real fancy, but they sound like shit. That's mostly what you find here. The prices are staggering.

My hope of finding quality speakers was short-lived and we elevatored up to the six-floor of the same mall I have been visiting every time. The first store was a knock-off Columbia store called Kolumb. I thought I would save some money and go for the fake brand at the same quality, only to find the boots were priced about five times what I expected them to be priced at. $200 for no-name brand boots that were "just ok". Then we went to some place I couldn't pronounce that sounded like Molzeks, and the boots there were also about $200. Next was Caterpillar. $185 for their medium quality boots! What a steal! Next, the real Columbia (I couldn't resist). Yea, now getting into the $300 range. Did I add that Kolumb offered a 15% discount if I bought a second pair of boots, and that they don't have any half size shoes here – only full digit numbers like 9, 10, and 11. Alright, I really need boots because my running shoes are like wearing socks and its Winter and dropping outside, so do I go with the Caterpillars and accept that there is a 20% don't-die-of-frostbite-tomorrow fee? I just can't do it. When I left my place in Virginia, I sold most of my belongings and I sold them at about 20% their retail value. Now for everything I need, stores are asking up to 400% of their retail value in Virginia. This is becoming a real concern to me. What do I do? Ask someone at home to mail me some boots? But those boots are made in China, so this can't be real! We give up on finding boots and try to find some underwear and socks. The same problem arises.

Underwear is selling for $25 apiece and socks aren't far behind. That's just H&M store-brand. We go into a supermarket and I buy a pair of underwear for $10. I figure that I will try them and if they stay in one piece after I wash them, I will come back and buy more later. I start to see things that I remember I also need, like a robe and some warm pajamas. There's a reason that my room was vacant when three other guys live here. It's freezing at night! Mozzy has lost all energy and I don't blame her. There is nothing like shopping for hours and making no progress. It has been my theme since I've been here. I spotted some Playboy brand boots that looked similar to the others I had been trying on and asked the clerk to bring out my size. Mozzy said, "You are trying those on now?" and after I put them on and they hurt my feet, I couldn't find her. I paid for the underwear and had to call her twice before she would answer. She was at McDonalds on the other side of the mall. I immediately felt hurt that she would leave and not even tell me. My whole walk over to McDonalds I am agitated that her, or anyone, would not tell me they are going to leave.

I spotted her before she noticed me and stood behind her watching her message people on QQ messenger on her iPhone. I couldn't read the Chinese, but I can read emoticons. Someone just winked at her while sticking out their tongue. I'm betting it wasn't a female. This was the fourth time today I found her messaging on that damn phone. I can't help but think how the other girls I have spent the day with doing the same thing have been so patient, kind, and not occupied with their phones. Mozzy turned and caught me reading her phone, so she immediately became defensive. "So, did you make up your mind yet?" I walked her to the subway entrance and hugged her goodbye. She had to work later and I was thinking that maybe it's a bad idea for me to see her if this is how it's going to be. Instead of turning around to walk to my subway line's station, I went back into the mall. I was determined not to go home empty handed again. I remembered there was an electronics mall across the street. As I crossed the street, I saw that the sun was going down and I spent another day shopping, seeing astronomical prices, and not being able to get some simple crap that I needed to live here.

Electronics store: walk through; floors 1, 2, and 3. No computer keyboard. I want to retype my résumé and it's a matter of standards that I use a normal-sized keyboard. My desk is supposed to arrive today and I want to sit down and work the way I have for the last forever. This store, like the one with crappy speakers, doesn't have any keyboards either. I continue to walk down the street and find another electronics store. Floors, 1, 2, and 3 = no keyboards. In the distance I see a Best Buy. I walk four blocks to get to it and find that its doors are locked and it's not in business. I walked back in to one of the electronics stores and into its connecting mall. There, on the second floor, I found computer keyboards. A woman stuck by my side as I had my first experience of realistic shopping. You know, the kind where you know you will actually make a purchase but you are weighing your options. She stayed with me and I went over to check out their audio speakers. I can't believe it, but they are asking hundreds of dollars for speakers that don't produce clear sound and they are asking over a thousand dollars for high-standard name-brand speakers. I don't mean to let the cat out of the bag, but someone really, really, really needs to educate the Chinese consumers about sound quality and value.

I went around the store to find a computer monitor. Normally, my computer ability limitations are device-related and I know a must-have item for me is a computer monitor. Unbelievable, the store sells 300 kinds of flat screen TVs and 200 kinds of computers, but no monitors. I am struggling with my translator application and telling a group of clerks that I want a computer monitor. Finally, I find out there are two monitors for sale that are nearly identical. Hey, it's a miracle in Shanghai – I think I found something priced at its value. I struggle with the clerk trying to get answers about the monitor and asking to view some photographs on it, but finally decide to purchase it. I gave him my order write-up from the last clerk and he typed something into the computer and nodded. I went back to the last clerks and they told me to pay upstairs, cash only.

I have a credit card that I really want to be using for these initial set-up belongings, and this is the second time that I have to present a store with cash. On my way back to the store from the ATM, I walked into a Bose store. I thought, finally, some quality sound! When the clerks are wearing suits, you know the prices are going to be embarrassing. I went straight to the smallest item in the store, the computer speakers. I did the math while the clerk came over to press play on some ubber loud opera music. $480. Man, it's just hopeless. I started to seriously consider having a friend ship my professional studio monitor speakers to me, even though it would cost hundreds of dollars. Those speakers would be priced at thousands of dollars here. That's no joke! Mao deprived these people of choice for so long that they still haven't discovered more than one kind of speaker sound. One brand name you might appreciate here is the name, Awesome. That's pretty awesome, except they sound unawesome and probably brake fast, which is definitely not awesome and may, in fact, be considered Shitty.

I paid for my new stuff and knew right away that the monitor price wasn't included. I saw it coming. I had to go and find the clerk that new some words in English and wait for him to finish with a customer. I think he was sick of being grabbed for me. That's okay, cause I was sick at looking at his eyes through his lensless glasses. I don't know what the hell happened, but we went back to the other clerk and they spoke for a few minutes and pulled something up on the computer. I gave them my receipt and thought to myself, "It's hard enough to be in China and not speak Chinese. And it's hard enough if I don't know what you guys are doing. But if you guys don't know what you are doing, then I really don't stand a chance." I had to go back upstairs, pay again, get declined a bag to carry my purchases in, and go back down to the second floor to show the clerk my recipient before getting my new monitor. The guy was nice enough to take it out of the box and test it before I left with it. Some guy on the first floor tapped up my boxes together and made a Tape Handle. They must have figured out that I wasn't going to be able to leave if I didn't have a way to carry everything.

It was dark when I got off the subway and I was getting hungry. I knew I wasn't going to go out again once I got to my place and I was trying to mentally prepare for being hungry later. Then I saw a tricycle with a grill on the back and a lady grilling kabobs. I really wanted some beef and tried to tell her that. She sold me two beef kabobs, but as I was walking away, I noticed the beef looked like pieces of a sick hotdog. Actually, I have seen this beef in China before and it looked like undercooked cow intestine, or bladder. I thought about eating it for 20 seconds before deciding it was better to go hungry then to go sick. At that moment, I saw a kabob stand. Well, I can just consider that last purchase as a donation. It only came out to about a dollar and people give money to beggars all the time. At least she did something for the money I gave her. I gave the kabobs to a lady behind the next kabob stand and ordered some real beef sticks. I ate them at a park on the way home and watched a big group of old women dance to modern pop music. Another one of those cute little dogs, that more people have here than should, came up to me to beg for some food. When I walked into the condo, Patrick was sitting at the table. I started to vent about another day of shopping at the ridiculous prices Shanghai asks for. An advanced conversation ensued.

I love learning about the magic of Asia and Patrick has been around. He grew up in Taiwan, worked in Hong Kong, was educated at Cornell in the US, worked in Miami, and travels around China for his job in Real Estate Investment. It's a small world, because he lived in Reston, Virginia for a period of time too. We talked for hours about the markets of Shanghai, Hong Kong, and the US. We discussed a lot of things that have been bugging me that I have been writing about. He took the conversation as a senior in high school would give a breakdown about the new social scene to a freshman. Patrick didn't have all the answers. He knew what was much more expensive in China than in the US and he knew what kinds of items are a rip-off in China, but he couldn't tell me why. We were discussing other cities in China when suddenly, Adrien came in the door. I got up to shake his hand and finally meet him. He joined us at the table and jumped into the conversation.

Adrien has been in Shanghai since April and spent most of his life in Paris. He is about 5 years younger than me and he came to Shanghai by chance when his uncle found him an internship here. He is enjoying the change, but doesn't expect to learn Chinese proficiently for another 4 years. We shared our shopping stories and at some point we all were doing currency conversions to our native currency. Mine is 6.3, Adrien's is 8, and Patrick's jumped back and forth from US, to HK, to Taiwanese, which is 4.5. Patrick laughed and said the US' is dropping. I asked Patrick what his take is on the "currency manipulation" that the US is claiming China is doing. I said, "I think its bullshit. The US just wants more advantage." Patrick said he doesn't know, and from the look of it, doesn't really care. How can the Chinese RMB be undervalued when the cost of goods here is multiple times higher than in the US? It's the same product, but I have to spend more money to purchase it.

That is, by definition, not a surplus of cash. Also, most stores run your cash through a machine to make sure it is real, and banks won't accept bills that have tears or rips in them. Do you know which country prints money when their country thinks they need more cash? All of them!

Patrick is right about one thing, Shanghai is a great city to live in for short-term. I will thrive here. When the thriving grows weak, I will exit stage right. He has seen many English teachers come and go here. Two years, and then poof. There is a lot of China that I want to see, know, smell, taste, touch, and listen to, so I don't know what the time frame is for me. Thinking about going back to the US eventually is similar to the feeling that a hot cup of tea is waiting for you in the house while you're walking through a blizzard. People bicker and bitch and invade sovereign nations, but all in all, it's a really nice place. No one hardly lives there, it's fresh, and you can organize. I have the feeling that here, if you organize, it has to be okayed by the government. So, I think that is a good firm fact I learned about the US by being here. By character and by allowance, you can organize for just about any purpose in the US. You can be socialist, anarchists, racist, religious, striking, into wife swapping, running for office, running for community council, living in naked communes, and so on. That's really awesome. If you're not a part of an organization, you should be. Maybe, when I return, I will start the Money Doesn't Make Any God Damned Sense Organization of Virginia. Our first item of business will be investigating why prices are higher in China for Chinese-made products than they are in the US. I'm still pissed off.

Fairfax, China

Everywhere you go, there you are. After wasting even more time searching for shoes, this time online, I decided I would go to a Rockport store and buy whatever boots worked best for me. I used my VPN to search online stores in the US and every time I tried to make a purchase, shipping was only within the US. I wanted to watch some Late Night and Late Late Night shows from the US to hear the latest happenings, in joke form– the best way to hear news. My internet connection kept failing, so I called my VPN provider. I had to upgrade to an Open VPN, which requires software installation and connecting will connect to multiple servers in the US at random. It's more difficult for the Great Fire Wall to track, but I am finding that if I am streaming TV, they must be able to track high volumes of data coming from a single connection overseas, and after about 30 minutes, my connection starts to freeze up and slow down. I had enough of this relentless low-price search shopping and needed to seize the day, or at least the afternoon.

The living room in my new place is big, so I wanted to do a little bit of stretching and dancing. I found a computer stereo system behind the TV that was super dusty and forgotten.

I transferred music from my PC to my iPhone and connected it to the speakers, and laid out my yoga mat. It's a great mat to bounce up and down on when the floor is so hard and I am barefoot. When you're dancing around a room to familiar music, it makes no difference where you are. You're home. I went up to the roof and did some light shadowboxing. For being an enormous building, the roof felt like it was going to cave in at any moment. There were some empty bottles of Chinese wine up there and a giant box of fireworks remains that I assume were lit for New Years. The first hostel I stayed at here had a sign that said, "No Fireworks", and I thought that was kind of funny. But it turns out, I have heard fireworks going off every day since I have been at this new place – and at all times of the night. I was excited to go running in my new park and grabbed my iPod to accompany me.

There were hardly any people in the park at all. The path is rounded laid bricks with little gaps separating them, which tore my shoes up and eventually tore my knee up. It's unfortunate, because the pathway is long enough to run that one jog around takes about 13 minutes. I ran around it two times and then started to do some kungfu stances. There were a few other people scattered around the park doing their own private kungfu. Cameras were everywhere, like the rest of Shanghai, so I am sure the guards were having great enjoyment watching the foreigner on live broadcast. I did that for 20 minutes and then ran a bit more before doing some more intense shadowboxing on the river. It's a really weird feeling to be looking out across the river to a wall of high-rises, and still not having anyone

145

around. When I was walking out of the park, it was turning to dusk and I could see the moon between two high rise buildings. I stopped walking and just stood there staring at it. It's the same moon alright. There was something about seeing it here that was hard to understand. It's still hard for me to understand.

I hadn't eaten all day, again, so I headed towards a nearby mall here. I was feeling pretty good and I wanted to check out all of the stores in the mall before sitting down to eat. There is a European café restaurant in the mall, but I actually really wanted Chinese food. It's something about the nutrients involved with Asian food that you can come to yearn for and crave. Of course, there is never enough meat in any of the dishes here. I'm pretty sure the statistic is if every Chinese ate as much beef as every American, there wouldn't be enough available cows in the world. I looked in every store and eventually got to the top floor of the mall where I had heard from Patrick a gym was located. The manager showed me around. Take the smallest commercial gym you have seen, and then subtract most of it. It was clean, and there was an aerobic area and a yoga room. The classes included had plenty of Zumba and Yoga, but no kungfu. Shanghai reminds me of my visit to New Orleans.

New Orleans was the birthplace of Jazz music. It was a mixing ground amongst mixing grounds. When I visited it a few years back, hurricane Katrina washed much of it away. The Louis Armstrong Park was closed, but I jumped the fence because I had to see his statue. He is one of my greatest heros and when I saw his statue, he wasn't even smiling. Louis

Armstrong became the Louis Armstrong he is known for in New Orleans, but even at the height of his career, he was not allowed to perform on stage there alongside any white performers. He was so hurt because of this, that he chose not to be buried in his hometown and the place that started it all. A year after Katrina, the central park dedicated to him was still an abandoned forgotten shithole. It is the first thing that the community should have come together to clean up, to represent all of New Orleans. I know there were plenty of other things to worry about, but the symbolic meaning of the park is of the New Orleans that changed the world and made it a place never to forget – and it was forgotten. Are you getting the analogy?

The monthly cost of the gym was the equivalent of $35 a month. When the Manager asked me if I had any gym experience, I got cocky and said, "I'm American". I guess I felt like it was asking me if I had ever eaten at McDonalds. At least, I'm pretty sure that the commercialization of membership gyms is an American invention. I walked into a restaurant at about 6:30 PM for my first meal of the day. I have been eating this way for over a week and even before that I wasn't eating remotely normal. My first week here was much like many people's college experience, eating a lot of Ramen-type noodles. My Chinese phrases are starting to be there when I need them and I was able to call the waiter, order my food, ask for everything I needed, ask where the bathroom is, and ask for the bill. Actually, the bill often comes before the food. It's part of the magic of not having to pay for a tip, which is starting to make a lot of sense to me.

I got back to the house pretty late and cued up The Simpsons on my laptop and connected it to the flat screen TV in the living room. Weird. I was having a day almost exactly like I would have had in my hometown. A totally normal day. There was one thing about walking around after exercising and still having my headphones on. Suddenly, Shanghai had a soundtrack and it was absolutely fantastic. Everyone has seen a movie where the emotional response gets to you and you start to throw up happiness. It's kind of like a sneeze, except it has less suspense, and then you can't decide whether to laugh or cry and you retardidly do both at the same time. That feeling started to come over me and I thought, the thing that can really define how a great a city is, is its art movement and its music. Wherever the most music is being performed, that is the greatest city in the world. Wherever that may be. I decided that I shouldn't have come to China to have the exact same day, so I pulled out my Chinese study books when I got home and started examine them.

The books are difficult for me to use because the directions and questions are often in Chinese and I have to look up many words in the accompanying dictionary. After messing with that for 30 minutes, I decided there has to be someone that will work with me, someone other than a prostitute. I remembered seeing an advertisement for a private teacher when I was searching for English teaching jobs, so I looked her up and sent her an email. We are meeting tonight at the equivalent of $8 an hour. One course at the community college in my hometown was priced at $225 plus $185 for books for a single one-hour class per week for 14 weeks. I am so eager to study now and I want to use this time before the next semester starts to get in a ton of Chinese studying. Like my neighborhood, Chinese is getting more and more comfortable to me. I have shed most of my shyness because I'll never get anywhere if I don't try. Plus, there are some beautiful people in the world that are very gracious and will make the extra effort to communicate with you to help you get what you need.

When I woke up this morning, I messaged with the Chinese teacher and we are meeting somewhere in public to study this evening. I searched for her email online, she is a legit and educated teacher, but meeting somewhere in public is safer and more convenient for both of us. Her advertisement said that she is happy to teach about Chinese culture, history, and cooking too. It sounds like a good match, except for that she's pretty in her pictures. I take that as her being smart to get business, but in the past, I searched for the oldest women I can find that teach, so I won't get too distracted. After all, we are learning to communicate and have conversation – the basis of any relationship. OK, except SOME relationships. She has a cool name too, Shiny.

I went with Patrick over to an enormous supermarket this morning. We had to take a taxi to get there. Take Wegmans and multiple it by 3.8 and then stack a Walmart on the second floor, then you have this supermarket. It's actually owned by a German company and I am starting to realize Germany seems to own a lot of grocery stores around the world. Check that out and you might find your neighborhood grocery store is owned by Heinrick Germanschtik. I was going to stick around and do some shopping after Patrick went back home, but he called me from the house and told me the first floor door isn't opening and asked me if I could come home to bring the groceries in. I have keys to the second floor because my room is upstairs. It's okay that I came back because now I have time to write, otherwise I was going to continue the quest. I still want to go to the Rockport shoe store, so I'll probably do that now. I think these posts will begin to thin out. I might start to fill more time with study, but I'm still not sure what I will do for Chinese New Year's because everyone I know will be going back to their hometown. The coming days will be filled with a lot of job searching, but I will report anything interesting and certainly when Chinese New Year's comes.

If the Shoe Fits,
Wear It

After doing some light exercises, I went off to the only Rockport shoe store I could find online that is located near me. I had to text message Ginger asking her to text me the word Rockport in Chinese, in case I couldn't find the place. Right next door to Jing An Temple is another seven-story shopping mall, and the 5th floor is for men's shopping. According to Patrick, shopping is one of the main activities to do in Shanghai, so there are giant shopping malls scattered around everywhere. When I returned to Virginia after my last visit to China, my roommates and I discussed communism and I asked if they could; A) Explain Communism, and B) Describe how China is communist. That is a little like asking someone to describe the nature of galaxies.

During that conversation, Randy asked me if there was any noticeable business competition in China, assuming there must not be very much. In many of these shopping malls, like this one, multiple brands share a floor and have their own isle with their own sales clerks. That means, when you are trying on shoes, for instance, you will be test-walking them down isles of other brands, with other sales clerks welcoming you, and seeing a variety of shoes similar to the ones you are testing. Therefore, the competition is brutal amongst dealers. Most shopping malls here are designed so every store selling a particular type of product are placed next door to each other. There is no hiding behind convenience, personality, or locality. In addition to that, you have imitation knock-off stores, fake copies, and neighboring stores selling your same product – and on sale.

I picked out a few different shoes to try on, that's after I told the clerk how expensive the shoes were and made a sickened face and grabbed my stomach. I had already seen some of these shoes searching America's websites, including rockport.com, which was offering free shipping. I told one of the clerks the price for the same pair of shoes in America amounted to 25% of their asking price, even at their discounted rate. Even though I told myself I would buy a pair of shoes at this store no matter what, I was having doubts. I was thinking, "Okay, my parents would ship me some boots for my birthday for less than these prices. Then it would probably take more than three weeks to get here, and then maybe a week to go through customs. Assuming it would pass customs, I would get my boots nearing the end of winter. Fuck!" Before the lady went to find me my shoe size, I made sure that she would accept credit cards. No more paying in cash for me, especially at these prices.

As what has been happening at other shoe stores, she came back with sizes like 9.5, even though I asked for 10.5.

Strangely, the shoes were too big for me. The clerk went and fetched a smaller size 9, again they were too large for my feet. By the time she was fetching size 8.5 for four different pairs of shoes, I started to mentally justify paying such a high price for the boots. This lady was working hard. Nope, 8.5 was too big and here comes the size 8's. They are feeling pretty close, and actually feeling how a size 11 boot would normally fit me. Just my luck, there are no size 7.5's for the shoes I like most, only 7's. I thought I would try the 7's anyway, even though I haven't worn size 7 since I was 10 years old. Strangely enough, they fit perfectly. What a relief. Finally, I have soles that won't let me feel every bump and crook on the street when I'm walking. It was 6:25 and I had to meet my Chinese teacher in five minutes a few subway stations away.

I couldn't find the exit number that Shiny asked me to meet her at, so after texting her, she came to meet me. She walked up to me, very seriously, and her appearance reminded me of a stereotypical female Russian spy from a James Bond movie. Her hair was combed in different directions, pulled tightly back, and tied in a small bun. Shiny is about a foot shorter than me, has light green eyes, and stands very erect with strong posture. The neck part of her jacket cupped outward and upward, to cover her neck entirely, and the rest of her long jacket was wrapped around the length of her whole body. She started to lead the way to a place she wanted to sit down and she wasn't sharing much friendly emotion. She just started speaking to me in Chinese, and speaking faster than I speak English. I quickly started to appreciate that she said everything in Chinese to me first and waited for me to respond, before repeating what she said in English.

We sat down together at a Starbucks, one of the hundreds that are located here, and I quickly inhaled a sandwich because I hadn't eaten all day. Shiny had a deep and loud voice, even though she was a young, small lady. As what typically happens with me, she started to teach me some basic pinyin, which I already knew well, then she moved onto some other things I already knew well, so I had to interrupt her and ask her to look at the text book that I brought. As usual, my teacher doesn't want to use the text book, but she at least used the dictionary and we started to practice phases with some new words, including sharing typical introductions that I haven't had much experience making. I have been forgetting some key words and I am learning that there are sometimes ways to say things polite, and sometimes not. We made some correlations between Chinese and English. You wouldn't say something in Chinese a certain way, just like you wouldn't say it in English a certain way. She burped once, and sneezed later, so I taught her some Western customs, like, "Excuse me" and "Bless you". It felt very western to explain the God factor of the "Bless you" story.

Our meeting went very well and we worked out a price to continue lessons three times a week for two hours a lesson. I was able to practice some survival phrases that I wanted to know here, like for when the taxi driver wants to drop me off too early and I want to tell him to continue driving straight. Shiny got more comfortable with me, as it was an objective of mine to get her to laugh sometimes. She walked me to the subway station in the bitter cold, even though it was many blocks in the wrong direction for her, and she asked to treat me to a lamb breakfast in the morning with her friend. She said they would be speaking mostly Chinese. I told her that it sounded good to me, even though I don't really crave lamb before noon. Then we went our separate ways.

Sunday morning was wet and dreary. I was thinking of a way I could exercise. On a day like this in Virginia, I would ride my bike fast and hard for an hour though a bike path in a park, and then jog for 20 minutes. I stood looking out our window here wondering if there was some way to ride a bike fast and hard, or if there was a place I could run. Those god damned bricks ruined that greatness of the park. Shiny called me, but the last thing I wanted to do was sit down to a dinner at 10:30 in the morning. I told her I wanted to find a gym or a dance studio and she recommended a famous dance studio to me. It turns out that this dance studio is only about a 20 to 30 minute walk away from my place. I checked the membership prices and decided that I should look into that more after I have a job. I called to see what Shauna was doing and she told me that she just ran up the stairwell in her building for exercise. Perfect! I told her that I would do the same and call her afterwards.

I didn't grow up in an urban jungle, so climbing stairs for leg strength and endurance is not one of my first activity preferences. I spoke to a lady on the elevator ride down who seemed excited to meet an American. I think that is still a neat thing for elderly people that can remember a China that was empty of Westerners. I was running at a rate just a few steps faster than walking and by the 9th floor, it felt like my heart was going to beat through my chest. I had to stand for a minute and hold my chest before continuing, this time only walking. By the 13th floor, I started to skip every other step, so as to use more climbing power. By the 19th floor, I resorted back to walking up the stairs. I checked the view at some point and saw that one of the condos in this building is three floors and they even have a balcony. I continued to the top of the building and stood resting on the roof for 10 minutes. It was so quiet up there. I spent more time walking around the roof to see the many views and pay more attention to the details. If there was just one skyscraper here, I would be able to note all of the details of it, but there are so many that you can overlook the majority of detail. I went back in the building.

I was going to climb up the additional three floors in the tower section of the building, where the elevator controls and some water storage tank is. I went up two flights, before finding a ladder to climb another few stories to the very top of the tower. I couldn't do it. I was already losing my cool and starting to flutter. It's funny, but I wanted to get back to the "safe" 33rd floor as soon as possible. My first two nights sleeping here, I would stay awake thinking about how high up I am. I was trying to sense the sway of the building, or feel some vibrations from the ground floor of any heavy activity. My bed is so hard that I started to dream of sleeping on a 33-story slab of concrete, just balancing in the sky. Even going down the elevator, my ears would pop passing the 9th floor. I washed my window on my third day here and if I focused my vision through the window at the ground, I would get dizzy and clung to the wall. It's comfortable for me now, I guess. I think Vertigo is nothing more than the brain rationalizing distance with gravity. The natural reaction to assess height can make you dizzy and give you the sensation of free falling.

After finishing my mountain climbing, I felt like I could take a nap, so I called Shauna and told her that I would rest a bit. Mozzy texted me asking if I could make dinner. She texted me the day before that she was sick, as usual. I told her that I would take care of her if she came over, and she said she would. She had been messaging me in various ways at random times and then often dropped out of replying. I guess this time, she really was coming over, so I bundled up to go meet her at the train station. I kept thinking to myself that I hope she isn't going to complain a lot and make me feel like shit, while I could be with ultra-delightful Shauna or meeting some other nice people. I called her when I got to the station and found out that she got off the subway at the station before mine. She misheard me on the phone when I gave her directions. I asked if she wanted me to come to her station to get her or if she wanted to come while I wait. She said, "No, I'm going back home," and hung up the phone. I waited a few minutes and called her again and said that it was just a mistake and pleaded for her to come, after all, I just walked 15 minutes in the cold to meet her. She said the same thing again and hung up.

It was just as I feared. Mozzy made me feel like shit again. I had enough, opened my phone and deleted all of the contact information I had of her's. If I wanted people to highlight how unimportant I am to them, I would have stayed in my home town. I was feeling ultra-low and, even though I was hungry, I thought I would go back to my room and call it a night. When I got to my complex, I continued walking passed my building. I didn't know where I was going, but my feet were finally warm and I thought I would explore my neighborhood again. Just across the street and around the corner, I discovered a narrow alleyway with a few vendors spilling out of it. It was dark and scary, but I thought it might be a shortcut or there is something else back there. The alleyway is literally a space between two buildings, but there are a series of plastic roof coverings at a slant connecting the two buildings. I could tell this was a place that few foreigners have ventured. After walking about 30 meters, a space opened up with more hanging lights and the stench of a funeral home and farm hit me all at one time. I thought I might throw up and wanted to keep calm and find a way out. This was a hidden, underground marketplace right across the street from me that none of my roommates told me about. There was everything here you need for grocery shopping.

The ground was black and made up of all kinds of material, including flattened-out waste, and it was muddy and leaky. There was way too much to see and I really wanted to get out of there. It reminded me of the people that used to live in the subway system of NYC, the Mole People. These were humans of another kind and even though I was playing it cool, it was obvious that I was an outsider. A young woman smiled at me and said, "Hello. Welcome." Surrounding her were dozens of chickens, roosters, and ducks. She was the axe woman. I thought, "This is amazing. How come Patrick takes a taxi to another district to go grocery shopping in a chain store? This place has everything, and he even speaks Chinese." I have slowly, but surely been able to figure out why Patrick is less interested in discovering and interacting with local Chinese here. If you think there is still hostility between a Yankee and a Confederate in the US, try being Taiwanese in China. Taiwanese have deep southern accents and it wouldn't take too much imagination for a local to figure he is from Taiwan after speaking with him. I thought, if I was in a heavily confederate town in Georgia, instead of embracing the culture and visiting the local stores, I too would go out of my way to avoid them. Patrick and I are in Shanghai for different reasons.

I finally got out of that underground market. It was a shocking discovery. Then I noticed a few other stores on the main street that I hadn't noticed before. Two more places had living, and dead, chickens and ducks. After further examination, I concluded the ducks weren't resting. Their necks are broken so they can't run off, but still stay alive and fresh. I am not 100% sure if that's what I am seeing, but I can't stand still staring for long or I will never get anywhere in China. I continue wandering and wondering if I can really get used to the amount of walking it takes to do anything here. I learned that Adrean uses a motorized scooter here, even though he doesn't speak any Chinese. At first, I thought that is really ballsy, but then

I remembered he grew up in Paris, so riding a scooter in a crowded city should be first nature to him. I suppose I could handle riding a bicycle in some of the less crowded areas here. That will make living here 10 times easier. It's too difficult to get exhausted because you need milk, or god forbid, you have to run two errands in a day. I made my way passed the bridge they recently demolished here. There is a bridge crossing the river on each end of our block and one they are rebuilding.

There are some buildings and restaurants that are lit up with colored lights and bright spot lights, so I walked in their direction. I kind of wanted to eat a steak, so I let that goal ease into becoming a part of my undefined mission. I walked along the sidewalk looking into each store and restaurant, trying to figure out what they offer. More often than not, it's mysterious. I discovered a number of hole-in-the-wall hardware stores and begin to realize that searching the internet for stores is going to be useless for finding things I need that are nearby. I walked into a plaza that I didn't know was here and on the second floor was another market place. This one was for consumer goods and I started to check out the audio speakers when Shauna called. She said she would treat me to dinner if I met her in her neighborhood and started to countdown from 5 for me to make a decision. I was still feeling terrible, nowhere near a subway station, not very hungry any more, and Shauna lives far away. However, Shauna is so delightful that I knew it would be a good decision to meet her, so I said yes and flagged down a cab. We drove for at least a half hour and looking at a map now, it was only for 10 miles, but still there was never any break or decline in tall buildings or enormous building structures. Shanghai never really ends, it just runs into other cities. The driver dropped me in front of a busy Soft Rail Train Station and it made me feel that I was in the wrong location.

I called Shauna and she asked me to give my phone to a Chinese person so she could figure out where I am. I walked into the train station and it was bustling with travelers. It is nearing Chinese New Year's and you can tell these Chinese were not the Chinese I had been seeing on the subways in their fancy clothes and fantastic footwear. Some of these Chinese were wearing pajamas and carrying sacks for luggage. I gave the phone to some official guy and Shauna said she would come to find me. A shopping mall connects to the train station and it's a good place to eat that is near to her. I told Shauna that I was in the mood for steak, so we looked at a menu in a western style restaurant. Their steak dish looked unsatisfying. When I asked Shauna if we could look at some of the other restaurants, she got excited. She had a preference, but I had to figure it out. The modern hot pot restaurant she had a coupon for was loaded with people and a line of people were waiting to get in. We put our name on the list and then looked at some of the stores in the mall. Finally, some quality shoes and book bags priced moderately low. I investigated them and even found the same book bag on the first floor was in the official Swiss Army store in the second floor at double the price. I actually did buy some wool socks and a knit cap earlier when I was wandering the streets and I still needed a book bag and some underwear, so I considered buying them after dinner.

I took a few video recordings of the modern hot pot place. There was loud house music playing and the servers were moving around quickly. We each had our own personal pot that was full of spicy liquid and on the burners as soon as we were seated. Shauna started to try to speak to me in Chinese and laughed because she felt like she was talking to a baby. Three enormous platters of fresh produce and sliced beef were delivered to us. Now all we had to do was pick up any ingredients that we want and drop them into the pot, one at a time. You can wait 10 seconds and start fishing out the food, or wait longer. You can't see through the water, so you don't know if you will get anything when you start reaching to pull stuff out. Then you can dip what you discover into a peanut butter sauce mixed with cilantro before bringing it to your mouth for a taste of happiness. The food is hot and spicy, so you eventually get a buzz more powerful than caffeine from coffee, where your whole body is warm, your forehead is sweating, and you feel a dazed high from eating such healthy and delicious food. That reminds me, at some point, my Chinese teacher the day before asked me if I like delicious food. I should have said "no" to see how she would react.

I ended up buying that bookbag and some underwear and putting my socks and hat in it that I bought earlier. The cashier made me sign my receipt twice because my signature looked different than the one on my credit card. This happened to me last time I visited Shanghai when I was exchanging money at the bank. I guess it would be like if someone here scribbled Chinese two times. If the writing wasn't exactly the same, I might think they were different words. It's a little amusing though because they can't read signatures here and for them to tell me that it's not my signature leaves me with little to say to defend myself. I want to tell them that I know people that just draw a check mark or a circle when they sign their receipts. At least mine is a crafted signature that I designed when I was signing more important contracts for my business venture. You can't write my signature fluidly unless you have a lot of practice doing it, so the fact that I write my full name in a series of swoops should be enough evidence that it's mine. Another clerk saw my signature and laughed telling Shauna it looked like I was writing in Arabic. Shauna and I walked in big circles outside in a littler park that actually smelled like grass and trees. What a wonderful smell.

We were going over some Chinese words and I was trying to tell her in Chinese about the dance school near my house. I told her that I especially want to tap dance and I started to tap dance around in my new boots. She laughed and joined me in spinning around and I said, "Hey! Do you know _Singin' In The Rain_?" I started to sing it from the beginning, "Dady dah dady du da dady du dady dah…" and tried to sing and dance the routine as much as I could remember, even swinging around the light post. I explained the scenario of how the guy was just love stricken, it was raining outside, and he closes his umbrella and starts to sing and dance. Shauna said I should teach her some English songs and it started a thirty minute solo singing extravaganza. I wanted to emphasize the lyrics to her to share the beauty and meaning in American and English classics.

I sang:

- Somewhere Over the Rainbow

- I Got the World on a String

- A Kiss to Build a Dream On

- What a Wonderful World

- Ain't Misbehavin'

- Summertime

- Feelin' Good

- Hello

- Imagine

- Here Comes the Sun

- Yesterday

- Daniel

Shauna didn't realize that she asked the wrong person to sing some classics. Or the right person. She walked me back to the subway station and I took a 25 minute train ride back to my neighborhood. My walk home was nice. I was wearing my puffy jacket on top of my leather coat, wearing my leather boots and new book bag filled with some items I had been searching for. My stomach was full and my spirit was too. I bought a slice of cheesecake and milk tea in a convenient store and slipped the milk tea bottle into the bottle pocket of my book bag. I ate the cheesecake while walking passed and observing the street food vendors' cooking their personalized styles of food. I just had to Unfriend Mozzy on Facebook once I got home, then I could sleep peacefully knowing I had another great day in Shanghai.

Treating Opportunity
to Dinner

I packaged a number of electronics in my carryon suitcase when I left home and one of the devices I brought is an old external hard drive that my Mother gave me for Xmas years ago. I have about 100 gigs of files backed up on it all the way back to 2006. Computers die if you use them often enough and hard enough, so I have about a dozen document folders scattered throughout my digital folders and I have been dreading searching for various versions of my résumé to revise for applying for work here. My second day in Shanghai, I plugged in my internet radio device that Randy gave me to me before I left, and within a few minutes, the AC adapter was smoking and burned out. It turns out that China's outlets pump out 200 volts while America uses about half of that. I was really worried that I might lose 6 years of personal data that I can never replace and I have been looking for electrical converters in every electronics store I have been going to.

I decided that I better cut the crap, because there are some good jobs available that I might fill if I hurry up and send my résumé to these people. In my situation, being in Shanghai already and being from the US, I should be able to grab a pretty good job without very much combing over my resume. I did a little research and found some AC adapters can use both inputs, so I checked the sticker on the adapter and found it will work here. I plugged it in and after an hour of searching folders, I pulled off about 30 versions of résumés. There was one that I was particularly eager to find, the one I did in Chinese language and in Chinese format sometime within the last 2 years. I dragged them all into a folder and decided to go over them the next day when I had more time. I was really dreading having to revise and update the résumés, but I was really hoping that I could find that Chinese one. I think that one will make me stand out and appear a bit more special. Why shouldn't it? It's the truth! I had to hurry to Pudong to meet Ada.

Pudong means "East of the River" and I don't know that area as well as I know this side of the river. I believe that, historically, many of the Western concessions occupied this side of the river and so there is a lot of western appeal here. Pudong is generally modern buildings from new construction and it is where Ada lives and works. Ada was the last person to contact me from my personals website subscription before I let it expire and she was very honest with me when I asked if she just had a "white guy" fetish. Her previous boyfriend was Spanish and if you spend a few minutes to think about what it must be like for a Chinese to date a man from outside of China, as well as to travel to his country with him like she did, it's not hard to see the difficulties of going back to a fellow Chinese. It must be a real thrill and something that is hard for an American to really understand. Ada is the person whom I exchanged singing songs with online previously and I wanted to meet her.

I arrived at the station that she asked to meet at exactly on time, but I forgot to write down her number. Luckily, she texted me soon after I arrived and we met. This felt like my first date here because the other women I have been seeing have only had the intention of being friendly and hosting me in Shanghai. I consider Heena and Shauna particularly good friends of mine. Ada was so shy and so delicate that it was captivating for me to watch her. I found that I kept staring at her when she wasn't looking. We sat down at a Dutch café nearby the station and I treated her to a salad while I had some tomato pasta. Ada would take a few bites and stop. She would freeze up and her eyebrows would suddenly sink and her head would slightly tilt. Then she would take a few more bites. She was thinking about what she wanted to ask me and then not letting herself ask me, over and over again. If I waited long enough, she would speak.

"What is the average salary where you come from?" She asked me.

"I think its a hundred thousand dollars. I think my county has the highest salary on average in the nation." I could see she was thinking and doing the math in her head. "Don't worry, it's not like everyone is happy. They just spend the money they have and don't have time for anything. It's not healthy or anything."

"Why do you come to China? China is so poor."

"Oh, here we go again." Sorry to say, I don't have any easy answer for this, so I didn't answer her.

Before agreeing to meet with me, Ada told me she was concerned that she couldn't speak English well enough for me. I asked her to please say everything in Chinese first and English second. She appeared so sweet, innocent, and delicate that I couldn't stop staring at her. All of her questions were internally vetted six times before I would demand that she tell me what she was thinking about. We left the café and slowly walked the streets of Pudong. There was music playing around every corner and I had an overwhelming impulse to grab her and start closely dancing with her. When you get that feeling, you can either fight it and feel terrible, or you can accept it and go with it feeling great. I asked her to dance every time, over and over, and danced around a bit by myself, but she was way too shy to dance in public. We stopped in an electronics shopping mall, and you guessed it, I checked out the speakers. I tried to explain to Ada how to spot phony speakers, but I don't think she believed me.

I will try to see Ada again this weekend and she will be here during Spring Festival, so I think we will join in with some local festivities here during that two week period. We saw each other off and I came home to sleep. I checked my email when I woke up and found that I received some praise for my blogs. Positive comments and gratitude for my blog writing is the only reason that I am continuing to write at all because I dread having to record my days and then have my Mother send me an email criticizing them. I just wanted to have some kind of morning food or American lunch food, and I don't totally know what that means, but it seems like Chinese just have three courses of dinner every day. I checked Google for some western fast food restaurants and saw there was a McDonalds over a bridge nearby that I hadn't been over before. Even though I designated the morning for revising my résumé, I had to eat something and knew I was about to take on a journey.

I set out walking east and found some of the streets in that direction to be very quiet. I thought I might be able to run on some of the streets near here after all. I crossed over the bridge and kept an eye out, looking and looking. Like my time in Pudong last night, I was finding Shanghai to be amazing because everywhere you go, you feel like you are in the heart of the city. While walking, I started to seriously consider the financial ability to own, and the skill involved to ride, a motor scooter. There is a bus system here and there are plenty of bikes, but I was imagining what it would be like to get around all of Shanghai on my own terms. I was thinking about the advantages and disadvantages to wearing a helmet. Two-wheel vehicles here aren't regulated. You can ride on sidewalks, in the main street, or on the sectioned-off two-wheel part of the street. People are always skimming each other and the name of the game is to honk to let someone know that you are coming at them. There's a ton of honking. With a scooter, my trip to McDonalds would be a 5 minute zip around the corner and over the bridge. I took out my iPhone, shot more videos, and took the subway one stop back to my neighborhood.

I got back to my house with enough time to use my bathroom before having to go and meet Shiny at the station. She was a bit late, so I went to the ATM to get some more cash. When she arrived, she asked where we should go to study and I said we should go to my house. She looked a little nervous about it, so I said we could go anywhere, but I don't know anywhere else to go. We walked around and around and never found a coffee shop or a place to sit. Before long, we were at my building and I asked her if we could study at my place again. I was thinking to myself that if Shiny will never study with me at my place, I will need to find a teacher that will. Her, and every other Chinese, has no problem asking what I pay for rent. They all say it's too much, until they see the penthouse and the view. We studied for three hours and Shiny charged me half rate. I'm not sure why. Because she charged me half rate, I treated her to dinner and we ate at a JiangSu restaurant.

Shiny is always speaking Chinese to me and doesn't have a strong vocabulary in English. She really enjoys teaching me Chinese, so she is an excellent teacher for me to have. I don't get sick of it, even though it eventually starts to pass right between my ears. We had some kind of boiling cabbage with lamb. It was surprisingly flavorful. When I was pulling some of the fat off of the lamb, Shiny told me this part is good for my face. There is fat on every cut of meat everywhere I have eaten meat. Even when the kabob pieces on a skewer have no

171

fat, they will put bits of fat between the meat cuts. Seems like people should be fat with high cholesterol here, but they're not. We finished off every drop of the meal and the chef came over and sat next to us. He overheard us speaking Chinese and him and his wife lit up with joy when they spoke to me a little bit. The chef was a bigger guy ravaged by years of hard work and had a high voice, so he reminded me of Curly from The Three Stooges. I walked Shiny to the subway station and saw her off. I didn't really know how to walk home from that station and just made a directional guess.

Talking to that Chef in Chinese has been the driving factor of my desire to speak Chinese. The main reason that I am in China is to speak Chinese. And the main reason that I want to speak Chinese, is to listen to the stories of a billion Chinese people. Think how much can be learned from a third of the world in all of its little pockets and scatterings. Not only that, but to give some Chinese the tools to tell their stories to Americans that cannot speak Chinese. My American friends and family, and my Chinese friends, are all correct when they say that there are nicer places to live than just about everywhere in China. But, the people that know me best, even those that kid around with me about China, know why I am here. This is not a career move.

Interacting with Shiny for so long in Chinese gets my Chinese senses up and improves my confidence. I had no trouble asking for directions and having small conversation on my way home. Although, I still got lost. Being lost and far away is one thing, but I really had to pee too. I saw a taxi driver pulled over and he hopped over the fence and ran back into his car. I thought, well, I may never find a place to pee better than this, and jumped the fence to follow his lead. When I jumped back over the fence, my pants got caught and a hole tore where my ass is. Damn it! I got home eventually. I was able to find the Chinese résumé when I was with Shiny earlier and we touched it up a bit, but it was already up to date for the most part, so I have already sent it off to one of my contacts here. There are some heavy hitters out here for finding English Teacher jobs. They get paid a finder's fee of a month's salary, so this kind of job is big business here and I am nothing less than a walking sure-fire money symbol to them. I think my Father would be relieved to hear that.

Grasshopper

There wasn't a lot left behind in the room I moved into besides dust, dirt, and grime, but there was one interesting item. This morning, I pulled out the restaurant delivery guide book that came with my room and searched for brunch. I need to start making my own meals in the mornings here, but I didn't have anything to eat in the house and I know there is only one western restaurant anywhere near here. I started looking up the listed restaurants' addresses on Google maps to try and choose one nearby. It occurred to me to check the book's website and sure enough, they had an automated process for ordering from any listed restaurant in Puxi, all in one place. I ordered a chicken parmesan sandwich and gave Shiny a call. She told me that she would be at my subway station by 1:00, so I had about 45 minutes until my sandwich would arrive and 15 minutes to eat it. I really wanted to exercise and find places to send my résumé to, but I already asked Shiny to come to Qipu road with me to do some shopping. I thought it would be a good language experience.

On my walk to the subway station, I kept feeling really guilty about not spending the day sending my résumés out and I was thinking that I might walk back to my place with Shiny and do that for an hour before going shopping. I also decided that I didn't need to go to Qipu road today because I still needed bed sheets and groceries and I can buy them down the street here. I got to the station 15 minutes early and found that my Tiger Woods golf game in my iPhone had not updated properly and I couldn't play the game while waiting like I did the day before. I looked out of the windows of the station to the construction site next door and watched all of the activities going on for about 20 minutes. I took a few pictures with my iPhone and shot a few videos. It was interesting to see that hardhats were not a requirement, although some people were wearing them. Safety was not important at all and I saw some close calls. I even saw a crane lift a little trailer house and move it, WHILE PEOPLE WERE INSIDE OF IT. I have noticed that the skeleton of these buildings tend to look like gaps are filled with random size rocks. In the stairwells of my building, for instance, there is a bamboo ladder every couple of floors. I have no idea how that is supposed to substitute for a fire escape.

Shiny wasn't answering her phone and after a half hour of waiting, I decided to walk to a store. I was thinking that I have already wasted an hour that I could have been sending my résumé to companies with. I walked to a grocery store and started browsing. I had no idea what I needed or wanted and soon Shiny called me to tell me she will be arriving soon. I walked back to meet her and we took a tri-motorcycle to my place. It is probably a mile from my door to the subway and the lift only cost me about 68 cents. I could envision myself getting to know those drivers very well in the future. I just wish I had their phone numbers. We should have got dropped off at the grocery store because we ended up walking another two blocks to get to it. We stopped at a building I was curious about and I asked Shiny if she knew what the building was for. This big, Roman-type building that had massive Greek statues all over it and big columns in the front, is a Spa. I never know what anything like that means any more ever since I learned that every massage parlor in China will give you a happy ending and some of massage stores are actually entire buildings with fancy appeal. We continued on.

I knew this shopping wasn't going to be much fun for Shiny, but there were a lot of things I needed to get right away, like toothpaste. We were probably in that supermarket for two hours and it was a bit nerve racking. Even though a lot of my friends here have been extremely helpful, there are limitations to what people can do for you before you need to figure something out for yourself. For instance, when I told Shiny that I wanted to get some Oyster sauce, she told me that people in China don't use Oyster sauce. That's funny, because people in China are the ONLY people that use oyster sauce! She told me no-one in the store would know anything about that, but I found it on the shelves myself. I also had to find the Japanese noodles myself. I was able to grab Shiny and get her to tell me what a lot of the fresh meats and weird things were made from. I keep finding myself walking up to the live mammals and crustaceans and feeling bad for them. There are so many live crabs for sale around Shanghai that it's hard to believe. When I saw the turtles tied up sitting on ice, but trying to escape, I got really sad. I had to make myself walk away and I was thinking, "We go to incredible extremes to protect, save, and repopulate sea turtles, and we treat these turtles like this. Why?" I walked away from the living creatures and saw a roast duck behind a glass window that looked like he was walking around moments ago. And I think that's the god damn fish head and eyeball that I saw Emma eat before.

Shiny had been asking if she could cook at my place since yesterday and I finally decided that it was okay. She started filling the cart with ingredients before I had to count them saying, "1, 2, 3, 4, 5, 6 is enough!" We were both too hungry to wait for her cooking, so we stopped at a Sichuan Restaurant on the way out. Eating out in China is so cheap that it makes treating people to a meal no problem at all. In America, you have to decide what bill you will forego paying this month in order to treat someone to dinner. Shiny went over and chose all of our ingredients for separate dishes and the total came to about $7. There was tofu and vegetables in mine and it was spicy and hot enough to cause both of us to blow our noses. We took a taxi back to my place and Shiny helped put most of the food away. I don't know where everything goes in the kitchen yet, so it was really helpful. I told her that I needed to do some work with my résumé and she was happy to sit on the couch and watch TV. Our cable doesn't work, but we have about 600 DVDs, four times as many DVDs as Jay had, which means collecting DVDs is not too difficult here. I got her setup with subtitles and she watched the TV series Out Sourced.

After a while, Shiny came over to me and said," I don't like Indian people." I thought, oh god, here we go with some Chinese discrimination.

"Why?" I asked her in a tone that suggested she was being stupid.

"Because India is very dirty and very crowded." She answered like she was reading from a script. I was checking the room for the candid camera. Was it a joke?

"Don't say that about Indians, they are people like you. You are being like Americans and Europeans are about China. China is dirty and crowded." I am finding it hard to believe that a Chinese would call the kettle black.

"It's true. I had a friend that visited all of Asia and he said India is very dirty and very poor."

"That's China!" I exclaimed.

"No, no, China has very quality people." Racism is something China isn't very good at. The dominate race in China is Han and I don't know if they are the most populous race on the planet or not, but they definitely act like it.

"Ok, quality people, do you know what Shanghai means in English? It means to cheat!" I could see she didn't understand me, so I tried explaining what cheat means. I pulled up dictionary.com and very confidently entered the word "shanghai" into the search box. All of the words came up that I was explaining; "Swindle, Cheat, Hoodwink" and a good bit more. She started typing those words into my iPhone's translating dictionary and she couldn't believe it. I could see it in her demeanor, she was so hurt.

"Don't be sad," I said and rubbed her shoulder.

"But Shanghai is China, so that means the world doesn't like China," she said very honestly.

"No, no, no. All kinds of people built Shanghai, and I want you to know that you can't call yourself better than other people. You have to accept that people all over the world are just people," I tried to comfort her.

"Yes, just people. Every people all over the world is the same." I think she said that, but it seems she got the message lightning fast, or maybe her English wasn't good enough to say what she meant to say.

I continued sending my résumé out to companies and she went into the kitchen to cook. I don't know exactly how she was making her dish but I know there was pan-frying and water boiling. The ingredients were only vegetables and salt, so I wasn't jumping with excitement to eat the end result. Actually, the dish came out beautifully and somehow had good taste. We wear slippers in the house and she lost about 3 inches in height since we came in the door. I noticed her hair is not only weaved, but it's also folded back, so her hair actually goes below her butt in length. At the store earlier in the day, some man was staring so hard at Shiny that I thought he was going to zap her with his laser eyes at any moment. I caught him multiple times, totally uninhibited, staring at her. I told her about guys staring at her in the store and used my Chinese language to tell her what I should have said to the guy, "You want to take a photograph?" After I finished eating, I grabbed a beer out of the fridge and started going through the DVD's to pick something we could watch. While I was flipping through I came across something that I had to put on.

"These Americans hurt themselves doing stupid things because it's funny. I met one of these guys. Just wait, you'll see," I dropped Jackass into the DVD player. I didn't think it through or anything, I just wanted to watch a few minutes of the movie to show Shiny something that I was sure she hadn't seen in China before. I had only seen the edited TV version of Jackass 2 and maybe Jackass 3, so I hadn't seen any of these scenes before. Shiny was completely and utterly confused. She kept asking, "Why these people do this?" and saying, "This can't be real." The cruder it got, the more I started to feel like I was taking Shiny's virginity. We were laughing, but the sketches were getting gross. By the 5th skit, she told me that it was getting late and she better go. That's when I realized that I just subjected Shiny to some gross shit instead of watching a nice movie.

After dropping her off at the station, I was walking home thinking that I basically watched a pornographic film with her, minus the sexual arousal. At least I told her before I dropped her off that my Mom would have been upset that I showed her that film, which showed a little regret. Walking home, I also thought that it really was a meaningful example of American culture. Not to say Americans are gross and stupid, but that things must be so trouble-free and people must be so well-off, that putting yourself in harm's way and playing tricks on people can be a form of entertainment. I think, today, I was the teacher.

Trying it On
and Pulling it Off

The gym I belonged to in my hometown used to have an annoying message playing over and over again on the speakers in the locker room, "It takes 21 days to form a habit." I think I just hit my 21st blog entry since I have been in China and I found myself wanting to come home and write. I posted my résumé on some websites here and received my first phone call about 20 minutes later. I have a job interview tomorrow, the next day, and Saturday. I was trying to figure out how to put a non-interfering Facebook Like button on my blog site when my phone rang. A man was saying something to me in Chinese and I kept telling him that I was American and couldn't speak Chinese. It went on and on and I was curious to learn when the guy would start screaming at me, give up, or find someone who could speak English. I finally told him to hold on and tried to forward his number to Shauna in case it was about my desk delivery. I couldn't get my phone to comply and decided that I should check the front door to see if a note was left about the desk. When I opened the door, a man was leaning against the wall smoking cigarette in front of an "L" shaped cardboard compiling. He didn't seem to mind that we just had a 10 minute conversation about nothing and I had to ask him if he was the guy I just spoke to on the phone.

My desk is all setup and it's really starting to feel like home now. I was standing at my desk looking out of the park and I thought, "How the hell did I pull this off?" I spent the next two hours playing with code and couldn't get the "Like" button to not change the layout of my site. It burned me out and I laid back in bed. When I awoke, I saw that Tina had called. I met Tina when I visited Shanghai last September and decided to go to an English Agency to see if I could start a job right away. My computer is a database of contacts in China and I had logged into my MSN Messenger at the hostel when I saw the agency was online and they told me that I could come by their office. By the end of my interview, Tina had a job waiting for me the following Monday, and it was Friday evening. I decided to come back to Shanghai in a couple of months instead and I sent Tina my new résumé yesterday. She asked me when we could schedule an interview because she found a position for me at one of the first subway stops on the other side of the river teaching adults English. It was 4:30 and I still hadn't eaten anything. I got sick of experimenting and think I overloaded on vegetables the day before, so I looked up an American restaurant.

Over the last six years, I never stopped thinking about Shanghai and China. I didn't speak with Chinese people online or call someone in China maybe a handful of times in six years. At some point, I researched American restaurants and there was one I always wanted to go to called Malone's. The time was now. I wanted to cram an enormous hamburger into my stomach. Shiny wanted to meet me there because we were planning to have a lesson later in the evening and she was hungry too. The combination of failing at coding earlier in the day, wasting hours of my time and effort, not having eaten anything all day, and the lack of exercise I have been getting, put me in a funky mood. When I was walking to catch the subway I noticed my shitty attitude and let my face lighten up. I suddenly recognized that everyone was Chinese around me and this is what I had yearned for, for years, and my spirits lifted. I am starting to get good at not holding onto anything while standing in the train. I use an internal Horse Stance and play my Tiger Woods golf game on my iPhone.

I arrived at the station before Shiny and decided to try to find the restaurant before she arrived. When we walked into the restaurant, it was mostly empty. We walked past the music stage and it had all the equipment I need, A Fender Deville Electric Guitar Amplifier, a real drum set behind a sound shield, two keyboards, and two guitars in their cases. That was the first Fender Amp I have seen since I have been in Shanghai. It was a thrill for me. I want to play out of that amp badly. We ordered our burgers and I was not in the mood to have poor communication. I really wanted to eat my burger, drink my beer, and numb out watching a sports game on the flat screen. I didn't order my beer because I knew that wasn't going to help my ability to try and focus on a conversation with Shiny.

It was really tough to show any interest or not totally turn off talking with her. At some point I tried to tell her, "If it takes them 45 minutes to make two peoples' meals when it's not busy, how long does it take when they're busy?" She didn't get me at all. I tried again. She re-explained back to me, totally missing the point. I tried again. Nope. I wanted to quit trying, and at the same time, why go on to another point when that one will be just as difficult? I said, "It's just math, this isn't a language problem. You can do math right? Two people, right? No one else is here right? It takes them 45 minutes to feed two people, so how long will it take to feed all of the empty chairs here?" I don't know if she ever understood me, but our burgers finally arrived.

I ate my burger and half of Shiny's. They gave us each like 9 french fries. I couldn't help but think about making my own enormous burger because these were half size. After we ate, Shiny sat next to me and wanted to go over pronouncing the vowels, but I wasn't going to do that in a restaurant. I told her, "This is an American restaurant and that is not polite to do in a restaurant." Man, finally, I could be the native and someone else could be the foreigner. We left and needed to find a place to study. She was asking people where a coffee shop was, but I didn't want to practice my vowels around a bunch of Chinese anyway, so I wasn't looking for that. We started to walk into a shopping mall, the same one that I bought my Rockports in, and Shiny said she thought it would be a bad idea. We went up to the restaurant level and, as luck would have it, there was an abandoned Information Desk with chairs that we could claim.

Shiny had put together some dialogues for us to practice. Even though she is young, she has a real passion to teach Chinese. She would teach Chinese from sunrise to sunset if you let her. I am learning that I have holes in my foundation for Chinese language and Shiny is filling them. She makes me write the phonetic pinyin of our entire dialogue, which is a real pain in the ass, but makes me over-conscious of each syllable's tone. Great pronunciation isn't good enough for Shiny, I have to speak perfectly. If I can learn a half a dozen phrases each day with Shiny, I will be able to start being more of myself in Shanghai and having conversations and saying things to people that I would normally say. I like to get to know everyone I see on a regular basis and there a ton of people in my neighborhood that I see all of the time. It's painful learning Chinese, but the moment I step away from Shiny, I feel immeasurably more prepared to be able to communicate. We finished "Survival Phrases" (a term I taught Shiny) and went into reading and writing large numbers that Shiny would say to me. This is why learning a foreign language is fantastic. The "comma" (,) that English speaking people so desperately depend on for our "and" when saying big numbers, doesn't exist in Chinese. Rather, there is a number that Shiny referred to as, "Before the thousand," which was actually the ten thousand decibel place, and acts as a good indicator for knowing what to call a number.

The Chinese abacus is one of the wonders of the world to me. Numbers are really obscure when used for solving problems. There's so many ways to find the solution to a problem and the abacus appears to be the most optimal way to count and run quick calculations without a computer. I was thinking of the abacus and I was wondering how Chinese Accounting is done without the use of comas. I told Shiny this was the most foreign part of Chinese that I have learned so far. I could count before, but only to 99. They also have some other symbol here for discounting. Rather than taking 30% off a price, they use another term that requires some kind of backwards math and leaves you with the amount that you don't pay, rather than pay. I will explain it better when I understand it, but as of now, I don't get it.

Even if I become fluent in Chinese one day, I don't think I will be able to be obnoxious enough to use it like people do here. I can't shout at people, or interrupt people, or expect people that are busy doing something to care about what I need, but these are all characteristics of common Chinese conversing. They do not lack compassion, but obnoxious is ingrained into daily life here. I think of the tough bad-ass Americans and imagine them here. You want to be tough? Take the stairs. Or, get behind the other 200 people trying to go up the escalator. You have to work together, but you don't have to like it. The comment made about handicaps being forgotten in China is a little out of context because I think the biggest and most predominate problem here is people. All people. Maybe if you can accommodate people in general first, then you can start going into the bonus world of handicap, but it's phenomenal that anyone can get anywhere here. At the same time, these brail sidewalk tiles that take up 30% of every sidewalk everywhere seem like a bit overkill. If anything, they take away the ability for non-handicap people to be able to walk well or haul things on small wheels. I saw about two blind people in all my time in China, but I have walked the Great Wall in length of these brail sidewalks.

Rather than walking straight home when I got off the train, I stopped at the river to sit in the cool night. It was really quiet and the lights across the river were mesmerizing. I looked to my left and found my eyes wandered to my bedroom window of my building. Again, I was thinking, "How did I pull this off?" For the first time, I smelt a little bit of natural water from the river. There was a piece of God in that cesspool, overgrown, drain ditch after all. I have seen trash floating in the river in both directions, so I don't even know if it has a real flow direction. I noticed the lights along the river in the park were slowly changing colors, fading from one to another. I had never noticed that before. Then, at 10:00, most of the lights turned off. I have noticed different light patterns at different times of the night, and the spotlights on top of the buildings here sometimes are turned on and sometimes are not.

I came into my complex. The guard at my gate that I used to be so fearful of not letting me into the community, was staring blankly and I passed him with ease. I walked alongside another guard shining a flashlight around. I didn't know there was a night watchman. I can't imagine that he's watching for anything, since security isn't real most places here. Ken pays the security guards on his street every three months, but not for protection, just because it's an unwritten rule and might in fact have something to do with tax evasion. The riverside that I was sitting at was closed to the public, but you can walk in where the cars are driving, right passed the guards, and walk around the park at leisure. When I walked into the house, Patrick was sitting at the dinner table watching Animae on his laptop again. I'm finding he is a bit of a Debbie Downer. So far so good, on my end. Once I am employed with a work Visa, then I can say that I really pulled it off. I miss the blue sky, but my bitter longing to be in China is gone.

A Wonderful Shitty

It was my friends' birthdays here, but not yet in America. I gave Micah a call and we caught up on some things. He told me his girlfriend gave him a Grounding Mat, a way to plug a mat into the dirt outside to conduct earth powers into the house so you can find peace and heal quickly. I am sure that I have heard of something more absurd, but I can't think of anything right now. Maybe it's because I'm 500 feet in the air, but I don't think an "earth mat" is the missing link between a person and their salvation. Thank God for good marketing. Speaking of disciplined meditation, I blasted some Stevie Wonder this morning to get my serious dancing on and I made a self-discovery: Stevie Wonder has brought more happiness to more people than Mother Teresa ever did. Saint Stevie Wonder. I decided to forego dressing up for my job interview today for a few reasons. First, it's cold outside and you better be real with yourself about what will be separating you from the elements. Second, I only have one pair of slacks, now that my kaki's ripped, so I would potentially be wearing other pants to work anyway. Third, are you really going to take a native language speaker any less serious if he is not wearing a suit? Most importantly, instead of ironing clothes, I got to dance this morning.

I knew how to get to the English School's subway station because it's where I met with Ada just a few days before. I got to the school right on time. It was a little beat up, consisting of only two classrooms, but it wasn't too far from my house and I didn't have to transfer any subway lines to get there. I met with a lady named Kai, she was the person that texted me their location. I learned that Kai is from Taiwan, like Patrick, and she studied for six years in Texas, USA. I learned about four levels of English taught at the school, the teaching schedule, and the pay grade. Then we talked a bit about myself and how I came to Shanghai. I really wanted to make it clear that I didn't just put my finger on a spinning globe and chose Shanghai at random. I have prepared for a decade to come to China and I want to teach English. I told Kai that I believed it helps bridge the gap between our countries and it is a noble cause. I also added that it was easy to say that now, but I might have to rephrase it when I am struggling paying my bills. Actually, teaching English is a prestigious job here and I will not be struggling with my bills. Although, I did have one bill I had to pay as soon as I left.

A few doors down was a China Mobile and I received a text message on my phone that my minutes were running out. At least, I guessed that is what the message said, but I couldn't really read it. It's kind of strange – when I bought my SIM card, China Mobile texted me to send them the number "21" if I preferred messages to be sent in English. I texted them "21" and received a message that said something like, "Thank you, bla bla bla, we will communicate with you in English. Enjoy your visit." And that was the last English message that I ever received from them. I have been getting random texts from China Mobile and I don't know what about. I can tell you that it costs about $6 a month for a ton of minutes and text messages and some amount of time on their public WIFI. I walked in and showed the lady behind the counter my text message and she sent me to a booth. The guy at the booth was really disappointed that a foreigner came to his booth and he called someone over to substitute for him. The transaction took about two minutes. I probably gave them enough money to pay for service for a year because they said I could pay them as much as I wanted.

Riding back on the train, a pretty woman was sitting across from me. Our eyes locked and she was staring. I pulled away and got it out of my head quickly. That Sex Guide book ruined the great hope that every man has of a pretty woman coming up to him to talk to him. When your "guide" tells you that if anyone talks to you, it means they are no good, you can't even have that small beam of glimmering hope that gives all single men a reason to get dressed in the morning. She already lost. I wasn't going to talk to her, and if she talked to me, I was going to hate her. That's a great predicament. When she left the train, another pretty woman replaced her and I noticed the great divide between old colorless Chinese guys on the subway, and beautiful, shinning bright, sparkly Chinese women on the train. I thought, man, that must be rough to see for these guys. A lot of the big-city-getup in places like this, is wardrobe. You can almost create a person by getting all of the clothes they are wearing and hanging them mid-air to represent them. I'm not a chick, but I can tell you that you just can't hang if your leather boots don't cover your calves and raise your ass 3 inches. Me and Pretty Woman got off at the same stop, South Train Station.

I made the difficult decision to get off the train a stop early to find a western fast-food place to eat. I actually did have breakfast and was able to fry up some weird chicken patties that Shiny helped me buy the other day. Lunch was now or never. I figured out if I walk ultra-slow, I can get to where I am going without getting tired. I found some more shopping malls and found they were the old-school China shopping malls, where each store is the size of a bedroom and sells 8 million variations of the same crap. However, there was a McDonalds in the basement. I wanted to hit the bathroom first, but a lady was in there mopping. It didn't seem to stop other guys from going in there to take a leak, but I decided there was probably a bathroom on another floor that I could use. Peeing in the urinal reminded me how every fucking urinal in Toronto was 3 inches too high. If I was any shorter, I would have to take a Viagra to keep from peeing all over the wall.

After eating, I wanted to take a cab home instead of muscling my way back to the station. I hailed a cab and told the driver where I wanted to go. He shook his head no and drove away. No other taxies were available, so I did muscle my way back to the station and ended up having one of those tri-motorcycle guys take me home from my station. I was feeling really soar from dancing, which shows you how out of shape

I got in the last week. Normally, I feel super charged after dancing, but this time I was aching and fatigued. I decided to take a nap before my Chinese lesson. When I woke up, I wanted to hurry across the street to look at buying a chair because if the living room was occupied by Patrick later, Shiny and I would have to study in my room. There is a furniture mall across the street from me, but when I walked in, a guard told me it was closed. Walking in, I got another rape-stare from a pretty woman. When I see my reflection, all dressed up with my scarf, hat, jacket, and glasses, I do look like a pinup Euro Caucasian savior (relatively). It's just funny, because that's all it takes to look sauvé here for me, but that image will shatter as soon as I open my mouth.

Shiny was on her way and I was feeling really disappointed that the furniture mall was closed. It's weird, but little disappoints have been overwhelming me lately. I think because everything has been going so well and things move so smoothly here all of the time that when you have to wait, or someone doesn't have something you expect them to have, you get so pissed off. It all falls into the Theory of Relativity. You know how cranky old people get over little shit because it doesn't fall into their worn-down way of life? Ya, that's me, minus most of it but with the same end result. In fact, my birthday is tomorrow and I will be hitting 30. Officially out of date, out of style, and on the fast-track to the other side of the hill. I am going to have a little party here tomorrow and maybe follow it up by going to a bar to get sloppy. The only problem is that I only know women here. It's probably better to be with only women for my birthday than with only men, but it will be a first for me and I am not feeling very comfortable about it. I was thinking recently about how I have only shadowed women in China. I need to follow a guy around to see how it is different. But it's not like I was going to set up a date with guys to get acquainted with Shanghai. Even learning Chinese would be twice as difficult if my teacher was an old fat guy.

I went up onto the roof to scope the view on a Friday night when all of the lights are turned on. It's so awesome up there. It seems like I should be up there with friends all the time. When Shiny got to my door I asked her if she wanted to check out the view. She replied that it was too cold. It's noteworthy that she never checked the view from any of the windows in the penthouse and could care less. Shiny brought me a cake because she visited her Aunt today whom is a professional cake chef. We went over some new dialogues and I picked them up pretty quickly this time. I learned that you can call someone stupid by calling them the number, 250. I looked it up and there is no real reason as to why, only some theories. I was really tired again and after she left I crawled into bed to play some Tiger Woods and fade out. I switched off my light to find a peaceful sleep, but there was something missing that I had to do before I could achieve rest. This.

Hello 30

How do you celebrate your birthday in Shanghai? My last two birthdays, I invited my friends to go snowboarding. No one came. Actually, no friends did anything with me for my birthday last year. The year before, none of my friends came snowboarding, but there was a local Chinese group that was planning to go the same day, so I went along with them. For both dates, it cost me all the money I had to go because I was only making $20 a day walking a dog. I canceled going last year when 0 out of 40 people I invited wanted to drive 30 minutes north to snowboard for my birthday. It wasn't worth starving myself to make rent for February when no one was going to come with me. Instead, I tried to meet up with some of my friends that were having a party out in the countryside. I drove a half hour to meet them at a bowling alley that they told me to meet them at and, when I called them, I learned that they changed their mind. Then I drove to meet them at the bar they decided to meet at instead, called them again, and learned they changed their mind again. I drove for another 30 minutes back to my home on the evening of my birthday. Awesome.

Bitter, I took a walk and ended up at Fairfax Square and

checked the movies playing. Nothing any good was playing, so I sat down in a sandwich shop that was about to close and had a disappointing wrap. Someone upstairs was playing a good joke on me because at the table across from me was a young Chinese couple and sitting behind them was a white guy eating with a Chinese girl. It gets better. In walked another white guy and Chinese girl, directly followed by yet another white guy and Chinese girl. Wow man. Excuse me chef, would you mind pouring some salt onto my open wounds please? I remember thinking, "I don't have a damn thing to lose by moving to Shanghai. Zero people will even notice I'm gone and there's nothing here for me."

There were a few options for my birthday this year. I could have a little party at my place and we could play some games here and eat pizza. Or, we could go out to a Karaoke bar followed by eating a big Chinese meal in a restaurant. Maybe we could go ice skating like I wanted to for Christmas Eve. The only thing I really wanted to do was sit at a bar and drink a lot of really good beer until I got sleepy drunk, like I used to in my early twenties. I am glad I visited Malone's American Restaurant the other day because I learned they barely had any selection of beer and it was supposed to be a top American bar around here. Now, I knew better then to expect a western bar to have good beer and looked up breweries in Shanghai. I found three listed on Google and one of them looked exceptional. Shanghai Brewery opened last year, their Brewmaster is an American, and their restaurant looked awesome in the photographs pictured online. A two story, big place, full of American sports on TV, pool tables, and various places to sit and enjoy. That was it! I asked Shauna and Shiny to meet there around 6.

I had to hurry and call my friend Greg in the US because it was his birthday and I knew he was getting drunk quickly. I was having trouble calling him on his phone, but he saw I was calling and signed into Skype. We had a video conference call and he put me up on the big flat screen in his living room in the center of his house party. All of our buddies were there, except for Micah. It was Micah's birthday too and he was supposed to come, but he only shows up to 1 out of 39 events that he says he will, including his own birthday party. I showed them the view from my room and someone said, "Nice, nine million neighbors," while someone else said, "Look at all that smog." It was rain, actually. I walked over to Ken's room and showed them the view from his window and that same person said, "Ok, I grossly underestimated your number of neighbors." We all took a shot of alcohol together, myself included, and then I took out my guitar and played with them. It's really wild to be home and away at the same time and I am sure that writing my blog and calling my friends back home has made this transition a breeze. For anyone that thinks what I am doing is difficult, it is absolutely nothing compared to real adventurers and frontiersmen. My great cousin was one of the original ship captains to venture to Antarctica for Man's first visit. I feel like I only quit a crappy job and changed bedrooms. Someone asked me, "When are you coming back?" and I answered, "I'm not." I detest the thought of that long-ass flight and two more weeks of jetlag to be back at the beginning again, minus a thousand dollars for the ticket expense.

I texted my only guy friend, Jay, to come to the Shanghai Brewery. I spoke to him earlier in the day for the first time since I got here. Shiny said she could bring a guy friend and I thought that would help balance the female to male ratio. When I showed my taxi driver the address, he said, "Lao Wei, Lao Wei," which means, "Foreigner, Foreigner." I said, "Yes, I'm a laowei." I thought that was a bit odd, but I learned latter that the name of the bar street was called "Lao Wei". I sat in the front seat of the cab, for the first time, and we drove a long way in the rain before reaching my destination. I was poking my eye the whole time to adjust my contact lens, only to find out later that there was no lens in that eye. Sitting in a comfortable passenger seat in traffic in the rain, I realized that I keep forgetting that I am in China altogether. I guess that is bound to happen, but it wasn't something I ever thought about before. I am writing a blog about my story here and contrasting the two cultures. How can I do that if I forget where I am?

The bar street was really cool with many lights and places to sit on the street. It is a pedestrian street full of indoor/outdoor, rustic bar restaurants. I got held up looking for the Shanghai Brewery because one of the restaurants had a marching band blocking the street to blast some crummy marching band tune in the rain. It's really common in China for a Manager to lineup his staff out front of their building and do some kind of motivational speech followed by a song. When I got to the restaurant, Shiny was waiting and handed me a box of

Chinese tea as a gift. We sat down and I ordered a beer sampler. Shauna arrived and she brought me a cake! She asked me a few times before what I wanted to do for my birthday and all I said was that I wanted to eat cake. I am indebted to her and look forward to helping to make her next birthday a special day.

I loved sitting in this restaurant and drinking some quality beer. It felt great to be in America and in China at the same time. The only weird thing was that there were foreigners at different tables, but this time when I say foreigners, I mean non-American and non-Chinese people. "Excuse me, this is not a Switzerland restaurant. If you would kindly make your way to the door, I am sure there are some Euro cafés down the street." Other than that, it was perfect. I let Shiny try all of my beers and she sipped them like she was sipping poison. Well, it is poison, but still… She told me she doesn't like beer and she asked the waitress what she should order. She ordered a Mojito and Shauna was coughing, sick with a bit of a cold, so I ordered her a warm Whiskey. After maybe six sips of the Mojito, Shiny turned to me with a red face and said, "I'm drunk! You got me drunk!" Shauna had about three sips of the whiskey when she decided not to drink any more of it. This wasn't going to work. I wasn't going to be able to get enjoyably drunk sitting next to two sober girls that don't know each other and aren't talking to each other. A billiards table opened up. Thank god.

While chalking my pool stick, I was wandering the skill level of an international bar. Normally, billiard halls in America are local joints with a local billiard scene. How was I going to rank amongst Australians, Germans, and whoever the hell else was here? I guess it didn't matter and we made a three player game work. When I took a leak, I found that they kept ice in the urinals. That's a first. After my fourth beer, I decided that I better end the night soon because Shiny and Shauna weren't going to have any fun watching me drink. We lit the "3", "0"candles on the cake and one of the waitresses got excited for me. Shiny had her guy friend waiting for us on the street in his new car and Shauna hailed a cab. There was a car accident on the bridge that made the ride home take super long and I really had to pee. I talked to the driver in my broken Chinese and I learned that Yao Ming owns Shanghai's basketball team. We are going to attend one of the games after Chinese New Year's. That will be great and I am sure the tickets are cheap. I was eyeing dark shadowy spots from the window and starting to let the driver know I really had to pee.

When I was finally dropped off, I was breathing like I was going to give birth because I had to pee so badly. The elevator was on the ground level, praise the lord. I took it to my bedroom floor, 33, and set my cake and stuff down at my door and pulled out my keys. I wasn't going to make it. This condo just had a second door added to the existing door and both doors are kept locked, so I have four identical keys, four doors, and numerous turns to make even when I get the right key. Plus, I was going to have to take off my boots from all the wetness, and I had already been holding it and holding it. Believe me, if I was driving, I would have pulled over. It was dark outside, if you know what I mean. So, one thing about being in an urban environment is that it's not such an awful, gross, disgusting thing to pee against a building or something. Sorry ladies. Indoors, or in the elevator, ya that's bad, but big cities are usually filthy and if there are no public restrooms around, you do what you have to do. I know my roommate, Patrick, disagrees. I walked up to the roof and peed in the ditch gutter. It was raining! There you go world. Before you condemn me, I had three options; pee on myself, pee in the hall way, or pee on the roof. So I don't know what *YOU'RE* talking about. Don't worry, the next three hundred times I had to pee during the night, I went in the toilet. Hello 30.

Internal Thoughts, External Farts

I'd be lying if I said race doesn't contribute to a society. I think one reason Chinese are not walking around with big heads about global policy is that it doesn't have to do with them. Besides the hard, ongoing hustling and bustling, there aren't any outsiders in a 9 out of 10 Han Chinese country. It's difficult to think of any reason for common people here to be concerned with any other country or continent. In the US, everyone comes from somewhere and people are stepping off their one-way ticket flights onto US soil every day. Washington is won by votes and votes are won by people. It's the American common folk's duty to have an opinion on world affairs and the media constantly is reminding you of world problems and critical thinking. Here's your contrast; let professionals decide matters on world affairs and not poll common folk on their opinions. In the context of China, why is it so important to have an opinion on any foreign country and its workings anyway?

My job Interviewer was over an hour late today, so I left to eat lunch at Subway and come back. For whatever reason,

Chinese here aren't as fast as Americans at making Subs or pouring coffee. The lines for Subway and Starbucks are always short, but take a long time. I'm pretty impressed, or surprised, with myself because I haven't had Asian food in the last five days. Somehow, I have managed to eat mainly western food, even if that often constitutes of only one meal per day. My Interviewer was a Chinese man, only a few years older than me and he had a strange Austrailianish accent – even though he studied English in Texas. I liked the sound of the job and all of its aspects. This job would mainly be teaching adults Business English. The guy was so late that I wasn't nervous at all and was able to interview with a second company at the agency before they close their doors for Chinese New Year's.

In between interviews, I talked to an American guy that works at the agency. I heard him talking with some of his colleagues there and learned his name was James. I pretty much always make conversation with strangers if I want to talk to them and kicked off the conversation in the restroom while trying to bend my glasses back into shape at the mirror. James came to the sink to wash his hands after taking a leak.

"I think these have reached the point of no return. I bent them so much that they're pretty much fucked."

"You can get glasses here for really cheap. Just get some Oakley's and change your lenses into them. That's what a lot of people do."

I broke the ice and already got the impression that it was another young, cocky American. James moved from Washington State after graduating University and he had all the answers and knew everything. This guy was going on his second year teaching in China and he started in Qingdao, the city that I visited this past summer. He said teaching English was easy. Of course, he was teaching Kindergarten in Qingdao. We chatted more and his cockiness was burning on turbo-drive until his next Chinese student came to interview with him. I did get to learn about the payment and policies of private English teaching as well as his decision to rarely use language books. I can't help but think that maybe I would have been cocky if I came to Shanghai sooner, so maybe it is a good thing it took me so long to get here.

A native English speaker was about to leave the office and he was talking to Tina about negotiating a better salary for the school he just interviewed with. "If they aren't going to supply a place for me to live, then I need at least 15 thousand. We can talk about it after the demo," I heard him tell her. I learned that these schools want us to come in and conduct a demonstration class for their staff about anything that we want. I don't know how to fill the time allotted with teaching English to a class because I've never done that before, but I'm not too concerned about it. I heard him talking about the iPhone Unlocking problem and as he was leaving I stopped him and asked him, "Are you talking about the iPhone?" He had the same problem that I did a few weeks ago. He was even more of a geek about his iPhone than I am and he talked for

10 minutes about it. His name was David and I could tell from the way he spoke that he was from Canada. David just came to Shanghai from teaching English in South Korea. He spoke a bit nervously and seemed a bit strange, like many of the Expats here. We exchanged numbers and I'm going to send him the contact information of the iPhone shop. Tina called me in for the second interview with another company.

I walked into a back room with lots of windows and two quiet Chinese men were sitting at a small round table. On the table was a copy of David's resume. One guy looked very Mao era, wearing a button jacket and having no emotion. The other guy, the Director, looked a little more modern, but didn't understand much English and seemed totally uninterested. They didn't say a word to greet me, so I just sat down at the table.

"So… you have an English school?" Me.

"Yes," Mao Guy.

"OK… do you teach adults, or…?" Me.

"Yes. We teach adults," Mao Guy.

"Uh-huh. Do you use text books?" Me.

"We use computer software," Mao Guy.

"So the students each have their own computer? And I

have a computer?" Me.

"Yes. The students take a computer lesson for one hour and then the teacher reviews the lesson with them," Mao Guy.

It went on and on like this but I was burning bright like a candle with charisma. I just caught my second wind from a coffee. It also helped that yesterday I did a great deal of stretching, Kungfu, dancing and running, so I was feeling great today. I can't remember which Chinese friend helped me write my resume, but the backside of my résumé was in Chinese language and it said that I met Shin Yan-Ming on occasion and practiced Kungfu. Finally, the conversation got interesting. They started to show some interest and some emotion. I started listing all of the elements of China that I am interested in and counted them on my fingers. The Mao Guy asked if I like Chinese food and I answered in Chinese, "I like". I used my Chinglish talking to them so the Director felt included. The Mao Guy brought up the Shaolin Temple and told me I should live near there instead of Shanghai. The New Orleans analogy came back.

The Shaolin Temple had been destroyed multiple times over the previous 2,000 years. It was a pinnacle civilization for all of mankind. For longer than the existence of the United States, Buddhism and Taoism commingled together in harmony and gave rise to Zen Buddhism. The Shaolin Temple was one of thousands of temples in the East devoted to the mastery of human living and human dying. More accurately, meditation and heightened living. The basic guiding principle for Zen living is that you know all of your own weaknesses and confronting your own weaknesses is a constant battle that requires the commitment of a warrior. A Monk is a person that sacrifices his independent life to spend each second in this committed battle and letting go of the one thing that we have that allows us to be who we are, our own thoughts. Meditation is often described as falling asleep while being awake and the religion of Zen has no more guidelines than this.

The Shaolin Monastery was one of the largest temples in China and was one of the most recognized temples by the State. Kungfu is no different than the Yogi's explanation of Yoga. Kungfu is rooted exactly in the same family and the legendary founder of the Shaolin Temple is said to have been Indian. Needless to say, the threat of religion throughout each change of dynasty, as well as more current powers, have eradicated the heart of the temple and the Kungfu that takes place at the monastery today is only modified sport. Shi Yan-Ming, who just opened a new temple in New York State, is one of the last (possibly *the* last) surviving Monks who was raised in the temple before its last demolition and he completely and totally represents Shaolin Zen Buddhism in spirit. Today, in China, the Shaolin Temple acts as an athletic university for Chinese sport and it is an enormous business with thousands of students. The Kungfu movements are hollow, empty of spirit, and the idea of being a spiritual warrior is not included in the criteria.

As someone who is deeply indebted to Kungfu and the Shaolin Monastery, I have more interest in looking at the Shaolin mountainside than the rebuilt "temple" tourist attraction. Looking at Mao Guy's grim smile while he started naming Kungfu movie stars to see if I recognized them, I knew my early introduction to China was a China that he never met. I knew right away that the previous school I interviewed with seemed a whole lot better, but I wanted to have a conversation with these guys. I was determined to make them laugh and smile before leaving. I got the point across. China is a big part of my life. I told them I had to get to my Chinese lesson and I would talk with Tina later about setting up a demo with them. I was at the agency for four hours and was beginning to feel like I worked there. It was time to go.

I didn't even have to leave the building to meet with Shiny. Yep, this is that big mall place I keep talking about. All of these buildings connect to each other here, including multiple subway lines, and this is also where Shiny lives. Shiny had to attend an English class later in the night, so we had to have a rushed lesson in a coffee shop. Waiting for Shiny to show, I had some time to think about the job interviews I have had so far and the amount of time required for each offer. These were all language academies that did not have summer breaks, holidays, vacations, or shorter work days. They are all eight hour per day jobs, Wednesday through Sunday. Before I left America, I remember telling someone that I didn't want to work full time in China. I said that I was coming to China to learn and I needed to spend half of my time learning or it would defeat the purpose of coming here. Full time jobs grant work visas and part-time jobs do not. I can get a work visa, because a Chinese once told me, "All Things Are Possible In China." That doesn't include everything, like blue skies, but it means that there is always a way around a legal obstacle and this is something I am considering.

I have another couple of interviews before Chinese New Year's, but I am leaning towards my first interview today. They would accept me as part-time or fulltime, six months or more. After my lesson with Shiny, I stopped at a book store on the way home and bought an English Learning book along with its Teacher's addition so I can prepare my demonstration better. I think it would be optimal for me to spend a portion of the day learning Chinese in a classroom, part of the day preparing and teaching English, and part of the day dancing in a legit dance studio with professionals. That sounds too good to be true, but if there's one thing I have learned in the last month, it's that dreams come true and things work out.

Man Overboard!

I felt like I was thrown over the edge, drowning, and no one could save me. I received an email from someone a few days ago that said they were forwarded my email and to meet them at some "Mansion" place and to bring my resume. I recognized the name of the company and was pretty sure it was for a job writing content for online English studies. I didn't really have any interest in the job, but I wanted to keep my options open. I asked the guy, Andre, where the place was and how to get to it. So far, everyone gives me clear direction when I ask that question. They tell me what subway lines to take, the station name, which exit to walk out of, and the exact street names and turns to take. Even with clear directions, it's easy to get lost. It took him a few emails, back and forth, before he gave me a cross street that I couldn't even find on Google, Bing, or Baidu's online maps. He was really making it hard for me to have any motivation to meet with him and he was even calling me "Perry" in his emails.

At 11 PM I opened an email Andre had sent confirming our appointment and I stayed awake until 1 in the morning trying to figure out where the fucking place was. When I went to sleep, I didn't set an alarm or anything and decided if I happen to wake up in time to attempt to meet him, I would go. I woke up just before 8 o'clock and called my Mother first thing to wish her a happy birthday. I told her and my Father what I was about to do. My Father pointed out that I could stay in America to do this kind of job, and my Mother told me to give him a call and tell him I'm not going. After all, I was exhausted and didn't even know how to get to the place. Those comments made it even harder for me to go and at least inspired me to sleep for another hour before leaving the house. I put on my stinky cargo pants and left with 45 minutes to get there. It takes about 8 minutes to get to the front street here and 5 minutes to hail a cab. In the end, I decided the only way I was going to find that intersection is if someone dropped me off there.

I texted Andre when I got in the cab because I confirmed our appointment so late that I wanted him to at least get ready to meet me if he hadn't already. Thirty minutes later, I arrived at the intersection he told me was near a Cosi coffee shop. He hadn't replied to my text message and I had the feeling that he wasn't going to. I couldn't find the coffee shop and was considering texting him a, "fuck you asshole," but deciding I have more maturity than that. Patrick and I figured that the guy wanted to meet in a coffee shop because he didn't have an office or a real business anyway. I walked into Fuxing Park and saw Shanghai morning activities, including; choir singing, ballroom dancing, slow traditional Chinese dancing, traditional Chinese music playing, some really strange spinning around while twirling something on a string game, and a lot of badminton.

I would have walked out of the park in another direction, but it looked like the previous street was the only one that had places to eat for breakfast.

I was walking passed the corner building, when in the corner of my eye I noticed the sign on the building read, "Sinan Mansion". I walked over and beside the building was an entrance to a European kind of a promenade and I saw a map on a sign. As I was spotting Cosi on the map, my phone received a text message that read, "I'm the only guy in here." I walked into the shop and an older balding man with an unshaven face wearing jeans and a t-shirt had his laptop and headphones sitting on a table. He introduced himself and had a European accent. He instantly started criticizing the European promenade as a failed attempt to build a Disneyworld here. I quickly finished my story about coming to Shanghai and asked about his story for coming to China. It opened a 25 minute story where I asked a ton of questions.

Audrey was from Switzerland and speaks Swedish, German, French, English, and Chinese. Through his comparisons and descriptions of places, I could tell that he had been all over the world. It's hard to believe how much time people can spend living in so many different places. He received his driver's license when he came to China six years ago and he has driven all over China. He told me that driving in Shanghai isn't bad compared to many other places. It was shocking to hear that. He wasn't just an HR for the company, he was the President and has employees all over China and the US.

His company is very innovative, using video conferencing from Harvard and Yale and holding English classes in China. He was looking to expand by adding some hands-on teachers here. I didn't remotely qualify. He asked me why I wanted to teach.

I told Andre how thrilling it has been for me to learn about China and Chinese and that I wanted to give that experience to Chinese. I said that I spent my twenties trying to engineer solutions and working behind a desk and now I wanted to be on my feet, tell stories, interact, and inspire. We talked about some of the challenges with learning Chinese and learning English and Andre admitted that his Chinese still was not very good. He explained that there is never any time to learn Chinese when you are busy working and I highlighted that I was aware of this and am currently considering working part-time so that I may have more time to study. Andre was sitting cross-legged, hunched over propping his head on his hand and I saw his eyebrows begin to sink.

"That's interesting. So how are you going to get your work visa?" he inquired.

"The employer will supply me with one, I just have to choose which company I want to work for," I couldn't reason as to why he was asking me such a question with an obvious answer.

"In Shanghai, and now just about all of the first tier, and second tier, cities require English teachers to have a Bachelor's degree in China," he was still waiting for my answer.

"What do you mean?" Colors started to become hazy around me like watercolor and felt I was dreaming.

"Well I have hired people in Beijing, Shenzhen, Shanghai, and I run into this issue sometimes. It's required law that all English teachers must have a Bachelor's Degree in order to qualify for a work visa. Six or seven years ago, it wouldn't have been a problem, but things change quickly here. You will probably have to teach far out in a third tier city if you want to teach English in China," he explained very matter-of-factly.

"Really?" I stumble asking him foolishly at a loss for any more words. A thousand flashes went through my mind. This was serious. Way serious. Way, way, way, way serious. This guy isn't just another expat. He drives around China and employs a ton of top notch people. He deals with this scenario regularly. If there was a way around this, he would know it!

"There must be a way around that, right?" I ask him implying that it's safe to tell me the truth now. If there is one thing about China that I know, it's that there is always a way to make something work.

"Ya, I mean, I don't mean to ruin your hopes, but I had to tell a guy recently that I couldn't hire him. I just don't have the ability. The government does a thorough background check and they will shut me down overnight if we don't comply. Don't worry though. You're young. You can get a Bachelor's degree in two years. I had to turn down a 50 year old man. What's he going to do?" He asked, trying to sugar coat the worst news I ever heard.

"So, what happened to that guy? Do you know?" I asked and was hoping to hear that he went to teach in Taiwan happily ever after.

"He had to go off into the boonies to some third tier city and I don't know what happened to him," he answered.

Not only don't I have a Bachelor's degree, but I didn't attend an Ivy League University, live all over the world, speak any other languages, or have any accomplishments inside of an institution in my whole life. It wasn't Andre's intention, but I felt so small, like I wasted my life and was going nowhere, and now I had to accept that I wasn't good enough to do the one thing that people want me to do and I was planning to do tomorrow! I got the feeling that this meeting was about over. A small fraction of the conversation was about my not even qualifying for the interview and the overall discussion was about my not qualifying to live in a remotely modern city in all of China. Fantastic! I shook Andre's hand, thanked him for the counsel, and walked into the street feeling paralyzed.

I felt numb and sick and wanted to call my Mother to cry. Mom was asleep in good 'ol America and I was going to have to take this blow alone. I let my feet walk, but I didn't really know where I was or where I was going. My plan, earlier, was to go to a store to buy some suitable pants. Now, I had some contacts in my head that I wanted to phone immediately. The problem was, their numbers were all stored in various emails, so I had to get to an internet connection. Heena was back in China and called me. I tried to break the news that I need to come up with a solution or I was going to be deported. She verified that she understood what I was saying and then said, "Do you remember Linda? Would you mind teaching her English?" It was not the response that I was expecting. I replied, "Yes, okay, if I can stay in China," hinting that this is a serious problem and any help would be appreciated. "Ok, would you mind doing it for 70 for two hour sessions?" she asked. Let's see, my Chinese lesson costs 100 for two hours and that is half the average rate and there a million Chinese teachers in Shanghai. That means that I am being undercut something like 80%, and even if I am lucky enough to stay in China, I would be required to work 8 hours a day on top of that two hour session. "Okay, we can try it," I told her because she was Heena and I wasn't going to say no. I hung up the phone and thought it was about time I saw the business side of Heena that I had been wondering about.

Drifting down the street sides, I was looking at every Chinese differently. I was watching their ability to live in China freely, making purchases, and going off to run errands. I was thinking, this was going to be taken away from me. I saw a McDonalds and regrettably entered to order a meal. I didn't even know what I wanted to eat any more. They had Wi-Fi, but it required entering your Chinese identification number to use it. I was digging myself deeper and deeper into despair. I didn't want to go home. I was in a different part of town, it was a nice day, and it's always a miniature trip to leave the house to go out again. I decided that I didn't have a choice. I needed to get to my computer and make some important phone calls. I was getting onto the subway when the phone rang.

Heena was asking me if I was going to be able to do the Demo tomorrow. She had been telling me that her friend has an English school here for children and I had already told her that I am interested in teaching teenagers or adults. Now, she was telling me that I must do the interview tomorrow at 3. I was becoming really surprised now because first she made me agree to teach her friend for almost free, and now she was demanding I go to do this Demo. I was feeling like shit and I asked, "Why do I have to do a demo for kindergarten?" That's when I learned that I was talking to Tina, not Heena. This was about the first interview from yesterday. I told her about the conversation I had this morning with Andre and she said, "It's no problem. This is a Chinese company and they have other businesses. They can get you a business visa. Don't worry, okay?" That's what I wanted to hear, but why didn't Andre tell me this? What about that 50 year old man that disappeared into the horizon?

I got off the subway after riding a subway line that I don't usually take. I wasn't exactly sure how to walk home from this stop, but I needed to learn. I was exiting the subway and in line behind a white man in his fifties, that looked like shit, standing beside a girl that couldn't have been older than 22, that

218

he was clearly renting. They were walking home the same way as me and I was right behind them. I couldn't even hold my head up high, just being close to that man made me feel despicable. It's hard to accept when I see white business men in suits with really young girls here, but this guy was a piece of shit and after my morning, I was angry that this guy had the right to be in China and I didn't. I thought a coffee might cheer me up a bit and stopped in a shop to order one. I had been texting Shauna how upset I was about my new situation and she called me. When I answered, she went right into an uplifting speech telling me that she read my blog and agrees that all things are possible here. It's hard not to melt when someone tells you that you have a great personality and someone will easily hire you. That really brought me up to ground level. I'm really lucky to know such a wonderful person.

When I got home, I pulled up one of the 600 emails that my Mother has sent me since I have been here because one of them was a forwarded email from her colleague. A friend of a friend of a friend's son works in Shanghai as Vice President of a business consulting firm here and agreed to see if I need any help getting situated. I was planning to call him today anyway, but now I had something worthy of discussion. I gave him a call and when he answered, "Hey Dan, how are you?" I replied, "Not good. I had a really low morning. I spoke to a dreamcrusher about teaching English in Shanghai." I gave him the short version of the story and he said not to worry because he knows two English school Presidents in Shanghai and told me the names of the schools. The second school he named was the one I just interviewed with. "Ya, I just met with Andre. He was the dreamcrusher," I told him. He let out a good laugh and said, "Tell Andre that John Slink told him not to crush dreams." He went on to explain that he is connected to Andre is ten ways and told me about some of them. John said Shanghai is small and everyone knows everyone. He was talking about the expat community.

I probably spoke with John for a half hour and never got the impression that he was trying to hurry me off the phone. We shared some laughs and some stories about Shanghai. It felt really good to talk with him and he told me to give him a call February 7 and we could meet. He gave me the name of someone that he wanted to introduce me to that was a clever American entrepreneur here. Before we got off the phone with each other he said, "Hey, don't take this the wrong way, but are you doing okay? I mean, financially? Are you alright?" Holy shit, someone here is really concerned about my safety – again! I just rocket-shiped into the sky with the feelings of compassion. "I'm okay. I should last another two months, I hope, but thanks for asking. I really appreciate that." He laughed and said it was no problem. He said, "You know, when you're Mom calls you and tells you to look up on someone, you know, I have to make sure." Lasting another two months here with what I have is only an estimate. In reality, I need this job to work out and pay me by the end of next month.

Shiny was coming over for my Chinese lesson and she was bringing me lunch. I had the feeling that I have really good friends here, a great place to live, and I don't want to go off to another city. We had our lesson in the sun room with the windows open. I shot a little video to share the day. It is unreal to lookout from above, in the only sun room in our whole building, while drinking tea practicing Chinese conversation. I could see a never-ending line of garbage floating down the river. A motorboat went up the river scooping up garbage with a net pole. It only picked up one or two things, while a thousand other items continued floating down stream. I taught Shiny how to pronounce her "R's" better and learned that she happened to be studying the same English book that I purchased. My phone rang. Another school was contacting me and I told them that I was uneasy about the Visa situation.

The lady on the phone, Jennifer, talked to me for a little less than ten minutes, telling me there are other avenues for me to stay in Shanghai. I could get a Residency permit or a Business visa and work as a "consultant" as opposed to a "teacher". She said they were granted by two different government bureaus and they don't work with each other, so if one denies you, it doesn't mean the other will. She told me their other school needs a teacher for children right away and her school teaches adults, but doesn't need a teacher until April. Jennifer offered me teaching children English and helping part time teaching adults. That would sound good to any newbie English teacher. She put me in contact with the other school and then Shiny asked me when my current visa expired.

I kept telling everyone that my visa expired in May, but

I wasn't sure of the exact date and went to grab my passport. When I opened it up to the Chinese visa page, I saw that I was only allowed 60 days per visit, even if my Visa lasts until May. I have already been here 30 days and Chinese New Year's starts tomorrow for a lot of organizations here and lasts at least 15 days. I wasn't even going to be able to talk to a company about my situation until February, so I got online and started to search for a Visa agency ad that I saw previously on one of my Shanghai websites. I had just emailed a company with all of my information when a local friend signed into Skype. I told her I was having Visa trouble and she messaged me a contact within seconds. She told me she was helping another American with the same problem. I copied the email I just sent to another company and sent it to the new contact. I received a call from the man an hour later and we spoke for 10 minutes. He assured me that I will be able to stay in Shanghai and that there is always a way. I will decide on a job and contact him in February before heading to Hong Kong to change my visa status.

Tomorrow I will figure out some kind of topic for my English demo and get some decent pants to wear. I have reached out to my friends living in Hong Kong and Shenzhen to try and plan my brief visit there. Some of them I have met in person, and some I haven't. I made plans to meet with Ada next Monday to celebrate Chinese New Year's by leaving the TV on the RMB telethon station and making special New Year's treats with her. She said I could invite Shiny and she loves to cook too, so I might get to experience a real celebration. That would really beat my previous attempts at celebrating Chinese

New Year's – changing my internet proxy to watch Chinese TV during the night, and going to a dead DC China Town to have dinner. Who would have ever thought so much could have come from a meeting that seemed so insignificant 24 hours ago? You don't always have to show up to a formal occasion for its stated purpose. There is always the opportunity for other things to happen that can make showing up worth it.

Professor Petie Holmes

All I knew about the class I had to teach today was that it was for Business English. It's hard to even know what that means. My students weren't going to be real students. They were going to be the staff members critiquing how I teach. One of the many problems with this scenario is there is no way to know what level of English they should already know and what they don't know. They weren't supplying me with any lesson plan and I wasn't going to spend hours cutting paper to design a game for us to play when I don't know if I will even like the place. Instead of getting to work on my very first English teaching class demonstration right away, I resorted to a technique that I learned from my last employer. I did nothing.

My previous job was a text book example of a middle aged, middle sized company on its way out. Each day, I would have five one-hour long computer meetings with the Managing Staff of different Associations to explain to them, and show them, how they can use our application for their business. These Managing Directors had already purchased our product and I was supposed to figure out how they can continue to do business as usual, but with our software. It was a living nightmare. The limitations of the software, more often than not, caused the Associations to have to discontinue many of their ongoing operations. As something as basic as adding a reasonable-sized image, or a file, to your own website was not included in the software even though website integration was the basis of our product's service. It was common practice for us to "jump" from one meeting to the next, without having any preparation and rarely any updates for answers to questions from the previous meetings.

I suppose that I could have copied a lesson from my new English book, or searched the internet for a play-by-play, but that's not how I want to teach. The last thing that I want to do is stand in front of people, with no personality, and read from someone else's creativity. I had a few ideas floating around my head when I was falling asleep, and I wrote them down. I woke up and followed my deeper beliefs that feeling good for the demo was more important than having a lesson prepared. I needed to exercise and make a plan to eat. I went down stairs to check the fridge. It looked like the meat I had bought with Shiny was gone. Patrick must have eaten it. I went to check the freezer and it looked like Antarctica, so I spent the next hour and a half deicing the freezer. I had about three and half hours until I had to leave to go teach my class and still had nothing planned, so I ordered a pizza and turned on the stereo.

My body was pretty beat up, again. I drank too much coffee, also again, and couldn't fall asleep until about four in the morning. I started trying to twist my body around to the music and throwing some punches. I was so broken that I was panting and it hurt, but I knew the success of my presentation was going to depend on me feeling upbeat. I got passed the initial warm-up stage and moved into some more solid movements before starting to get a good workout. I did that for over an hour, then ate some of my pizza and took my vitamins. I showered and pulled out my pants that I wore for New Year's Eve, a turtle neck shirt, and a long-sleeve black collared shirt to wear over top of it. Well, I felt good, I was clean, and I was dressed properly. Now, I just needed to take a nap. I only had one hour before I had to leave and as much as I wanted to take a nap, I knew this was my only chance to have any preparation before teaching a topic that I didn't even have. I took out my notes from last night, a few scribbled words, and sat down at my desk.

I decided that I was going to teach about business in the context of a Farmers' Market. I thought there was ample examples of terms and practice scenarios to use and I had some in mind. As I was writing down business terms and thinking about how they could all be used together in a short story, I remembered that I have a huge advantage in teaching Business English. I knew a great deal of business and economics terms from all of the reading and preparation I did for my own company. I definitely studied business more than any normal English teacher would have. This wasn't just going to be an English lesson, it was going to be a business lesson. I wrote the following words down on a piece of paper:

- Deal

- Rate

- Discount

- Bargain

- Negotiate

- Bargaining Power

- Dozen

- Turnover

- Term

After I was writing the definition of the last word, I checked the time. I had to leave. I didn't have a scenario or a plan for classroom interaction, but I knew that I needed those and they needed to be the majority of the class. I wanted the class to role-play as buyers and seller using these terms. I thought I was going to, at least, order the words in alphabetical order in my notes while I was on the subway. Instead, I sat next to a guy eating potato chips and almost fell asleep. I didn't have clear instructions to find the building and it was raining, but I found the building. It was exactly where I shot some video with Ada last week, in front of Times Square in Pudong. It was a really nice building and in the most central of locations. It was a big change from when I met Kai in a building that only had one classroom and no elevator. I got off the elevator on the 9th floor and saw out of the corner of my eye that there was a little deli or something beside the elevator. I went to check the room number and found it was the school, but they painted their walls neon green.

I walked in and told the ladies I was here to meet David. Luckily, the lady didn't wait to hear who I asked for and ran off to get the man, because around the corner walked Mao Guy. Wow. I thought I was going to meet with that Austrailianish accent guy from the first interview. This was a really nice place. I didn't think those guys were so clean and modern, but this place looked top notch. He walked me back to the conference room, and out the window was a view that reminded me of that MTV program that is shot on the second floor of a building in Times Square. There's a lounge/movie area just like that in this office, and there are many hip, modern computer desks, as well as multiple small glass classrooms. This place was pretty awesome! I met two other Chinese and one Canadian woman. I noticed later that she had big breasts, which was a bit of fresh air. They all sat down and Mao Guy said, "Ok, let's begin."

"So, I wanted to take us to a Farmers' Market today." I wrote FARMERS MARKET on the board and asked, "Is there something we can do to improve this title? Eddie, any ideas?" Then I added an apostrophe behind the "R" and asked, "Can we add the apostrophe here? Kris, what do you think?" They weren't speaking and I was pulling teeth. "No, we have to add the apostrophe after the 'S' because we are talking about all of the farmers having one market, not a single farmer having a market, right?" I thought this would be a good opener. It wasn't business, but it was pretty advanced English stuff. I was trying to let my charisma steer the ship. "Ok, so at a Farmers' Market, something we want to find is a GOOD DEAL. Does everyone know what a GOOD DEAL is?" Mao Guy nodded his head. "Ok, so a GOOD DEAL is when we buy something at a low price. And a BAD DEAL is when we pay too much for something. So we have GOOD DEALS and BAD DEALS." I went over half a dozen more terms and then asked two of them to have a dialog using some of these words. I never had the chance to play it out in my mind and I was totally dependent of them coming up with a dialogue. It made everyone laugh a little bit, which made it a success.

I had no plan for ending the lesson and I didn't know how much time they expected me to go on, but I had some more material, so I continued. "OK, does anyone know what TURNOVER is and how it can give us BARGAINING POWER? OK, so TURNOVER is the number of products that the seller sells and a TURNOVER RATE is the number of products that a seller sells against the number of products that he does not sell. That can be accounted for in a day, in a week, or in a month. In the case of Apples, we have a SPOILAGE RATE, right? Let's say an apple rots, it cannot be eaten, after one month, so we know the Seller has one month to sell all of his apples. Let's say he has one tree and he can harvest, get, 24 apples from it per month. So after 27 days, the Seller still has 10 apples to sell and only three days to sell them. He will be willing to lower his price, or offer a DISCOUNT, so he can sell all of his apples for the month and have a 100% TURNOVER.

Any questions?" Mao Guy asked for another example of TURNOVER and after that my lesson concluded.

The Director and Mao Guy talked in Chinese for a few minutes and discussed something about the interaction experience with the Canadian woman. The Canadian woman, Jeri, defended that activity for being highly useful and they asked me to sit and wait while they had a meeting together. On the way out, Jeri told me, "That was good. I never heard an ESL teacher try to tackle *turnover* before. The jury will convene." I sat and waited for them for 20 minutes, staring out the glass window into the rainy streets. I couldn't wait to get out of there. Knowing that I did well, I wanted to leave while it was still a success. The Director and Mao Guy came back and went over the terms of employment. It all sounded good to me. Some of the top notch English schools here would never hire me without a Bachelor's Degree, Andre made that clear, but this English school was founded by some previous employees of those schools and they were the competition. This place was innovative and wanted the teachers to design new methodology and be creative. That is exactly the kind of company that I can work well in.

My whole Kungfu shpeal during the interview paid off. The first thing Mao Guy asked me about was if I had done Kungfu this morning. Later, when I suggested they partnership with a Chinese school so I can continue my studies, the Director said he will teach me Chinese if I teach him Kungfu. For whatever reason, I beat out the iPhone guy that had already had experience teaching. I am to return on the 29th, after Chinese New Year's, to sign the employment contract. I told them about the Bachelor's degree visa problem, and they are confident that they can handle it. At least, it will not be a surprise when the situation arises. I will have to go to Hong Kong, at least twice this year. I am pretty sure that if I can get another kind of visa, I will have to go to Hong Kong every 60 days. Aside from the large financial setback, I will get to know a little more about south China and Hong Kong.

I left the office building and crossed the street to yet another enormous shopping mall. Ada was going to meet me for dinner and a movie because she worked nearby. I was checking out speakers for the 15th time and discovered some quality JBLs. My Chinese is better than a few weeks ago and I was having a good time in the sound room DJing American music to them at full volume. After dinner, Ada and I saw the new Sherlock Holmes movie because it was in English. It was very interesting to see an English film from that time period while being in China. It really was like seeing the context of "Foreigner" as an elegant, nice, classy thing. Their wardrobes and materials were all so stunning. The fight scenes made me laugh a bit because these contemporary British white guys were doing Kungfu sometimes. It was late enough to call home, so I told my Mom about the job. She listed me 100 things to be concerned about and reminded me that my parents love me like no other.

Less Opium Bars
and Pipe Dreams

Korean food in Fairfax blows away Korean food in Shanghai. I have eaten at a handful of Korean BBQ restaurants here and none have held a flame to the restaurants in my hometown. If you have never eaten at a Korean BBQ restaurant in Fairfax and you live there, shame on you. Shiny's car-driving friend had to go back to JiangSu the next day, so she was obligated to spend time with him and invited me to eat with them. The original place they wanted to go, a giant tea house, was closed due to Chinese New Year's. Instead, we went to the mall near my house and ate at one of the only open restaurants. We were the only customers. I miss meat so much. Actually, I think the portion of meat Chinese eat is regular, I just grew up in a country that eats it in abundance. I only feel that way because when you think about how many animals you have to kill, and all of the time, it's a lot. I personally would kill an animal to eat it, but I think I would kill a whole lot less of them if I was raising them and killing them myself. Nevertheless, I really miss big chunks of marinated meat.

It's weird that this enormous city is located so close to Korea and can't get a meal down. They bring out a fraction of the little pre-meal bowls before the BBQ begins, and the food is mediocre at best. The marinate BBQ sauce doesn't come close and has little flavor at all. The strips of meat, of course, are razor thin and sparingly served. They don't bring you rice unless you ask for it and there is no kimchi! The salad dressing is the same, but neighboring that is a purely Chinese mix of spices to dip your meat slice into. They also overcook the shit out of the beef and serve purely Chinese dishes along with the meals. I know Fairfax is one of the most densely Korean populated places in the world outside of Korea, but there are countless Koreans here as well. This one stumps me.

I chatted with Ken on Gchat the other day and learned he would be coming home later in the night and it was his bar's 8 year anniversary. That meant 6 to 10 was going to be an open bar and I had been wanting to visit, so I told him that I would go. When I told Shiny I was going, she got excited and wanted to come too. Shiny's friend dropped us off at my place and we were studying Chinese when Ken came home. After he took a brief nap, he threw me a beer and we piled in a taxi. Apparently the Frenchman didn't pay rent for January yet and he was already back in Paris for the holiday. Ken and the driver started to have a quiet argument and a few minutes later Ken told me that the driver wanted to drive to the bar another way then Ken suggested. The taxi drivers amaze me here and I believe they must know these streets in a very special way. I'm so impressed that Ken can tell them the best way to go somewhere and have the nerve to argue with them about it. I told Ken that it is a dream of mine to have small talk with the taxi drivers here and he said he doesn't like to and they mostly ask annoying questions. He meant, personal questions, which is okay for normal people, but Ken has a lot going on.

When I first moved in and was using his bathroom to shower in the mornings, I found it was pretty messy. I thought, I hope I'm not living like this when I am his age. Of course, I had no idea that he had so much going on and now I have no trouble aspiring to be him. He just got back from the tropics where he has a 32 foot sailboat at a resort marina and an apartment. He lives in the master suite of a penthouse in Shanghai and has his own bar where he goes to hang out 4 times a week. He speaks proficient Chinese, his place in Malaysia is mostly Chinese, and he has a number of adventurous friends there. Every few months he goes there. To top it off, his Mom lives on a converted houseboat there as well. He wasn't telling me any of this outright. I had to pry and he is absurdly humble about the whole thing. He mentioned wanting to sail the Philippines, which was a major pipe dream of mine.

We pulled up to The Otter and when we walked in the door, white guys were waiting to greet him. The bar was full of foreigners and I didn't see a single Chinese. It was a very basic half-circle bar with some stools around the edges of room and Shiny and I sat in the corner. I kept getting Shiny fruit-drink Bacardi's and she would down them quickly. I was drinking Brooklyn Brewery beer while the American music played louder and louder and the bar begin to fill. So, this was Ken's job. He stands around shouting to people over the music, drinking a beer, while people get a little crazy. Shiny was telling me that China had no bars before foreigners came, I think she meant alcohol bars because I'm sure there were opium bars. She wanted me to explain why people go to a bar, but I didn't have anything to say except to present the scene to her. The couple next to us were practically having sex and Shiny was staring at them. It was a cultural experience for her.

We took a walk in the night air afterwards and Shanghai was very peaceful. After a while of wandering, we shared a cab to drop her off at her house and for me to continue on to my house. When I was telling the driver how to get to my house, I was just following the lessons that Shiny has taught me. My pronunciation is so clear now because before each lesson, I have to say each Chinese sound. It's like the vowels and consonants. There's usually TV screens in the back of the headrests for the passengers to watch and that calmed my drunkenness on the long ride home. I heard Ken come home late. Real late. 7 in the morning late. I couldn't last more than four hours in that place once a month. Ken's a badass. He exemplifies an alternative to having a career with a retirement fund and carrying out a pretty awesome plan. Maybe I won't convert a ship into a house boat like Ken's parents, but I wouldn't mind converting a pipe dream, or two, into reality.

Half Full

Shiny scheduled another class in the afternoon and she has her English class in the evening, so I kind of got ditched today. I feel that I only have 9 more days to improve my Chinese before I just become another guy too busy to have a life, so I was bummed that we couldn't meet for a lesson today. I took it easy most of the day and by the late afternoon, I went across the street to the furniture mall. It seems like everything is closing and I wanted to see about getting a chair for my desk before the mall closed for a week. The fold out chair I am using now makes my ass cold and I think our maid likes to sit on it while she is hanging out laundry to dry. On my walk over to the furniture mall, Shiny texted me that she had 2 hours available if we could meet right away. I really wanted to scoop a chair before the place shut down for ever, but Shiny kept persisting to meet right away.

Walking around that furniture mall is a good indicator of what China is like. There's too much to sell and too little to buy. For instance, the first floor of the mall is Soft Furniture, the second floor is Nice Furniture, the third floor is Elegant Furniture, and the fourth floor is International Furniture. Each store is a display setting for a gaudy rich family setting with things like rime stone bed covers and a thousand different versions of a bed frame. I went to meet Shiny at that big mall at ZhongShan Park and ended up having to wait 15 minutes for her to show. A Chinese English teacher came over to introduce herself and ask me a lot of questions. She asked me, "What do you think is better, America or China?" I just looked at her like she was an idiot. "They're the same. What is 'better'?" At that moment, Shiny called and she was looking for me. The English teacher followed me and talked to Shiny for a few minutes. I am starting to find that teaching English here is a big industry. I'm going to get a lot of people asking for my school's name and what my 'major' was at university.

I hadn't eaten all day, so Shiny helped me find a restaurant where we could study and I could eat. I was so agitated that I had to walk so much for nothing and that I was so hungry. Shiny chose a Guangdong restaurant and I chose a dish that had beef. You might find me to be shallow for saying this, but maybe the thing I miss best from America is its meat! I am having serious meat withdrawal and not enjoying it. This wasn't going to be the first time I order beef with noodles to eat all of the beef without eating any of the noodles. Shiny had already eaten earlier, so she just ordered some kind of pudding. When her pudding came out steaming hot in a plastic bowl, she snapped. She was yelling at the waiter to bring her the pudding in bowl. It's a little strange for a person that wears the same shirt for a week and lives in such a dirty place to act like a plastic bowl is going to be the death of her. I pointed out that the lid said, "Microwave Safe", but it didn't help.

I don't know if it's because a younger woman is with an older man or if it is more acceptable in this culture, but Mozzy used to shout rudely to people when I was with her too. I can tell they shout more aggressively and rudely than everyone else in restaurants, but I can't tell to what extent. I feel very uncomfortable being with someone that is always shouting. The waiter was taking someone's order and she screamed at him, "Waiter! Hey, Waiter! He didn't get his food yet! That woman got her meal! Why hasn't he? He ordered first!" She was talking about me. I just looked at the waiter's face thinking, are you going to take that from her? They always do, so this is part of my confusion. I can tell it's rude, but it doesn't seem to be as extremely and utterly unacceptable as it would be in America. Part of the trouble is, in America, waiters come check on you to see if you need anything. Here, you have no choice but to shout across the room or you will never get anything you need, including the bill.

This is why I said before that I will never be able to speak Chinese properly. I will never unlearn politeness. Eventually, I will be with some other people when I'm with someone yelling rudely at a waiter and they will be able to tell me if it's a little over the top or not. After my lesson, Shiny went her way and I went to the mall. I need clothes for work, especially pants, and I have to take on one of man's most dreaded activities – trying on clothes. It seemed like a daunting task to do alone because my level of communication doesn't cover the questions I need to ask or measurement conversions. I was about to find another big problem.

All of the pants here are made for slim guys who have a small "package". I saw some pants were even labeled "Thin" and couldn't imagine trying to squeeze into them. I am 5"6' and weigh 165 lbs. I'm not obese, or a body builder, and when I put on these pants with my waist size (about 32 inches) the legs are always much too long, the pants are tight as hell, and the crotch inseam is way too small. By about the 5th store I got to, I saw a sight of beauty. In Dickies, there were three shelves labeled, "Japan, China, and America". Oh god, give me the pants made for Americans. I tried them on and they were OK, but still not comfortable. I was looking for a store with Dockers or even Ralph Lauren. Again, like my shoes, I was starting to find price was becoming less of a factor, and clothes that fit, more of a factor. I pretty much visited every Men's store that I had a chance of trying on clothes by myself in, and was about to give up. It seems to me that I need the legs hemmed on my pants, but I don't want to try and have that conversation. I walked in the H&M to see if they have anything else I need, like a sweatshirt.

H&M had jeans that looked remotely familiar. I know I just turned 30 and I can't make the dramatic change to skin tight jeans like the youngsters are wearing. I'm comfortable with my body enough that I don't mind wearing clothes that fit as tight as a woman would wear, but it's about 50 times more uncomfortable than wearing lose fitting jeans. Or how about back pockets that are larger than the size of a quarter? There was a photo chart above the jean section of the store displaying the different fit types of styles and I saw jeans that looked American. They were labeled, "New Standard" and I was trying to find them when I asked the clerk where they are. They didn't carry them. Of course. I grabbed another type, with a short crotch seam, and went to try them on. There was a sign on the wall that said that customers could try on clothes at home and bring them back within 30 days. The line was long and I was sick of changing clothes, so I paid for them and went home.

My friend, Ada, made two requests for Monday; that she could use the kitchen, and have the television tuned in for Chinese New Year programming. Our TV didn't pickup any stations. I was worn out when I got home, so I sat down in front of the TV on the couch to rest. I had built TV antennas before, so I wanted to see if I could get the TV to pick up any stations. Otherwise, I was going to have to pay a bunch of money for a TV antenna. Ken previously told me that the TV wall socket didn't work because of some problem in the wall. I searched the dusty cabinets and found a Chinese kind of UHF cable. In another drawer, I found another one and a double female extender connector. I ran the line from the TV to the window and I was able to pick up about 5 TV stations that were mostly clear. I thought, for the hell of it, I would try to plug it into the wall. I plugged it in, but didn't receive anything. I had to change the language setting on the TV to English, and run a channel scan. Then I picked up 9 stations clearly. So far so good, but the only thing working on the remote control was the power button. I took it apart and cleaned it really well. I had to do that two more times before it worked like new.

This house is really nice, it just hasn't been treated that way. I think, sometime in the past it was used properly, but somewhere along the line it got neglected. I assume it was from all the prostitutes coming and going before, or Ken just started to keep to his master suite more. He has his own large couch and flat screen TV in his lounge. I am slowly getting the place in working order. Patrick, by himself, leaves a giant stack of pots, pans, dishes, and bowls in the kitchen sink after one or two days. Our maid washes all of the dishes, but he doesn't leave room for anyone to use the sink or wash any of the cookware so we can use it. It's just been a free range, free-for-all, house with little communication. I did make a great discovery yesterday.

When I was showing my Mom the map of my neighborhood online, she noticed an open field close to me. Yesterday, I checked it out. It's a park called Suzhou River Park, but it was locked up. Ken said there is a secret way to get in there. It looks like they have a paved sidewalk! I can't really tell from the view from the street, but that would be miraculous. I could have a normal jogging routine. I will check it out when it's not raining. I am finding that the Chinese calendar makes sense. The weather is changing at the "New Year". The streets are emptying out too. No more food vendors. They all went to be with their family. This holiday makes the most sense to me, unlike Halloween, Easter, and Christmas, which are all perverted Christian holidays that don't relate to anything. Finish one seasonal year and visit your family before kicking off the next. I like that.

On my now working TV, I watched American Idol with Chinese overdubbing. It was really strange and I got really frustrated not being able to hear my own language. I think Chinese TV will help me learn Chinese faster. Especially if the American channel is overdubbed in Chinese.

I am about to start another day in search of pants. It's a real shitty day outside and getting to the stores isn't going to be fun. I'm still in my Honey Moon stage, but comfortable enough that I am forgetting that I am in China and even forgetting that I am in Shanghai. The thought of a Suburb sounds like a good idea, but not something I could visit in a thousand mile range. Blue skies, grass lawns, personal landscapes, unused sidewalks, the sounds of cars driving on a distant highway, obnoxious Americans, being able to ask simple questions; these thoughts flutter in my mind sometimes. I think about it the same way I used to dream about Shanghai. I won't get stuck here, even though it isn't hard to do. Believe me when I say that there is plenty of freedom and opportunity here. It's just different and my cup of tea is currently half full.

Fighting Fireworks
with Fire

I'm an asshole. You must be a real asshole if you don't even know you're an asshole. I was just doing the math. I still don't really have any guy friends here. I always figured, if you were a dude with only girlfriends, that you were either a homosexual or an asshole. The few times that I picked up some up-close gay magnetic energy from a guy, it literally felt like two positive magnets pushing into each other and made me feel nauseous. So, I'm pretty sure I must be an asshole. Then again, I only have dude friends in my hometown, so I take it back. I'm not an asshole. At least, I'm not calling myself one. I'm grateful that I have any friends here at all. I'm defiantly not complaining. I met Ada for round two of pants shopping yesterday.

I made a mistake and got off the train at West Nanjing, as opposed to East Nanjing, where Ada was waiting. While she was coming over to meet me, I walked the block and saw some English letters. I thought, maybe, with a glimmer of hope, it was a restaurant. Maybe even a restaurant that served hamburgers. It was, yet, another day without lunch, breakfast, or dinner from the previous night. Whoa, underneath the sigh "Carl's", the sign read, "Charbroiled hamburgers". I circled back to meet Ada and brought her over to Carl's restaurant. I guess this place is a chain restaurant on the West Coast of the US, but I had never heard of it. I ordered a double-decker with cheese and I was waiting in line when I noticed some Middle Eastern guy seated with an evil look on his face. It was scary. I was thinking back to my FBI's Most Wanted TV show days and was wondering if this was that Taxi driver that shot his two daughters for wanting to go to college and date boys. No one was going to recognize him here, or in the Middle East for that matter.

After I slammed my burger and Ada called Americans "fat" again, we crossed the street so I could get a coffee. Ada was patient enough to wait for me while I tried on pants – four times. It was raining outside, so we took the train one stop to Jing An where the mall was that I bought my Rockports in. On the Men's floor, I spotted a nice sweater and shirt and tried them on. They were great and I took a seat while the clerks were wrapping them up for me. Ada heard them calculate the price and she said, "Nine thousand." Head: shake, shake, shake; exsqueeze me? I pulled up my Calculator App and found the sweater came to $300 and the shirt was closer to $200. I thought telling the clerks that I didn't want to buy the clothes any more was going to cause an argument, but even the clerks knew the price was ridiculous. Ada preferred going to a grocery store, rather than going out to dinner, so we took a subway closer to my place and walked to the supermarket.

This was my second chance to get some things in the supermarket that I wanted. This time, Ada helped me to find some Chinese Chili mixes, more similar to what I could buy at the Chinese grocery store in my home town. They didn't have as much as my hometown's Chinese store, which I don't really understand. Then I went over to check out their spice selection. It should have been a cartoon. The rack was just as big as a spice rack in any grocery store in my hometown, except it was totally loaded with 5-spice and Chinese pepper. That's all. Some tall older Chinese lady wearing wavy hair extensions, flashy clothes, and a lot of makeup locked eyes with me. I had to have a look because of her outfit and height. She was shopping with two younger girls, also taller than me and wearing flashy clothes. Ada caught her look at me a few times and laughed. I am pretty sure that she is the Manager of one of these Massage Parlors and those were her employees. I could just be shallow, but I think that I'm on the right track.

I wanted to eat at a restaurant after being on my feet shopping all day, but Ada wanted to eat at my place. I thought she wanted to cook something, but she asked me to cook something. I had bought enough stuff at the grocery store to make a meal. I finally got some familiar pieces of beef. I didn't even recognized the chunks of meat that my slices of beef came from. I tried to ask for the translated word for "sirloin" and I think it came to "the belt of a cow". I still had Japanese Udon Noodles and half the ingredients that I would have had back in Fairfax to make one of my favorite dishes. I found a Teflon stove-top wok and prepared a sliced onion, green snaps, peppered beef chunks, a mix oil, and four different sauces. I was rubbing the cleaver against the steel rod when Ada told me that I don't cook like Chinese at all. I said, "Well, I don't cook like an American either, so who do I cook like?" After preparation, the dish only takes a few minutes to cook and it came out very well. I think it was good for Ada to see that a foreigner can have some Asian qualities.

Ada wanted to use my computer to help me purchase my flight to Hong Kong. While she was going through the transactions, I hooked up my electric guitar and started singing. I felt at home making up a song as usual, this time singing the hook line, "I'm going to Hong Kong" and asking Ada to start singing her line overtop of mine, "He's going to Hong Kong. Don't worry he won't be long." After she booked my flights to Hong Kong and back, she grabbed her purse and asked which way the subway was. I thought she was going to stay because it was rainy, cold, and late. As I was putting away my guitar, the sound of someone shooting at my building drew me to the window. It was yet another guy lighting fireworks, but this time in my building's courtyard and the fireworks were shooting into my building. I'm pretty sure you would go to jail for that in America. Car alarms were going off and it was late at night. Of course, if you set up fireworks stands for Chinese New Year's and 250,000 people live in a complex, someone is bound to be a jackass. I understand that tonight, Chinese New Year's Eve, will create a sight and sound like warfare. I'm pretty nervous about it, but it's such a shitty day outside today that I wouldn't mind everyone setting it on fire.

I'm tuned into the CCTV1 watching the New Year's Celebration. It's almost 3 o'clock. Ken still hasn't gotten out of bed, and his flight attendant girlfriend's shoes are at the door, so I guess there's no reason to. Plus, I don't think we're going to be able to sleep today. Our ceiling is a fireworks launch pad. CCTV is broadcasting a live event from Beijing. As an American, you would expect some kind of live news broadcast outdoors somewhere near a live event. Then you think about it and remember that outdoors is shit here. So, instead of some street side interaction, there is a ever-ending series of stage performances at an indoor auditorium with a lame crowd clapping to lip synching. It's not like "live" performance broadcasts in America are a whole lot better. There used to be a real career for talented people and a demand for them, but engineering a show seems to be acceptable.

Last night, the shows were all a certain type of comedy performed in traditional China. They remind me of Abbot and Costello pairing. It appears that one is the blissful idiot and the other guy is the elegant intellectual, so there is a constant joke setup and delivery. Today, it has been a lot of horrible singing and groups standing on an empty stage uncomfortably clapping along off rhythm. Then, there was the classic gathering of ethnic minorities and letting them wear their traditional wardrobes and chant their aborigine songs while waving their heritage flags. And, pretty much, on the hour every hour, there are some children talking into a microphone, crying, and close-up shots of audience members with tears in their eyes. Instead of being about God, or blessing the country, it's supposed to show the deep love and respect the children have for their parents.

When I bring myself to buy a guitar amplifier, I want to take it onto the roof. I've always had an urge to blow a wave of music over a town to wake them up and let them lose. You don't have to read a text book to learn that Chinese had been repressed for a long time. You probably won't see a staler audience in the world. The video clip of The Beatles performing "Don't Let Me Down" for the last time on the rooftop of their Apple building in London crosses my mind. I had a friend once that named his band "Smog" because he said he polluted the air with music. In my case, I think naming my band "Fresh" would be suitable. Or, forget the band. Just call me Fresh.

Shanghai's
Amazing Volcano

Ada was expected to arrive soon and I wanted to use my legs a little bit, so I thought I might try to meet her half way. I put a pair of spandex running pants on under a pair of windbreaker pants, and layered my leather jacket under a windbreaker jacket in the same way. We missed each other. Ada walked around to the front while I was walking out of the back. I had to circle back to meet her and found she had brought some more food from the grocery store. It was about 3:30 and we still had a long way to go until midnight, so I put a DVD in and we watched a movie together. At about 5 o'clock, we realized that if we wanted to drink wine later, we would have to go buy it right away, before the stores closed.

The majority of wines to choose from were Chinese and we selected one of the more expensive ones to buy. I asked Ada to take a walk with me in the park, but she said it was too cold. She was right. When we came back, Ada started cooking and I watched some more of the TV series <u>Outsourced</u>. After a few episodes, I went over to help Ada find some sugar and then started to rearrange the dining table for better feng shui. I hooked up my iPhone to the speakers and had it playing the jazz piano of Bill Evans while lighting some of the candles I found behind the bookshelf. Ada served what she had been working on for over an hour. It was chicken wings in a special sugar sauce, a type of goulash, and some dumplings from her hometown. It looked fantastic.

Right when I started to take my first bite, Ada was laughing. I had to ask her why she was laughing like three times before she said how I made the dinning environment like a western setting. I didn't realize it before, but she was right. And I loved it. Eating home-cooked Chinese food in an environment that took some preparation is something that I really love. Her food tasted awesome and it was a great mix of starch, vegetables, and proteins. I was starting to near the end of my pig-out fest when we started a fantastic discussion. I can't remember the order of the conversation or what spawned it, but we talked about recent Chinese history, modern civilization, world war, world religion, and how China and the US relate to each topic. I was impressed that Ada didn't build a wall around Chinese history and accepted some other perceptions of history.

After dinner, I put a DVD in for <u>Curb Your Enthusiasm</u> before realizing that the kind of humor it used was mocking details of American culture and English wordplay. I changed it back to <u>Jackass</u>, this time with the remote ready to fast forward. Eventually, I put on a comedic film about Noah's Arch and kept an eye on the clock. At about 11:20, the fireworks were ringing out non-stop and we got up to sit at the glass balcony in the front of the condo. They started to get more and more intense and I couldn't wait any longer, I went to put on my jacket and told Ada that I was going to the roof. She had been saying it was cold, but I wasn't going to miss this. I stepped foot onto the roof at 11:45 expecting to find a crowd of people on the roof. After all, Jeri from my new workplace told me that everyone goes "up" on New Year's Eve to see the fireworks. Not only was our roof empty, but I didn't see anyone on top of any roofs. Ken had remarked earlier that it's probably safer to stay in the glass rooms to watch, but then you can only see one view. Plus, it didn't look like any fireworks were reaching above our floor.

Luckily, Ada and I visited the roof for a few minutes earlier in the night and she discovered one of the champagne bottles hadn't been opened yet. Since our bottle of wine was finished, we opened the bottle of champagne and started scouring the rooftop. The day before, I was afraid of the amount of fireworks that were going to be shooting off because of living on such a high floor. Suddenly, I felt like we had one of the best views of the city and Shanghai was all mine. There were fireworks shooting out of gaps in building tops from miles and miles away, far off in the distance, with layers of fireworks exploding in front of them. I ran to the back view, then to the front view, then to the side view. I couldn't see them all and every few minutes I was checking the time. Ada was off video recording from her phone and I was recording from my phone. I felt like a reporter on the front lines of the biggest event in the world and I was the only one that could capture it.

Ten until midnight, I was feeling one of the biggest thrills of my entire life. I have never seen anything like it. Was the city designed for this? Am I in Disney World for grownups? What is this?! I had seen fireworks before. Most July 4ths, someone somewhere is lighting some fireworks off and sometimes I have been lucky enough to see some good shows with fireworks purchased "south of the boarder". Some of the best fireworks shows I have seen have been out in the countryside, in a big field. They usually start with streamers and move into more flash as the show progresses. Some of the finale ones make shapes in the sky and flutter. But what I was seeing was a cityscape that was alive and erupting like a volcano.

It was five minutes until midnight and taking into account that it only takes a few seconds for a firecracker to rocket off into the sky and explode, I was thinking that there can't be any more fireworks going off at one time. Maybe for Chinese New Year's, midnight isn't as important as it is like western New Years. I was wrong. Somehow, the rumble that I was shouting over to Ada increased. It became so loud that Ada and I had to use sign language to communicate. We didn't have to say much though. I gave Ada a giant smile and shouted, "Whooo hooo. This is fucking amazing!!!" It really felt like Shanghai was built for this occasion and my building was built to observe it from. I should say, experience it from.

It was cold on the roof and we had been up there for a half an hour, so we decided to come down into the sunroom to watch the volcanoes begin to calm. We shared a German beer sitting on some bar stools. It made me feel like we were on a cruise ship, or a space ship, with a view that is always of exploding lights. The sound of fireworks coming from the other side of the building started to overpower our side, so we switched rooms to continue watching. An hour later, the fireworks sounds became more distant and Ada and I could lay down. We watched some more RMB entertainment TV until we fell asleep. Somehow, this was just a normal day in America. I am interested to see how well these dates align with seasonal change. Ada stayed over the following day and we finally got that walk in the park that I wanted.

A Little Skinny
on the Little

I haven't written in a few days and because of that I cannot recall the details of my past days. I know going forward I will not be able to write frequently. My job starts Sunday, assuming we can agree to some terms that weren't previously discussed, such as a six month contract and/or allowing leave. I spent a lot of money in the last few days using my credit, but they were for clothes that I had already been shopping for and just have to finally give into the price. I don't want to have to go trying on clothes at different stores before or after work. I don't know what my work schedule will be, but I imagine I will be working in the evenings and have Monday and Tuesday off.

Last Tuesday, Ada and I were leaving my building together and she was going to walk to a friend's house and I was going to try running in a secret park. I needed saline liquid for my contact lenses and hadn't been able to find it anywhere since I have been here. So, I asked Ada if she wouldn't mind going to the store with me quickly to help me find the stuff. The grocery store didn't have it and neither did the pharmacy. The pharmacist told us to walk 10 minutes in another direction to buy it at a glasses store. I started to complain to Ada that "This isn't running," so she invited me to jog there and she joined me. Since a simple purchase turned into an excursion, I was hungry, so we ate at one of the Japanese chain restaurants here that I have eaten in a half a dozen times now. After that, we did finally split ways.

The next day, I searched the internet to find President Obama's State of the Union Address. Just like last time, I just missed it and it took me an hour to find a website that had it posted online already. I rigged my laptop to display through the TV and connected the audio to the speakers. I made a big country style breakfast and listened to the speech. Midway through, Ken woke up and came downstairs. It was the first time that I sat beside a non-American watching a State of the Union Address. You have to realize that nothing the President is going to say could possibly excite an Australian. Not only that, but you realize how silly it is to have Nations because in the speech everything is always referring to the citizens of the United States of America. Like, the world is pretty big. It's just strange to divide people, basically at random, and then say there is "us" and there is "them". Maybe it's not strange on the surface, but it's definitely strange when you listen to the competitive aspect of who is better. We're all born the same, living within the same laws of nature on planet earth, and no one decides which nation they will be born in.

Ken hung out in the living room and I showed him the

video I made of the fireworks display for Chinese New Year's Eve. It was good spending time with him and he helped me book a hotel for my first night in Hong Kong. He had to travel to Hong Kong dozens of times for the same reason that I have to. The other two nights, I will be staying at a hostel that a friend of mine booked for me. I don't know how she was able to do it, but she said that it's already paid for. The first night I will be staying on Hong Kong Island and the remaining nights I will stay in Kowloon. When I have to go back to Hong Kong again, next time I will fly into Shenzhen and see some friends, before taking the train into Hong Kong. That is said to be a little cheaper as well.

Yesterday, I finally made it to the secret park. I call it a secret park, because the nice gated street entrance is closed off. However, if you go around to the quiet side street, there is an entrance to a car park where a lot of busses are kept and there is a dirt path to that park that way. It's called Suzhou River Park and it's pretty darn big, running about a mile along the riverside. It looks like it is a 400 million dollar project that suddenly had funding pulled. The walkway is very flat and good for running. It's made-up of the same kind of rough marble that you would find used as the walkway material for many outdoor monuments in DC. There's a bunch of sculpturesk walkways, docks, non-working lights, and empty fountains. There was only about three people in the whole park. Its right across the street from my complex and it was the most remote I have felt since I have been here. Sure, there are dozens of high-rises everywhere that people could see me from, but no-one was probably looking.

The air must tunnel in from the ocean along the river, because I could smell very clean air. There were a lot of trees and a field of unkept, overgrown grass. I could hear Warbler birds and see them zooming in to a tree for their landing. It was the first completely clear day in Shanghai that I could remember and the weather was warm. I did some slow exercises in the relative silence and relished in the feeling of being far away from a big dirty city.

When I came back to the house, I texted Ada and she wanted to get out of the house. I had to return some clothes at the big mall and she said there was a giant park next to the mall, so we could go there next. I got to the mall on time, but she was running late, so I sat down at a western restaurant to have lunch. Sitting at high tables is perfectly fine for eating Asian food. In fact, it's helpful for bringing the chopsticks from your plate to your mouth. But, for western food, it's a real pain in the ass to use silverware on a surface that is neck-height.

I was wearing a baseball cap and it feels very American to do that. On the occasion that I see a Chinese wearing a baseball cap, it actually feels very comforting to me. I don't know why. Some Chinese guy must have been visiting Shanghai, because he gave me a cheery pump of the fist when he saw me. The hat must have made me look American. And that reminds me, when I got on the subway earlier, there was a Chinese couple holding their luggage studying the subway map on the train I was ridding. It was interesting, because in this context, they were the outsiders.

After returning my clothes and commending the clerk for having a tattoo of a treble clef on her index finger, we walked over to the park. I was feeling great and there was a skip in my step. I was asking Ada for Chinese word after Chinese word. My learning is starting to stick more rapidly and my range of communication is starting to open up. That is the feeling of China opening up to me. We walked passed some "stinky tofu" cook stations on the street and I thought I was going to puke from the smell. Finally, a big park with giant trees welcomed us.

The park weaved around a moat, small streams, fields, pagoda-type buildings, and stone walkways. Around every corner was some kind of music being performed. At one of the music stops was some real talent. The man playing the erhu with another guy playing an accordion and small choir of older Chinese singers were fantastic. He made his erhu sound like the voice of a human being. The singers were very passionate and it sounded like they were singing some Mao era, propaganda songs. It was so great that I stood there watching with a big smile on my face so everyone performing could see it. Ada told me to record it on my phone, but I assured her that recording it in my brain would be far superior. I told Ada that it was the most Chinese thing that I have seen in Shanghai and I fucking loved it.

After walking the park, we went back to the mall so I could get a few things. I wasn't going to be home in time to meet Shiny for my lesson, so I asked her to meet me at the mall. Ken had told me that this night was the second most important day of Chinese New Year's and his bar was having some kind of event. Ada wanted to come, so we tried to plan for her to walk around the mall while I had my lesson with Shiny. The problem was that all three of us were very hungry. When Ada first met Shiny, she said hello and quickly left before formally meeting Shiny. Shiny asked me why she scared Ada and I said I didn't know. Really, I knew Ada was a little intimidated with me having to pull away to meet with another girl, but I knew she would be fine with it if they got to know each other. I called her to come back so we could all eat together. They started talking and before long they got along fine. We walked to three closed restaurants before finding one Shiny liked.

Before the food came out, Shiny and I got out our materials and reviewed our previous lesson. Ada had a big smile on her face because I can imagine that seeing a grown man have a child's lesson is very amusing. After we finished eating, we continued our lesson for one hour. The restaurant wasn't busy, so one of the waiters sat down and listened to my lesson. He finally got up the nerve and came to sit down next to Ada. I don't know what they were talking about, but I was glad Ada didn't just have to sit and wait for my lesson to be over. The waiter was one of many that shared with me that he wants to learn English. It always reaffirms my commitment to coming here to hear that. It was a good lesson and I learned a lot of useful phrases and words. As we were leaving, another firecracker was lit beside the exit, and we had to cover our ears. Actually, the fireworks here are starting to really piss me off.

I guess everyone is used to it, but in the context of my country, if someone was to light off a million of those popping ground-fireworks in front of my restaurant so that it sounds like a drive-by shooting is taking place, I would go out there fuming mad and threaten to kick the shit out of the person who lit them. People here don't mind. A couple times during my lesson, we had to stop and wait for the sound of explosions to stop so that we could hear each other. We walked Shiny back to her apartment and I asked her to come to the bar with us twice. I really wanted to try and meet some guy friends this time and it would be better for Ada if Shiny came so they could talk while I talked with some other guys. She thought she would be interfering. Jay texted me asking if I had any plans for the night and I invited him, so I really wanted Shiny to come.

We got to The Otter bar around 10:30 and it was pretty empty. I bought a beer and each of the ladies a glass of red wine. I almost didn't tell either of them about it earlier because I knew I wasn't going to be able to afford buying everyone drinks. If I went alone, I could actually drink some beers, but if I had to buy everyone drinks, I wasn't going to be able to have more than a beer. They told me I was a very good guy, which means thanks for making everything free. At least up until now, I have needed the company and wasn't concerned about treating meals or drinks. Ken showed up and came over to take a shot of vodka with us. He told us a "bar crawl" group of 45 people would be showing up just before midnight and he will light fireworks in the street then. The girls were having a good time and playing some funny Chinese drinking game. Jay wasn't showing up.

The other day, Ken told me that lighting fireworks off early was like premature ejaculation and a schoolboy error. I kept an eye on the time and we were throwing some darts and checking out the pictures on the wall when suddenly the sound of fireworks came from the street. God damn it, Ken lit off the fireworks five minutes early. What was all that "schoolboy error" bullshit from the other day about? We ran out there and just as we got outside, he lit those ground poppers off that just about shattered my eardrum and were shooting off into our bodies. We had to run back inside. The new crowd was pretty rowdy and drunk, so I pulled up my sleeves in case I had to get a little physical. It reminded me of years ago when I was in a bar and was displaying my arms to someone and pulling up my sleeves saying "safe" and pulling them back down and saying "unsafe". I practiced a really defined style of Wing Chun Kungfu pretty intensely for a couple of years when I was younger using my arms with other people and some Wooden Dummies. It makes you really comfortable in crowded areas where you are pushed up against people in tight spaces. The street fireworks were dying out, so I suggested we take a walk. We got half a block when the girls had a new idea.

"Let's go to Muse!" Shiny said. Ah fuck. I spent all this money getting us drunk and the party just started to get crazy. The music playing was dance music and people were dancing all over, now they want to get into a taxi and drive to an expensive stuffy club to dance? This coming from the mouth of the girl that didn't want to go out and then said she would, but only for two hours. There was no talking sense into them. They were being drunk girls that had never been to a club before and suddenly had the inspiration to go. Girls can get into any club any time, but I was wearing a windbreaker, cargo pants, and a baseball cap. Even if I wanted to go to Muse, it defeats the purpose of going to a club if you are going to wear everyday clothes. The club is supposed to take you away to a fantasy land and I didn't want to spoil that for everyone, even if my clothes were acceptable in China. Plus, I had taken them to my friend's bar and we were both hospitable to them, and they wanted to leave right when it was starting to get fun. They still had their wine glasses in hand and asked me to bring them back to house later to give to Ken. The reality set in. They were going to go to Muse, and I wasn't. So, I went back inside The Otter, pushing through the dancing crowds just like you would find at any club, and took a final leak. I came back into the street and looked at them and said, "Okay, be safe. I'm going home. Goodbye." There was a cab waiting in front of the bar, so when I turned around, I jumped in and sped off.

On the drive home, I had that feeling you get sometimes when you find that you only have yourself in the world. You can't depend on other people to make you happy and if you invest too much in happiness from someone else, you will fall that much farther into unhappiness. That night I spent a lot of money in pursuit of the goodtime that I never got, so it was a sunk investment. It was the first money I spent in Shanghai that felt like a total loss. I only spent about $35 on their wine, but it goes to show you that I should be going to the bar with guys and that I need guy friends. If Jay showed, I would have kissed them goodbye and stayed having a great time. This was a Chinese New Year's party, but to me, it was my last night partying before starting my new job. I had to shake it off and start thinking about the next day. I live in Shanghai now and will start having commitments and obligations to fulfill. I'm looking forward to being paid instead of paying.

As my most-likely last entry before I start my new job, I want to capture a few of the thoughts I have been having since being here. I have been in Shanghai for over a month and already think of Fairfax, Virginia as a rural place, even though it's not. I feel like I will be in Shanghai for at least this year and that I will be able to carry on a reasonable conversation in Chinese by the end of the year. I am becoming more familiar with the culture here and I could imagine that it would take at least 48 hours to adjust back to an American city. I have discovered that North America is like a giant resort. As far as climate and nature go, I think that is the real wealth of North America because there is still so much untouched land there. I imagine Europe isn't far behind China with its land usage over the past couple of thousand years. I don't know much about the other side of the equator, but I doubt there is such pristine and vast changes of land as there is in the United States. I really hope that I can make a long-term goal to live in such a place. Considering that I am already American, I think that goal is obtainable.

What is the Chance?

It's funny. Some time ago, Mozzy asked me to install an App on my phone called WeiXin so that we could talk there. It's a newer Chinese application designed to allow text chatting with audio walkie-talkie capability. It has some additional features for meeting strangers, such as opening a "drift bottle" or shaking your phone to match up with someone else that is shaking their phone at the same time. When I came home from my bad night ending at the bar, I signed into WeiXin to get my mind out of the weeds. There is another feature WeiXin has to meet people, called "look around", that will access your GPS location and display a list of people nearby sorted by their distance away in meters. I played with that for a little while and started chatting with someone when I received a message. Someone else found me and started to voice chat with me. It sounded like a cute girl practicing her English. I only signed into WeiXin for a couple of minutes the following night and when I signed in the next morning, the same girl sent me a "Good Morning". I told her I was about to go to the furniture store to look at office chairs. Little did I know what was in store for me.

The lady's English name is Villa and I told Villa that I

was probably going to go to the furniture store a few subway stops north of me, but I might check the furniture store across the street from me first. Villa recommended Yue Xing outlet and I told her that was the same outlet across the street from me. She asked if I knew her line of work and then told me that she works at Yue Xing. We planned it out so that I would go there around noon, we would have lunch, and then she would show me where the chairs and mattresses were. I wanted to look at mattresses too because I have woken up with my back in pain every day since I have been here and sometimes it hurts all the way into my stomach. I was hoping I could get used to it, but I can't be working a full time job with the equivalent feeling as sleeping on the floor every night. Villa told me her x-boss sold mattresses and I said, "So what?"

When I walked into her store at the outlet mall, ironically called NOVA (the same name as the area that I am from), her colleague told me to have a seat while she got her. I was a little nervous to meet her. I had never met someone this way before and for all I know, she was a 17 year old little girl. Around the corner walked a lady about my height and my age with a big smile on her face. We said our hellos and quickly setoff for the in-mall restaurant. The restaurant was primarily built for all of the employees of the outlet mall and I had never seen it the past few times I visited. Villa ordered us one of the dishes that cooks in front of you and I am starting to feel more familiar with the selection of Chinese food restaurants. Villa has a very pretty face and had her hair perfectly pulled back with a barrette on. She had a silky scarf around her neck and a tight-fitting green and while big-striped knit sweater on. I was probably one of the first foreigners she has eaten with because she asked me to write words on paper when she couldn't understand what I would say.

Because of her industry, I thought I would have the chance to try and solve the mystery of expensive goods in China. Using math and pictograms, I showed how one speaker in the US can cost $200 and in China it can cost $400 or more. It took some work, but she finally understood me. She wasn't familiar with prices in America and didn't have an answer either. Every time that she could not understand me, she got a sad face, her face would blush, and she would cover her mouth with her hand. When she spoke, if she said a word similar to what she meant to say without saying the correct word and she knew it, she would instantly stick out her tongue and bite it smiling. That happened a whole lot. I think I surprised her because I knew her home town, which was small and not very famous, and I could use chopsticks and speak some Chinese. I am a little determined to not be a stereotypical foreigner here. After we finished eating, she took me to look at chairs.

When we walked into the store that had chairs, it was clear that everyone was familiar with her and I followed her through shortcuts for employees only. It reminded me a lot of my experience at Beijing's International Terminal at the airport. I spent so many hours in that airport on many occasions and knew it so well. And when I missed my flight because they wrote down the wrong gate number for me, the airport personel walked me back to the main terminal through a series of "employee only" passages and eventually to an underground employee office building. I had been in this store, and this mall, a number of times. Now, I knew people in a store that would hold my goods for me while I shopped and grant me VIP access in the bigger store. I shopped for a while and ended up getting two kinds of their cheaper chairs. Villa had a coffee waiting for me when I came back to her store, which was great because there isn't anywhere to get a coffee around here and it was raining. I had some small talk with her colleague and then we went off to look at mattresses.

Villa told me to say "I have to go home and check with me wife" to any of clerks that would be pressing me hard for a sale. She took out a calculator before we left and showed me the price difference of what she can get me if she calls her x-boss. She told me to just find the mattresses that I like and she will know what to order for me. We tried a number of mattresses in a number of stores before walking into a "Science" mattress store that sold memory foam mattresses. The clerk came out and started giving me the prices. I have found that just about everyone I meet for the first time here does not show any friendly emotion. I read some years ago in a book about doing business with Chinese that Chinese culture has become used to hiding emotion because of their repressive years. China changes every day and the meaning behind that bit of advice some years ago may be obsolete soon, but it has been my experience that people open up after a little while of talking. That's when you will start to gain their interest and provoke bigger smiles.

Villa learned the kind of mattress that I wanted and we walked back to her store. She told me there was no way for me to use a credit card to make the purchase, so I told her to wait a while until she hears back from me about the mattress. I want to make sure everything pans out at work tomorrow before making that purchase and scheduling a delivery date. I was incredibly lucky, but I have been very lucky since I landed here. Villa told me she was off work now and she would help carry one of my chairs to my house, in the rain I might add. She finally found out how close I lived to her job. I kept telling her, but it wasn't clear until she could see for herself. It was an incredibly ironic series of events. We put the chairs in the house and I followed her out the door. She demanded to walk to the subway stop by herself, but I insisted that I had to run errands in the same direction. It was true that I needed to go to the bank and stop by the grocery store, but I didn't have to go right away.

On the walk over to the bank, Villa embarrassingly told me that she had a secret. Her secret was a method for me to grow the hair back on the top of my head. She said to cut up some ginger root and rub it on my head and asked if I was angry at her. It was pretty funny. We tried to get some bearing of when we would see each other again and then split ways. After the bank, I went over to the bigger grocery store here and bought some items and food. I bought a bag with wheels that is similar to what a golfer would use to roll his golf bag. I concluded that taking a taxi home from the grocery store every time I had to grocery shop would be the same price as paying for the bag after a few rides. I could fit all of my groceries in the bag and walk home, and I could use it over and over again. When I shopped for food, I mainly revisited all of the same stops that I had with Ada and Shiny. I got my chicken squares, beef cuts, Japanese noodles, eggs, yogurt, and a handful of other things. On my walk home, I thought that living anywhere else wouldn't feel right. It's my perspective of trying to get here for so long that I need the relief of actually being here to continue on. I had to carve out a special line for the transport home so the wheels of the cart would avoid the most textured terrains. As I got onto my elevator, I received a text message from Shiny that she would be over any minute.

I had enough time to put the chairs in my room, turn the heaters on, and use the bathroom. By the time she walked in, I just started putting away my groceries. That was followed by a two hour review of everything I have learned so far. Nearing the end of the review, my head started hurting. It was brutal. As soon as Shiny left, I popped open a beer for instant relief. I called up an old colleague of mine from my previous job to see how he's been doing. The IT guy from the last job in the U.S. forwarded me an email written by the CEO about management changes that he made that made my stomach turn even though I no longer work there. I knew my colleague's position at the company was substantial, managing a team of almost two dozen people in multiple locations and I wanted to hear his feedback. It was great talking to him and he was eager to hear how everything has been panning out for me since I arrived here. We shared many lunches at the company where I discussed my plans to move to Shanghai and he was thrilled to hear everything has been going so well for me. The problems with his company persisted after I left and it sounds like him and another of other long-time employees are looking for the exit. There is no winning there.

I'm really setup now. Ken left to start his "day" around 8:00 PM and I had the place to myself, so I rolled out the yoga mat and went to town. It was true, what I told my colleague. I was extremely lucky. I found a great place with a great roommate. I don't have to worry about my laundry or cleaning the dishes. I am probably the only person in the whole building that doesn't have anyone sleeping above him or below him (at least that knows it), my place has is adjacent to two different outdoor parks and one of them is basically vacant, and my roommate owns a bar with one of the best beer selections in Shanghai. My job, if all goes well, is with an advanced English company in a prime location. My role at the job is important with a job that is fun, yet challenging. I have half a dozen friends here that have treated me with compassion, I am learning Chinese every other day with a great teacher, and I am staying connected with many people in my home town. In fact, this blog has allowed me to take my friends with me and that is extra comforting. I would say, don't be afraid of something better. Take the chance. Mainstream is lame stream.

A Hard View
on Fast Times

It didn't start off great. It didn't even start off, preliminarily great. I set my alarm on some free iPhone App that ended up chiming on the hour every hour, waking me up at 2 in the morning. I got up early enough and downed two yogurts, trouble pursued. I was all ready to hit the road when I noticed my glasses were sitting slightly crooked on my nose. I went to bend them and the screw holding one of the lenses popped out and vanished. God damn it, I had to look around for the screw for a minute, and then revert to trying to put on my contact lenses. What a night mare. I suck at putting contact lenses on. Then, I lost one of the lenses and spent three minutes searching the floor for it. I grabbed an older lens and got it in my left eye, but I couldn't see out of it. I thought I would fix it on the subway train. My legs felt like running, so I jogged to the station.

I was dropping eye drops into my eye and spinning the lens with my finger, but nothing I did was clearing my vision. After 15 minutes on the train, I started to feel sick to my stomach. Could it be that I was getting dizzy enough to feel sick? When I got off the train, I immediately pulled the lens out. I felt better right away. After I explained the glasses and contact lens situation to my new boss, he told me to go across the street to the mall to have my glasses fixed. When I put the fixed glasses on, I couldn't see out of the left eye correct. I took them off and looked at a sign. Strange. I could read the sign clearly without my glasses and when I put them on, I couldn't. I was sure I took the lens out of my left eye. What happened? Did the lens reshape my eye somehow? Did I scrape the surface of my pupil accidently correcting my vision? Was I wearing two contact lenses before? When I got back to the office I checked my eye. There was a contact in it alright. Somehow, I was wearing two contact lenses before. I didn't even think about it before, but maybe I never dropped that first lens in the morning after all!

The day was unbearably slow. Mao Guy sat me at the computer without any activities to do and sat beside me. I would have rather been solving a nuclear war crisis than sit at a mediocre computer desk in a cold room all day while letting the circulation to my feet come to an end. I was over dressed too. I sacrificed comfort when I didn't have to. Not until late in the afternoon was I presented with the work contract. I noted my questions and found a typo in the Appendix. I pointed out a clause where it said that I would not be able to do unrelated work on my own time. I pointed out that it should say, "related" work and that it needs to be changed in case I want to get paid to play guitar or something. Mao Guy found that surprising because I am sure that the last half dozen English teachers signed it without a complaint. I also pressed for a six month contract with an "option to renew" and I had to explain what that means. In the Appendix, there are a number of lines referring to the Chinese Government and one of the lines makes me promise that I will not interfere with the Chinese Government. That, in summation, is the golden rule here.

That could be classified as communism, maybe in a modern context. But think of it this way. I saw a really cool scooter a few weeks ago, parked at the station. I thought, "Man, I want a scooter like that. That thing is awesome." And therein lies the problem. That guy broke one of the golden rules that is turning into a bronze rule. Don't tote shit that people will envy. Not because it is immoral, but because you just made your transportation the most coveted item around and increased its "being messed with" by a multitude of 1,000%. A good scooter to have here is one that will be where you left it when you get back. Don't stand out with things that you cannot wear. On the other hand, if you want to wear some crazy outfit with mismatching colors, sparkles, fur, and flash, then that's totally fine. I, personally, have grown really attracted to this kind of living art and it is especially provoking in this new era for China.

I got up to walk around a lot because I felt like I was dying in there. I circled my floor in the building and then went up to the floor above us to see what kind of offices were there. In America, I can assess a company and its viability pretty quickly. You know, the customer base is usually American and the industry is usually relative. I know most of the numbers, like population of the market, the state of the economy, and what people expect and want from a company. I can make some conclusions by floor space, rent estimation, the number of employees, location of the company, and a feel for how much capital it would take to be in their position with some assessment of salaries, margins, and demand for the company. Here, I have no idea. If someone told me, "We make plastic ears for frogs in Germany" I wouldn't skip a beat, nod, and say, "Oh, that's interesting." I can't tell what most of the offices do because there is no hint or the signs are in Chinese.

All of my colleagues today were Chinese, so it was nice to hear Chinese conversing. I saw on the schedule, there was a day in the week labeled, "Salon English". I tried to explain to Mao Guy that Salon was usually associated with Beauty Salons and a place where women talk. I did some research and told them that "Saloon" is originally a French word for a big room where people can talk. Eventually, in English, "salon" came to reference a place where women talk in a beauty parlor and "saloon" referenced a place where men drank alcohol and talked. Mao Guy was really surprised and my new colleague, Chris (Chinese woman), laughed out loud. Nearing the end of the day, I couldn't resist. Mao Guy and Chris were just browsing the internet, so I invited them to check out my websites. Chris was really taken by all of my presentations of artistic whatever. Who doesn't laugh when they see my dance videos? So, by the end of the day, they got a much better feel for who I am. I'll probably never get to see as much of someone as I am willing to share.

There must be investors in the company, because it looked like all five of us spent the day surfing the internet. If it was their company, I imagine we would have just stayed home. I haven't been in the position to have to kill time in a long time. In fact, it's a problem that only people with salaries have. It's nice to be able to take your time and relax, but people like to be challenged as well. Just from knowing myself and having so many previous jobs, I expect that I will try to reinvent how language is taught in the coming months. I know me, and I will probably think that I have the world's first idea how to do something, or I will dig up some old way and try to push that forward. I can already tell that I don't support the teaching software that the use. That's why I know I'll resort to pushing some far-out theory of learning onto the school. I'll probably be making my students learn the alphabet in reverse. Not just the order either, but the sound of each letter.

Maybe it's because I hated having to kill time all day, or because I was cold all day, but I was feeling happy to talk to strangers. For lunch, I went to KFC and it was very busy and there weren't any photos on the wall menu. A few weeks ago, I wouldn't have waited in that line, knowing that I would slow the crowd when I tried to order. Getting used to being a foreigner is no different than getting used to being fearless. You just don't have care if you understand people or they understand you. Like, Villa's look on her face when she can understand or knows that I can't understand her. She got really flustered and uncomfortable. That is normal. After a while, you won't even blink when someone is talking to you that you don't understand. You just look them in the eye with compassion and don't say anything back to them. Or you can completely ignore them and say whatever you want when they finish. You don't have to do an inch more than try, but it's more fun if you try to be creative. I think a lot of the words that I use I can also use sign language for. So, you don't have to have a big vocabulary, you just have to be clever. I got out of work and called everyone I know in China.

Mao Guy and I shared two trains part of the way home and there was one of those tricycle taxis waiting for me when I got to my home station. This guy loved that I was a foreigner and I say the Chinese words that I know now with comfort. The driver was so happy to say "Yes!" in English and when I stepped out of his back seat, I patted him on the arm and thanked him. He was laughing and said, "Yes!" again before he sped off. I decided to walk another two blocks to my neighborhood supermarket to see about buying a pair of really cheap loafers. My feet were cold and sweaty all day long. Even though my boots are great for outdoors in Shanghai, in the office they are horrible. I saw a pretty awesome polo shirt for ultra-cheap and tried it on. That was the first clerk I spoke to. Then I went over to look at the shoes and came back to the same clerk to ask her about prices. It wasn't her department and all she could tell me was that no-one was in the shoe department. Damn, isn't that just my luck? Well, fearless mode continues on and I checked the centimeters of my Rockport shoes under the tongue. It said 250, but when I when I tried a pair of 250's on, they were way too small. 265 fit me just right. I knew the sizes are all wack in these shoes. I was getting ready to get in line with a pair of shoes to ask the cashier to tell me the price of the damn shoes.

Suddenly, a lady was looking over my shoulder, leaning down on me as I was packing up the shoe. I gave her a strong "Ni Hao". The whole "rude" thing here is starting to rub off on me. Actually, rude is a culturally defined behavior. If everyone decides something is not rude – guess what? It's not rude. I guess there is a slight version of that in New York City. People from the West Coast would say New Yorkers are very rude. In my opinion, they are just straight forward. Therein lies the dilemma. I was having a conversation with the lady, never mind that I only understood half of what she was saying. Then, from the amusement of me carrying on about the shoes I wanted, another couple of clerks came over. I went from receiving no help at all, to suddenly having half the store bending over backwards to find the shoes that I wanted at the price that I wanted. I know it was fun for them to figure out what I meant, and I wasn't the least bit embarrassed. In fact, I played along. I was poking them and trying to tell jokes. It does take some balls to do that because some of these people are tough as nails, and to go into a joke, you better mean it. Just don't get embarrassed and you will be totally fine. Don't be afraid to throw some punches back.

I checked out of there and went a few stores over to a buffet type of restaurant. Fearlessness ensued. I didn't even want anything in the buffet, but I wanted their acknowledgement that I was interested in their food. I finally grabbed (literally) a guy in line and asked him in Chinese what food was good. I pulled him along the buffet and he tried to tell me what stuff was in English. Then, once I decided what I wanted to eat, none of the clerks were ready to serve. I had to go over and call one of them. One thing about me is that I will make some elaborate funny faces. In reference to yesterday's post, Chinese don't tend to make faces upon greeting. Me? I try to speak with my face before my mouth, so I made a helpless face and told someone to help me. There seems to be a lot less asking in Chinese than in English. There's a lot more demanding. Then, like the last place, four servers all tried to help me at once and I think I got a free soup out of the meal. That was fun!

I was thinking on my way home about the race issue again. It's not racist to make observations based on the lack of race diversity, especially when I am not a part of the majority. Therefore, I think it's safe to point out that most of the "clicks" I have witnessed in American society are race based. Maybe that's some really primitive analysis, because it is probably primarily cultural based. I guess that's the thing. What is the difference between race and culture? I guess race is just the easiest way to make an assessment by only using your eyes. It's just really different for me to be surrounded by so many people and not witness any strong segmentation at all. There is no sign of over aggression or sign of outsiders in the mainstream view of Chinese. If there were four major races/cultures that made up Shanghai, with distinct differences, then I am sure there would be obvious pockets of separation. But there aren't and there isn't.

Last week, Ada told me there was a gunman in her hometown that shot and killed someone for their money. She told me to be careful because he might come to Shanghai and think I am rich because I am a foreigner and he might shoot me for my money. I don't think it was a joke, but even if it was a joke, it is hard to imagine a world where that is such an extremely rare occurrence. Her hometown is probably a hundred times more populated than my hometown. In fact, we viewed each other's hometown on Google Earth last week and her home city had one park and in mine, it was difficult to tell where public and neighborhood parks end and where private yards begin, as well as the gray area of sidewalks and neighborhoods carved through forests. The picture of this gunman from a million miles away in a country five times more populated than the U.S. is hanging in stores here in Shanghai. Can you believe that? I can't remember the last time the local news wasn't updating everyone about a local murder, and often a shooting. Of course, I never liked to watch the local news because of that anyway.

Finally, China through American eyes. Our whole lives we are completely stuffed with American's acts of freedom. We sing about this land is your land, this land is my land and everything we ever had to memorize about history was about someone improving our freedoms. I'm pretty damn sure that the same thing is true in every country about their history. Everyone is fighting for freedom. Even oppression can be a kind of a freedom. The view of China is focused on Human Rights. The other side of the coin is that Chinese are kind of left to govern themselves and conduct themselves in society. You just get removed from society if you try to impact it. Otherwise, there is a lot of gray area. I don't think you heard me, so I'll say it again. There is a lot of gray area. America is developed to the point of over development. America's "problems" cannot even qualify for problems in other countries because it's like Warren Buffett would always say, "I know a lot of people that would love to have these problems". The best way to assess whether China is right or wrong about something, is to turn back the clock on American history. We've been there. And what will happen is, America will cycle too. China had greatness many times, and lost its greatness many times. China is America in two thousand years, in some ways. I can foresee Chinese characters symbolizing luxury items in the future. Not European letters.

Chrome

I wanted to write the other day, but sometimes it's hard to share what I am learning publically when it can put others at risk. Basically, my second day at work was better. Jeri was there and she explained to me a lot about the school. It turns out that the Chinese Director and Mao Guy don't really call the shots. There is an owner in another province that calls in and tells them all what to do and Jeri kind of makes strong suggestions. I got to talk to her about Shanghai. She has been here for 4 years and it sounds like she has been to every bar and venue multiple times. Believe it or not, she teaches horseback riding outside of Shanghai on occasion. She is from Niagara Falls, the Canadian side. After work, I went to check out a Gym a few blocks away from my office. I ran in the morning. The car park entrance was closed, so I had to go down the street to find another way in. There was a pack of wild dogs that came to snap at me, but once I got passed them, I had an entire park to myself.

I had a tour of the Gym and saw what I was looking for: a large aerobic room. The guy giving me the tour told me the room is locked when they aren't having a class. When he walked me down to talk with the big Chinese guy about a membership, I told him there was something that I hated. He tried to spice up the membership and defend locking the room, telling me that I could rent it and he would assure it would be clean for me. I wasn't interested. I don't need it to be clean, I just need it to be available. After that, I walked through one the malls in search of a shoe horn. It would help me get my boots back on at work when I slip back out of my shiny shoes. I didn't find one, but I walked into a clothing store and stood staring at a clerk that wasn't paying attention. When she turned and noticed me, she laughed because I had been standing there watching her for so long. She came over to me and stood almost up against me. We talked for five minutes in Chinese and I asked about a flannel hooded vest I saw. I think she was asking me to eat, but I thought if I got any more excited talking to her I would have started to drool, so I got her contact information and got out of there.

When I got off the train at my subway stop, I came down to meet my "Yes!" driver. This time I tried to ask him to drop me at the back of the complex, closer to my building. Another caddy driver came over and read my map because it turns out that my driver can't see clearly. That's good to know. We are developing a relationship, and thanks to my lessons with Shiny, I am able to direct him where to go and when to stop. I spent the night catching up with Ken. He rarely stays home in the evenings and the more we talked, the more lingering questions about the house came up. We solved a lot of problems I was having and I learned a lot more about how things work here. I still stand by him being a good guy, even though my colleague says that she got punched in the face at his bar and he saw it happen and didn't help. Ken proclaims that it is hard to believe that any guy wouldn't react to a woman getting punched by a man and he has a good point. Then again, unless you're piss drunk.

I didn't have enough time to run the next day, so I just did a few quick exercises before taking off for the train. I listened to my earphones on the walk over and it truly is the ingredient to make the city beautiful. I decided that a great description for Shanghai is that it is chrome. It's gray, but shiny. Music gives it the color it needs to make it beautiful. When I was walking out of the station, I noticed one of the girls that works in my office was right in front me, so I tried walking fast enough to catch up. People walk really fast here sometimes, and I was barely able to. She is one of the many people here that wear big glasses frames without any lenses. I got to my desk and got the routine down. At least, I understand that it is up to me what I do in my free time, as long as I am here. My computer had a virus and I had to solve a number of issues that the IT wasn't able to. The IT guy loves me. I speak a lot of Chinese to him and talk about a lot of stuff that he finds interesting. He is so gentle and kind that all he can say half of the time is, "Wow! You are awesome!" I went out to eat and found a place called Food Inn. It's actually a mall, a 12-story mall that only has restaurants. I can only tell that the first 8 floors have restaurants, and it has no impact on the restaurants on the street. There are still a hundred on the street. That is what makes the location of my work so amazing. I can't imagine any place in the world that has so many places to eat in such a short distance. It's strange to me that Jeri keeps telling Chris to call a Korean Hot Pot restaurant for delivery every day and being disappointed that they still haven't reopened from Chinese New Year.

At the end of the day, I wanted to get a number of things done in Pudong. I had my pair of paints with the hole in them from my peeing incident in my book bag and I wanted to drop them off with a seamstress somewhere. I had two wristwatches that were in a drawer here that Ken said weren't his and just needed a band and a battery that I wanted to drop somewhere to get fixed. I wanted to check out another Gym a block away and I also wanted to check out the "stadium" that was only a few block away because I heard they have indoor basketball courts. Mao Guy helped me figure out the bus system on a map because a few blocks here can still be a long ways. In fact, it was three subway stops away, but it required a transfer to take the subway. When I was leaving the office, I found out that Chris was going to the stadium too because she lives there, so I thought to join her. Even though I wanted to go there last, it was good that I went with her because she took another bus line that is less crowded than the one I was going to take.

The stadium, itself, was closed. When I looked behind the gate, I only saw a running track and less than 50 rows of stands. It was a weird stadium. There are restaurants on the outside of it, and a hotel, and they were open. I saw basketball courts next door and walked over there. There is a place called "HooPark". Sometimes I noticed signs don't include double letters, like this one should have been named, "Hoop Park". It cost 10 Yuan to play basketball all day and you can rent a basketball for 200 Yuan. There were about 40 baskets there and plenty of open courts, but it is outdoors and pretty cold out now. I walked over next door from there and into another open building. I climbed the steps and looked over the edge to find a bunch of badminton courts. The HooPark had some indoor badminton courts as well, but these were nicer. On the next floor, behind some double doors, was a large room full of Ping-Pong tables and it looked like a father had a bucket of ping-pongs that he was severing to his son to help him practice his ace return swing. Instead of taking the bus back to my office location, I walked to the subway and took that line with the transfer.

I was really tired and my legs started to shake. I am not used to having to sit behind a computer for 8 hours and not accomplish anything. That, and the sudden lack of exercise I can get with the 40 hour a week job and an hour commute each way. Instead of going to check out the other gym and visiting wristwatch shops, I was dying to get to a bar that had good beer and I had some in mind that I walked past the day before. I shot a little video with my iPhone and then went into a German Beer House. The beer was probably the best beer that I ever had in my life and I drank my beer quickly. I ordered a special breadbasket and a steak dinner. I couldn't wait. I was going to have a large piece of beef for the first time since I have been in China. The steak was tiny, but it was delicious and so were the steamed vegetables that it came with. I told the waitress that I knew it sounded crazy, but I wanted to order the meal again. It wasn't cheap but I was feeling so weak and tired early that it felt like I was consuming the life force that my body demanded in order to go on. I spent a lot of money, but nothing crazy. I can say it is a lot of money only because eating at restaurants here can be so, so inexpensive. When I went to take the subway home, I put my iPhone's iPod on shuffle and out of the 1,500 tracks I have on it, the track of a hypnotist's directions started playing. Needless to say, it put me to sleep and I was damn lucky to wake up right as the doors were opening for my home station. God damn that alcohol mixed with moving warm beams of sunlight from one leg to another in the clear sky after I "let go" and continued taking deep breaths, felt awesome.

The next morning, today, I got to work with a mission. I needed to write a lesson plan about poetry in the format that Jeri has requested. Apparently, the owner wants us to have a standard format. I learned that there are two big English schools next door to us and I get the feeling that we are a business and they are schools. Think about it. The owner doesn't know English and neither does the Director, yet, they are in the business of teaching English. Get it? For lunch, I went over to a place called Moo's something that has a picture of a cow on the sign. I ordered the supersize hamburger, just because it was offered. That place had the American meal down. The coke had ice cubes, and there were more than five fries on the plate when I got it. Of course, it costs four times more than if I ate at the Japanese Ramen restaurant. I just thought I should stuff myself full of beef in the last 24 hours to see how my body reacts. I feel like a meat sack, but it's kind of nice.

Back at the office, I worked on finding examples of different sound devices and rhetoric examples for my poetry lesson plan. I am familiar with almost a dozen famous poets and their work, but I really wanted to include Eminem in my examples because I think just one piece of his uses every poetic tool that I have to cover. There are probably some songs that have great lyrics too, but Eminem's work is more word focused and less melodic focused, so I wanted to stick with written poetry. Keeping all of the tools that I needed to find in mind, I found the piece, Infinite[2], and it blew my mind. It's nice to have your mind blown at work. Sorry that it's 2012 and I don't know any other great poets, but I can't imagine finding a better example of poetry writing techniques from any other English speaking rapper. It's nice to spend time getting acquainted with my own language more and appreciate its use in art.

I asked to sit in with Jeri's class at the end of the day and she grabbed me when it was starting. It was just her and one guy. I learned a lot from the meeting, but not from Jeri. I learned that it must be that I love China, Chinese people, and Chinese language that makes me a great teacher. I really want to hear Chinese use English and demand them to improve their speaking. Jeri has been teaching for five years, but she started in Vietnam, then went to South Korea, and finally ended up here. I think she likes to tell, which is a little different than teaching. I want the Chinese person to talk to me and use new words that

---

2   Eminem, *Infinite*, Infinite, Web Entertainment, 1996

I have given them. I learned that it must be a major factor to teaching that I am also a student. I admire the Chinese that come to learn English. Not just a little bit, but I completely admire them. I don't want to preach to them about cultural items, my personal stories, or words that most English speaking people don't know. I want them to feel like I am their best friend and that I am genuinely interested in what they have to say. That's where my advantage lies. I am genuinely interested in what they have to say and their speaking progress. That meeting lit a fire under me. I have been speaking to Chinese for eight years already. Can you find anyone more interested in their improvement than me?

After work, I went across the street to one of the malls and found a wristwatch store for one of my wristwatches. They told me that I need to call their service center and I got a pamphlet from them. Then I walked over to the other Gym that I wanted to check out. The wind was blowing and it was bitter cold. Unlike the other Gym that had its own building and catered to westerners; this Gym was on a three-story walkup and is entirely Chinese. I'm telling you. I love talking to Chinese. They know it too. No matter how we first start out, by the end of our conversation, we are best friends. The gym was small, but the exercise room is available when there are no classes. I think this is the one for me. We went over the class schedule and the room is usually available at lunch time and the cost of the gym is about $30 a month. I bought a little gym bag from the Manager and saw a guy training a girl in some boxing techniques. I saw a little list for a boxing class sign up.

I made the Manager take me over to the boxing instructor and I mimicked throwing some punches and gave him a thumbs up. I can tell that the people at this Gym aren't prepared for me to come in and start kicking some motherfucking ass with my Chinese and Western boxing exercises. I know people are going to want a piece of the action. The beautiful thing about it is that it is Bruce Lee's legacy. Combining the East and West.

I worked out some pricing plan with the Manager and explained to him my situation. I can't pay in their system with an American credit card, so I might hold off until I am back from Hong Kong and can see about opening a special bank account. I got all of their information and headed out. One more stop. I walked into another giant electronics mall and continued going to clerks that sold iPhone stuff and asked about a Bluetooth keyboard that works with my iPhone. I don't want to bring my laptop to Hong Kong, but I want to continue to write for my blog, so I have been thinking about getting one of these keyboards for some time. The first group of guys couldn't help. I went into an Apple type of store and they didn't think such a thing existed. I told them it does. Then I was looking at some devices at another counter when a guy asked me about it. I told him what I really wanted and he called over some other people. A lady brought over a keyboard and I agreed to pay $80 for it if it worked. We tested it and it worked. They started off distant and uninterested when we first started talking. At the end, they were my friends. One guy said the girl was single and to call them if I had any trouble.

It seems like a great position to be in. Chinese girls like you because you are from far away and therefore are special. Non-Chinese girls like you because they have some cultural issues with Chinese guy's treatment of women (although I don't suspect it is as different as I have heard them say it is). And, because it is a city, there are a million young and single people everywhere. Sometimes, I walk around looking at people here and thinking, "You're not allowed to leave and I'm not allowed to stay". Staying in China as a foreigner is just a tricky thing to accomplish. No doubt about it. I like it here. Americans think there is no freedom here. The same Americans that cannot smoke in a pub, smoke marijuana in the closet, get drunk at home because they can't carry an open container in public, have to hide their sandwiches and drinks on the subway, and masterbate at home watching porn. I think the definition of a free society might not be as American as Americans are lead to believe. It's cool that provinces and people can be so different and it's cool that prices can vary depending on the situation. It's choice. It's freedom.

I got off the subway at my stop and my "Yes" man was waiting for me. I missed him yesterday because I got home so late. This time he drove me all the way to my building. He insisted. I walked in and Patrick was home. I caught him up to speed with my new job and he told me it was 78 degrees in Taiwan. Ken called me and told me he will be bringing home some different beers for me to sample because I told him that I wanted some good beer for the fridge. My old colleague from my Boston days called me and asked about my Hong Kong plans. He lives there and wants to spend some time with me when I visit. I didn't have any of my flight information, so I am glad he called to remind me to get it. Ada sent it over to me and there were some unclear things about it that Tony helped me to straighten up. He recently quit his job and he is working on a new venture, so he will have time to spend with me when I visit.

I stayed up late yesterday trying to tell some of my hometown friends to visit me. I feel like I hit Jackpot here with the location of my home and my job being so special. You can see the tallest building from my office building. Not far off in the distance either. It's the closest skyscraper to view from one of the windows. They are building the second tallest building in the world beside it. It just recently started to pass ground level, even though it has been under construction since 2008. The building will be 128 stories tall and will be one of the first "green" skyscrapers ever built. An American company is building it, but partnering with many Chinese-based branches of theirs. It's pretty crazy. It will actually have insulating space between a glass shell and the core building itself. I have absolutely no idea how the three tallest skyscrapers can be next door to each other here. If it was Sim City, you would be required to put a power plant and another sewage plant next to it. I will never understand how Shanghai is possible. I think that is what I have in common with the 40 million inhabitants here (28 million is only the registered number), no-one can understand how this place works, but we all use it.

Writing About Life in Shanghai

This morning I jogged the park again. There was a new addition to the wild dog pack, a big black Saint Bernard-looking dog. I ran fast enough that my lungs burned and the air was so awful this morning that it didn't really feel healthy to be breathing like that. I recalled the "Code Orange" warning days we would get in DC when the air levels weren't safe. They would have to come up with a whole new color system here and it would have to be with neon colors. Someone told me that there was an avid runner living in Beijingthat would run 10+ miles every day and he ended up dying of lung cancer. That's great. By exercising to be healthier, you're just harming yourself more. I was thinking of bringing some dog bones and treats for the wild dogs to try and befriend them. I don't know though. They might follow me more if I do that. And I don't have time to get to know them or pet them. Of course, they probably all have fleas. But you never know, because my apartment doesn't have any cockroaches and I thought those were standard in all apartment buildings.

There's a flock of birds that you can watch from the front sunroom of our house. Maybe there are 100 of them and you can see them ever so often flying in a flock around in large circles. The first time that I saw them, I thought they were stuck between all of the high buildings. They do appear to be trapped, flying at half the height of the skyscrapers that surround them. You can catch them circling off in the distance, looking down from our 32nd floor living room. There's some other birds around here, but no pigeons. Peoples' pet dogs run around without leashes, no matter where or how busy the traffic is. In the environmental park next to my house, there are parties of wild cats that vary in color and type. Interestingly, they all look pure bread, as if they only mate with their own type. Other then that, there are no other animals, only animal fur for sale sometimes on the side of the road in the form of jackets or rugs. Ken found a dog fur rug in our closet that a previous roommate purchased. No squirrels, no noticeable rats, no crows, and I will be interested to see if I hear crickets as the weather warms.

I found that the treatment of foreign English teachers is highly respectable. They gave us some of the larger desks in the office, while the other Chinese use smaller desks. They allow us to use our spare time how we see fit and taking a nap is acceptable. Since asking Mao Guy to speak to me in Chinese sometimes, his personality has lit up. He is more at ease and excited to talk to me. I showed him a picture I took of an advertisement I saw in the subway station. There is a cartoon of a guy standing next to a little girl at a school desk and he is wearing a baseball cap with the "W" from the Washington

Nationals baseball team logo. He read the Chinese and with a lot of effort, tried to explain to me the meaning. He said, outside of China, these words mean something different. In China, it means that this is a troubled man that had a bad childhood of being a delinquent. He said, in this picture, he was supposed to be seated beside the girl, but was shown bothering the girl. He said the girl is supposed to be mentoring the man. How interesting is that? The troubled man that led a bad life is clearly an American cartoon charactor, and wearing my hat. I showed Mao Guy the pictures of me wearing the same hat.

Yesterday's alarm clock was Ken talking to himself in the hallway at 7 in the morning. "I am so worried... I am so worried." He sounded wasted. Finally, he made it to his room and shut the door. I called him the next night and told him about my wake up call. He said that he went to a place called Hollywood and they kept giving him free Champaign. He blacked out at some point and couldn't find the keys to his bar.

Shiny came over and started to write my new dialogue lesson. I asked to practice making an appointment over the phone for a haircut. The Chinese grammar used in the dialogue was really complex. I literally had to move six parts of an English sentence around and rearrange it to be spoken Chinese. I love learning it though and I can't imagine staying China for as long as some people here do without wanting to learn any Chinese. My roommate back in Virginia used to tell me that people become fluent in a foreign language within 9 months. I think that is a heavy underestimation for Chinese, considering I have heard of people that have lived here for 14 years and still do not speak Chinese. I met an Austrian in a restaurant the other day that said he has been here for 4 years and cannot speak Chinese. Screw that! What a waste of opportunity.

The best suggestion I have for learning Chinese from America, is to practice pronunciation and tone. Just concentrate on those things, because without perfect tone, Chinese will not understand you. You can say the words correctly and even pronounce the sounds correctly, but if one tone of one word is incorrect, the communication will not work. I want to convince at least one of my friends back home to start practicing these elements in preparation to their visit. It should be exciting and very helpful. No tone, no chance.

I don't think I have much available time to write in the evenings when I am working. If I run a few errands and have a Chinese lesson, it's already about midnight by the time I am free. I already have to stay awake for an additional two hours every time I write a blog post. It looks like I can write sometimes while I am at work – like now, for instance. I thought that I might be able to write on the subway with my new keyboard and iPhone, but it is too crowded in the mornings and there is nowhere to sit. I imagine it would be quite difficult even if I could get a seat. Some things are best shared in story because at times, like when I am jogging a big empty billion-dollar unfinished park with wild roosters and a pack of dogs barking behind me, weaving around different terrain and abandoned unfinished marble statues and sculptures, I know there is no way to share the experience any other way. A 360 camera lens on an HD camera wouldn't come close. You have to be here with me and I can take you the best way that I know how. Perhaps, sometime I can add some sound recordings. Even still, written word is best.

I did get the thought yesterday, walking back to the office from the restroom, that it does seem difficult to have moved to Shanghai without a plan. To have sold all of my belongings and hop on a plane. I hadn't viewed it in this light until yesterday. I finally could see it from the eyes of some others, like my parents. I suppose it is because I am comfortable now that the idea of doing that seems very uncomfortable. The thing is, when you are unhappy, you are uncomfortable, so it really wasn't difficult at all. I can say that my life is now interesting, whereas before, I was caught in a stagnate cycle. I'm sure I'll return to that cycle again, but I have a lot of time left before I'm there. This time, I know that it truly is possible to relocate to a place where learning is wedged into every hour of every day. Getting older is a blessing, but only if you are growing all the while.

First Life

I used to think there were two kinds of foreigners here. Then, after further examination, I decided there were three kinds. Later, four kinds. At my most recent estimation, I was up to about six. Last night, I just gave in. I only had one student for the day, although I don't like to refer to them as that. I should say, English speaking enthusiast, or ESE. I was supposed to lead an English Corner where a number of Chinese ESEs come to play in a round discussion about whatever I want. The goal, of course, is to get them to interact. The other teachers were supposed to be available to join in and help me, but due to miss-scheduling, no-one was available. In fact, the whole staff had plans to go to a university to do some promotional activities. So, I was left to make the Big Room here a place to interact with the ESEs. The problem was, the chairs and room weren't any good for interacting and there were only two ESEs expected to come. I spent an hour rearranging the furniture until I found something harmonious that would work – or at least comfortable.

I projected an outline of the map of China onto the whiteboard and then traced it. My first ESE showed up, and I received word that the other one wasn't coming. My ESE's name is Joy and she is probably about 26 years old. We instantly started drawing on the map, filling in some of the provinces and the missing islands. Once I found out her home province, I pulled up the map from the internet and projected it on the board. I asked about her hometown, exactly the same way I had for years online in "Second Life" now. I was living my Second Life in my First Life. The first time I entered Second Life, I couldn't understand what it was for or what to do there. I explored around different places until I ended up on some guy's yacht sitting in a bubbling hot tub with him while he was drinking a margarita. I asked him what Second Life was for and he told me, "It's for living out the fantasies that we cannot achieve in our first life." Remarkable. I had an early start. A virtual start.

I had another 5-star haircut Friday night from the same guy that cut my hair before. I can't emphasize enough the level of detail that he gives to cutting my hair. He must have sniped each one of my hairs no less than 20 times each. I left trying to avoid him seeing me put my hat on and forgot about my book bag. I walked over to a big cafeteria that I noticed on my way out of the subway earlier and sat down to a hot Korean stone pot meal. It wasn't as good as the Korean food from my home town (as usual), but it was good. They had Wi-Fi there so I called my Mother and we spoke for a long time. We spoke for so long that all of the food places shut down, everyone had left, and the security guard was locking the door when I ran to the exit. I walked back to the haircut place to get my backpack, but it was closed and everyone had left.

When work ended the next day, I really wanted to have another one of those amazing German beers. I think the six-day workweek might have caught up to me. However, I had to get my backpack as soon as possible because my new Blue Tooth keyboard was in it along with those nice wristwatches that I have been meaning to get fixed. I met Ada half way there at a subway station. By luck, I was waiting for her at the exact train compartment and door that she arrived at, so I walked into the train backwards as the crowds of people were exiting before she noticed me. We exited the training walking shoulder to shoulder and when she turned to fine me beside her, she jumped back surprised. I think she saw my feet walking out beside her, so it must have been a good gag. Boy, that was a good one. I was really happy to see her because I hadn't seen her for a week. Shauna is back in town and I want to hang out with her this weekend too, but Ada has been upset with me lately and I'm not sure why. I wanted to make sure she was okay and she seemed fine.

It was lightly raining and I couldn't get my bearings after we exited the station. We walked in a bit of a circle, but we eventually found the hair cut place and I got my bag back. Since I wasn't going to be able to drink that amazing German beer tonight without going all the way back to my work, I wanted to go to a place called Boxing Cat. I saw it while I was staying in French Town and I heard they brew their own beer. We weren't far north of French Town and could walk there. The only problem was that it was raining and I wasn't exactly sure where it was. To get out of the train, we walked over to Malone's, the

American Restaurant that I went to before with Shiny to have my first hamburger. We sat at the bar and I got Ada some kind of apple beer and I drank a Guinness. Ada told me that she had never been to a place like that before – the kind of place I have been to over a million times. We figured out that Boxing Cat was on Fuxing Rd and after we finished our drinks, we started to walk in that direction.

The rain was too much and the distance was too far, so we walked to the closest subway station to see about taking the train one stop. Ada told me that she was going home, which was really disappointing. Some of her frustration with me lately has been that I am not including her enough, or something like that, and she was leaving me to a Saturday night. It kind of let the air out of my tires, but I decided that I would still go and try one of their beers before going home. It was Saturday and it had been a long week. It was a really nice feeling to walk the same streets that I was walking when I stayed at Jay's when I first came here. In a strange way, it was like being back home, at the beginning again. I knew the area well now and I started thinking how many streets that I now know and how far I have come along. Thanks to my writing, I can recall things that I would have otherwise forgotten, such as the feeling of crossing streets and the crowded bombarding of people. All of that is natural now and I don't notice it any more. I walked past the hashish dealers that were so dedicated that they had umbrellas standing outside in the rain. I said aloud to myself, "That's awesome. Real dedication. Pushing in the rain."

I walked into the bar and found an empty stool at the bar beside two bar girls. Some women here get paid to sit at the bar and talk foreigners into buying drinks for them. Beside them were a row of white guys; two students beside two businessmen. I ordered a lager and listed to their conversation. The first student was boasting to the prostitutes about knowing the name of the band playing and demanding that they try to pronounce it. He couldn't understand any Chinese and asked them if they were saying the word, "Beautiful" at some point. Unfuckingbelievable. This jackass doesn't know the word for beautiful, he is studying in China, and the word for his own country is "Beautiful Country". He didn't know these were bar girls either, because he asked one of them if she wasn't going to drink the beer he bought her, if he could have it.

Beside the jackass was another student and he was telling the businessmen that he decided Chinese was the way to go. He had been learning Chinese for a whole year now, but hadn't been successful in using it. He was talking like he was so brilliant for making the decision and he was so dedicated in learning Chinese. It made me feel like the fact that I am here shows how badly I want to learn Chinese. I could only have dreamed that I could have been sent here to school. If he really wanted to improve his Chinese, he wouldn't be spending his night at a Western Bar talking to westerners. Meanwhile, the businessmen were talking about manufacturing and dropping place names like India, Japan, and Korea. I couldn't take it anymore. I had to get out of there. I know there are other visitors here like me that want to absorb as much Chinese education as they can, but where are they? Every foreigner that I see or hear is either with a prostitute or boasting about himself. I am lucky to know Ken, because he speaks fluent Chinese and seems to have his head on straight. I now feel like the ultimate hypocrite. I already didn't like most foreigners here, but I think that I might have snapped.

When I got home, I told Patrick about my feelings. He doesn't like foreigners either and I could tell that since meeting him. Actually, he didn't even come over to meet me when I first looked at the apartment. The last roommates really ruined his view on foreigners and I don't blame him. It was still a bit early, so I rolled out a mat and started exercising to some Chinese television. I ordered a pizza and after a good bit of Kungfu, I sat down to have a few slices before bed. Sunday will be last day of work for the week and the next evening I will be taking off for Hong Kong. Inti and Tony are excited for me to visit and that makes me thrilled. Its one thing to know some good people in a place you are visiting and it is another when they are excited for you to visit and want to spend time with you when you arrive. I might get lucky. It is the Chinese Lantern Festival and I may be able to see many fireworks and floating fire lanterns as my plane descends over Hong Kong Island. That would be something.

The Dragon's Layer

I had to conduct an English "salon" class on the subject of American Culture. Jeri made a slide show and asked me to play it and talk about each slide in relation to "culture". Only one ELE showed up and her name was Wendy. Wendy was kind of adorable and looked like a Chinese girl that wasn't allowed to do much growing up. I can start to imagine what it is like growing up in a box with no escape to a park, forest, mall, or any normal thing I grew up with.

I wasn't comfortable doing anything with anyone paying money to improve their English by standing up in front of them and talking. I just said, two posts ago, that I didn't want to spend all my time talking about my culture to them. So, this time I drew a map on the white board of the USA, with all of the states. I just started by asking Wendy what places she knew about in the US and let that snowball into an amazing session. I extremely enjoyed talking about America and helping Wendy to learn about culture related to regions and it was extremely fulfilling for me. Wendy may never meet another American again and may never set foot in the US, but that day she memorized the habits of the inhabitants of another great body of land. The one that I am an authority for.

That night I met up with Shauna at a famous park that my coworkers told me is the most popular garden for celebrating the lateen festival. I thought the lateen festival was when they light miniature hot air balloons into the sky and push paper boats into the river with lit candles on them. Well, I was mistaken. I paid for us to enter an area of streets with a million other people walking them and there were lit-up, kite looking material sculptures of stuff. There was a mass promotion for Pepsi, Starbucks, and McDonalds. I complained to Shauna about the branding and she said she likes Pepsi and McDonalds.

The food we ate was bad and Shauna's English wasn't as good as it was before she went back to her hometown for New Years. I must have walked 25 miles that night. There were some neat stores and things to look at. I shot some video that I will post. I had Shanghai street food there and then stopped on the way home to eat even more street food. My immune system is now treated for Shanghai. My stomach won't get sick if I eat something raw in Shanghai now.

The next morning, I laid in bed to rest. Shiny was coming over in the rain. I haven't been able to get my wristwatches fixed, or my pants repaired, in a week, so I was going to pay her to try and take care of those things while I am in Hong Kong. Ken was home and the landlord came by to collect rent, so I got to meet her. Ken suggested a way for me to get to the airport that was a bit quicker. I have been so lucky since I have been here. One thing after another. Shiny's friend drove me to a more convenient subway station and I took that all the way to an express train to the airport. It is supposed to rain in Hong Kong, so I really only packed gym clothes that dry quickly.

I packed my Blue Tooth keyboard and iPhone tripod and I am lying in bed typing with them now. My timing was pretty much exactly right. I got to my gate just before it was boarding and went and got a club sandwich from the cutest girl whose face would bush every time I spoke. Right as I swallowed my last bite, I checked onto the bus shuttle. It was so full of people that I had to literally push my way on. I was the last person to get on the bus.

Walking from the bus onto the airplane, I could see the wing of the airplane. It sure looked like a crack to me, and the engine sounded like an old car. That's not good, but of course I boarded anyway. An empty seat separated me from a trademarked Hong Kongnese lady. She was tall and thin and had a hybrid Asian face with her hair done-up so fancy that I couldn't tell what the hair style was supposed to be. Her over-sized sunglasses rested on top of her head, even though it was night time, and she was wearing fishnet stockings with a black tight leather mini-jacket. She tried to sit straight up and pay no one any attention.

When I was looking out the window towards Shanghai, I had the strong feeling of wanting to stay in Shanghai. I am really happy in Shanghai and you never know what might happen if you leave. Then the plane taxied past the view of Shanghai and into dark nothingness (the ocean). I got excited again. During the flight, I looked out of the window. I thought I saw tall building blinker lights below, and then I realized they were fireworks and people were celebrating the Lantern Festival for the last night of Chinese New Year's.

When I stepped foot off the plane, the air felt warm and damp. I walked backwards through security to use the restroom, and then went through customs. Everyone was friendly and kind. I found an ATM and pulled out a random amount of HK money. Here's the thing about Hong Kong: I don't know much about it. For all intents and purposes, it's another country. I have never gone to such a foreign country before without any real preparation or knowledge of it. I do know more than nothing, but on the face of it, I am empty.

I kind of know how to say "hello" in Cantonese, but I don't know anything else. I figured out where the express train was to HK Island and took that. I sat beside an Indian woman that was making all kinds of strange faces while she was texting. It made me very uncomfortable. I wasn't in Kansas anymore. When I exited the express train station, I waited for a taxi and was really surprised to see a car drive up on the wrong side of the road with a driver sitting on the wrong side of the car. I wasn't sure at first when I pulled open the door, if the door was light or if it opened itself. The driver did in fact have a button that opened the door automatically, as I found out upon exiting.

I slid down the back car seat and leaned over to show the driver the address of where I needed to go. In Shanghai, I would have been about to say everything, and if I couldn't, I would show them the address. I leaned over the seat to show the driver and he snapped at me, "Don't show me the address, okay? I speak English, just tell me where you want to go and we'll go there!" Well, I tried to laugh it off, but he sounded pissed off. I told him I was coming from Shanghai and he said I must be there for the money. I told him that I was there for the Mandarin and he said, "Fuck Mandarin." The streets were narrow and so were the buildings. It didn't feel safe and it sure wasn't Shanghai.

I had to read the addresses until we found my hotel. The driver could have taken advantage of me, but he didn't. He drove me there directly and gave me my exact change. I walked in to a young girl receptionist with her hair chopped up so many ways that I couldn't tell what was going on with it. She looks 16 years old, but like a punk rock boy. I asked some questions, like, where could I go have a drink. She told me that I could buy a mixed drink at 7-11 and I let out a series of laughter. I told her I would do that right after I dropped my bag off.

My room is the size of a large walk-in closet. I knew rooms are small in HK and I knew this one would be too. It's just different to be in one. However, this is the most optimal design for a small room possible. It's pretty awesome. I gave Inti a call. I don't have Tony's number with me, I have to pull it off the Net. We will meet in the morning. I left and walked down the street to the 7-11. When the Taxi dropped me off here, I had no idea how tall the buildings were. In New York City, some buildings are narrow too, but they are usually only three stories high. This building is 12 stories high. It's amazing how narrow and tall the buildings are here.

I picked out a pineapple and vodka drink, some nuts, Ramen noodles, and a bottle of water. I mixed some mandarin with English to ask the clerk if the noodles has chopsticks in the packet. He answered in Cantonese, but I could understand him. It sounded like an extremely accented version of Mandarin. Of course, I think Cantonese is an entirely different spoken language, but they share some common base words. That is my understanding of it. He gave me a pair of chopsticks and I went to walk back to my hotel.

I was thinking on the way out here. It's really special to me to come to Hong Kong. I saw a plane in the terminal with the name "Dragon" written on the side of it and it reminded me of what's going on. I was going to my hero's hometown, Bruce Lee. Bruce Lee's name in Cantonese means Little Dragon. Bruce Lee was born in the Year of the Dragon, the month of the Dragon, the day of the Dragon, and the minute of the Dragon. I was arriving to Hong Kong on the last New Year's Day for the Year of the Dragon. I think he died at about my age too, so I am letting my mind run with that. Walking these streets, it was easy to imagine gang violence and street fighting. It feels like a place for danger.

I am showered up now and ready for sleep. Interestingly, the shower really brought me back to being comfortable. I have to have the A/C on here, whereas in Shanghai I take every precaution I can to stay warm at night. It's really strange to be here. Suddenly, I have to be the kind of foreigner that I despise so much in Shanghai. I know so little about Cantonese. I do know a good bit about their history and industry, but I don't know hardly anything about the people here. That is what I will learn about in the next 72 hours.

A Big Slice
of Hong Kong

I don't know how it is 8:30 in the morning. I thought my window was clear and it is dark outside, but it must be painted or something, because I thought it was 5:30 in the morning. I hear people on both sides of my room that sound like they are still awake. The sound of a night rain pouring down has been continuing for the last few hours and I woke up on and off. I am in the room that Inti booked for me in the heart of Kowloon. It's about 10 feet by 10 feet, bigger than my last place, but less modern. I had a terrific day that I am going to try and do justice with sharing now – in a semi-hungover state.

The weather outside was warm when I awoke yesterday, so I only put on a t-shirt and pants to go outside. I wore my running shoes instead of my boots because the terrain here looked more consistent. I found the bathroom had everything I needed to get ready to go out. I shaved with the supplied razor and shaving cream and washed up with the body wash they supplied before putting in my contact lenses and calling Inti to come over.

I checked out of the hotel and felt a little uncomfortably dressed waiting out front. My shirt is really thin and it felt like I was wearing only an undershirt in a city center. When I took a walk, I found an interesting undershirt store and went back and forth with the store owner until we found a ribbed tank-top undershirt that I could purchase. I went back to my hotel and slipped it on before Inti arrived and eased my comfortability.

Inti walked over to me and continued passed me without stopping and I followed beside her. That was our greeting. I asked if we could walk over to the bay if it wasn't too far away. I could smell the air coming off of it and wanted to get a lungful before I return to the bubble of Shanghai. I was missing Shanghai a lot and was still having culture shock.

After checking out the backside harbor view, we walked over to an authentic brunch restaurant and Inti ordered some dishes. Looking around, I clearly wasn't in China. I couldn't stop thinking of Hong Kong's history and how this culture was the outcome. People weren't wearing outfits like they do in Shanghai, and they weren't necessarily cheap either. It was most like New York City's dress style. I once heard David Letterman ask a celebrity which city he liked living in more, LA or NYC. The guy replied, "I like New York, because I don't have to shave every day." The dress seemed to be scattered and a lot more Chinese appeared to be overweight. Women wear flats instead of heels. Their complexion is darker. As I told Tony later when comparing to the mainland Chinese I have seen in the North, "They don't wear the same clothes, have the same face, eat the same food, have the same laws, use the same money, or speak the same language. It seems like the only thing that is the same is the written language." Then Tony told me that Hong Kong uses traditional Chinese characters and mainland does not.

I had read about westerners seeking salvation in Hong Kong in the past, especially ones spending time in the south of China. I didn't feel that. Maybe if I was from England, I would have had some sense of comfort, but I felt totally foreign and out of place. In the restaurant, I saw many people eating rice and I told Inti that I only had rice one time since I have been in Shanghai. I wasn't counting the Korean food that I had eaten, but it was fairly accurate. She ordered some kind of stewed chicken with mushroom, fluffy steamed brown sugar cake, shrimp scampi, and a familiar tasting piece of pork that was like Chinese food I had eaten in the United States before. Waiters poured hot water into our tea bowls and Inti poured them into our cups by holding the lid on the bowl with her index finger and leaving enough room for the tea to escape without the leaves. The beginning of the meals here seem to require a ritualistic hot water cleansing of the cups, bowls, and chopsticks and the remaining water is hauled away in a discard bowl. The men's room had a big ditch to pee in and the plumbing didn't appear to be working, so there was about 20 gallons of pee filling the ditch. I told Inti about it and she wasn't surprised.

After eating lunch, we walked over to the subway station so I could by a ticket for later and Inti could take the subway to her office. She is a journalist and I found her to be quick-witted and not easily grossed out. The culture shock was still hitting me and I was hoping a coffee would relax my brain and make it easier to take in. It didn't.

Before leaving my hotel room, I pulled out the gym bag that I packed and put the bottle of water that I bought the night before in it along with the Raman noodles, chopsticks, complimentary tea and coffee packets, the free razor, body wash, and shampoo. I had to transfer trains and I started to be able to discern some Chinese women that appeared as though they were from mainland China by looking more like the people that I have been around for the last month and a half. I had heard from a number of Hong Kong people that mainland Chinese are coming to HK like locust. I thought that was a little ironic because my friend, Mike, in Toronto said the same exact thing about Toronto and I yelled at him for using that word. He tried to tell me that he didn't mean it as an insult, but clearly locust are an unwelcomed pest. I figured out what train to transfer to and explored until I found the building's address.

In a tight "lobby" on the 6th floor, two Cantonese guys were scrambling to please their foreign customers that wanted to check in. They both had long hair and one was wearing his hair pulled back in a ponytail with an oversized dress shirt tucked into his low hanging baggy slacks. This was Hong Kong. The other guy was wearing glasses and would glance up at me looking through the top rim of his glasses, splitting his vision into two parts. He spoke with a quasi-british accent and I learned later that he studied in a remote location in England, overseas like many of the younger generations here do. He made a lot of funny faces when he was talking and gave me the impression of someone that did too many drugs at some point in his life (or continues to do them). We had to walk over to another building to check into my actual room. The guy told me that was how low budget hotels work in city centers like this one. I called Tony and we met at my building. It was the first time that I had seen him in over ten years. We gave each other a bear hug and set off.

Tony was letting me join him to run some errands, but I didn't realize that we were walking into a car garage to take his new luxury Mercedes to run them. I never sat passenger on the left side of the car before and it was great to be driving around Hong Kong. I was able to see the city scape change throughout the various areas of Kowloon until we drove deeper into the mountains and ran out of road to drive. We picked up Tony's old buddy, Jack, and they pulled over to take some inconspicuous pictures of advertisement signs. I don't know what business Tony is thinking about starting, but this was a part of it.

We dropped Jack off and parked the Mercedes back at the garage we first set off from. From there, Tony walked me around downtown Kowloon, showing me the prostitute street, interestingly named Shanghai Rd, and Temple Avenue where you could buy all kinds of things at a bargain. We made our way to weave through a shopping mall and ended up at Victoria Harbor. Tony walked alongside me with his hand around my back and on my opposite shoulder. It's not something that guys do in the US, but I remembered when I went to eat with him in Boston with all of his Cantonese buddies and how they were all doing that with each other. It felt uncomfortable and was difficult for me to stop thinking about, but I knew it was sign of endearment here and that I should be grateful for the brotherly love.

Victoria Harbor is awesome. It was night time and it was lightly raining. The Hong Kong skyline was lit up like a light show and as we walked toward a larger platform, I could hear music playing that synchronized to the blinking patterns of lights across the harbor. Somehow, maybe a hundred buildings are connected to some kind of switchboard to make them dance along with music played on both sides of the harbor. Spotlights and laser beams would shoot off and rotate around depending on the mood and timing of the music. One light would appear to race across a building in a zigzag and then shoot from one building to another. I had never heard of any skyline that had such a thing. We stood in the rain watching it with a crowd for ten minutes before continuing down the Avenue of the Stars.

The Avenue of the Stars is a take on the Hollywood foot prints in America, except these were prints of both hands of many famous Hong Kong and mainland actors and actresses. We had an eye out for Jackie Chan. Suddenly, there was the statue that I heard about standing in front of me. It was my hero and my greatest inspiration to be here in my life, Bruce Lee. I stepped around the statue studying how well they sculpted his kungfu pose and muscle structure. People don't realize how superior Bruce Lee was as an athlete. Arnold Schwarzenegger once said that Bruce Lee was the strongest man that he ever met. Kungfu continues to be misunderstood by those that never studied it, but here was Bruce Lee, the Hero of Hong Kong, forever in his peak performance standing in with his home city at his backdrop. The crowds came, posing and taking their pictures alongside the Great Bruce Lee.

Hong Kong has a population of only 8 million people, yet the Hong Kong movie stars are the movie stars of mainland China with a population of 400 times that amount. Bruce Lee started his acting career as a child because his father was a famous traditional actor. Less publicized is that Bruce lee is at least 25% Caucasian. I say at least, because one of his grandparents was an orphan from a foreign country and believed to also possess Caucasian genetics. I asked the druggy hotel clerk about a Bruce Lee tour or something and he told me that it is widely accepted in Hong Kong that Bruce Lee learned his Kungfu in the USA. Even though Bruce Lee is considered a representative of strength and power of the Chinese people, he was half-invested in the US for everything he achieved. In one of the only video interviews that he ever did, Bruce replied to a question about which country he likes more by stating, "It is not only the West, or only the East, but the combination of the two." No one has ever done so much culturally to bring our countries together.

Tony and I sat down to eat in another kind of Cantonese restaurant. He was going to order me something that I had before, but I insisted that he order something local for me to try. I had salty fish cooked in rice in a clay put over a fire so that the bottom rice is dark and crispy and the top rice is soft and just right. There were three kinds of sauces to choose from to pour into the bowl and I went with the spicy one. The meal didn't smell good, but the taste grew on me quickly. We shared a Qing Dao beer and talked about Hong Kong, continuing conversations that we had earlier in the day. We had talked about mainland China for hours and it was fantastic to learn Tony's understanding of the mainland and the mainland people. What an amazing pocket of independence Hong Kong is and how great is it to be speaking with someone about the language, culture, and country that I have sought to live in that knows it so well. Tony wasn't blowing my mind, but he was amplifying it.

We walked back to Tony's house to regroup and wait for Inti to get off work. The walk back to Tony's house took us through a big city park with some nature reserves. I saw a hundred flamingos in a pond and Kowloon's water park. Tony lived right across the street from the park in an extremely central location. His one-bedroom apartment was spacious, bright, clean and cool. He turned on a soap opera while I chatted with some of my Shanghai friends online using my iPhone. I got caught up in the soap opera and it brought on some discussions. I noticed an actor on the show was speaking Cantonese and threw in the words, "at least" in English. I confirmed it with Tony. I would imagine that both the English speaking people and the Cantonese people would be commingling phrases after a hundred years of living with each other, but it seems to be more rare than I expected. In fact, when I asked Tony if he ever met a white guy that could speak Cantonese well, he answered no. That was really surprising and disappointing to learn. It seems so counter intuitive to not integrate and cross populate.

I had been bugging Tony to take me to a bar street all day long and we finally were walking over to one nearby to meet Inti. The "Terrace" that Tony walked me to was a brick pathway lined with Euro cafe after Euro cafe, full of foreigners and expensive crowds with half empty bars. I complained to Tony that I wanted to go somewhere local with Cantonese people, so when we met with Inti, they walked me over to some more local bars. After three or four other streets of bars, they let me pick one and we walked up to the second floor. There was a full cover band in front of our seats consisting of a keyboardist, drummer, bass player, electric guitar player, a male singer and a female singer. There were fog machines, all kinds of lights, LED light patterns on the side of the stage, and a giant monitor playing art patterns beside the big stage that they were performing on. They started off singing 1980's songs and then went into some Cantonese songs. The female was half Caucasian, wearing red platform shoes and a one piece miniskirt dress. The male singer was Cantonese, wearing a mismatched suit with a skull design made up of Rhine stones on the back of his suit jacket. Some point later one, the keyboardist sang a song in Mandarin and it felt comforting to hear Mandarin again. I can hear, now, how clear and precise spoken Mandarin sounds compared to Cantonese.

I ordered a Sex Motherfucker off the menu for

myself, Tony a Corona, and Inti a Qingdao beer. I verified my knowledge of Hong Kong history with Tony and he gave me some additional details about it. On the table was some cups full of dice and Tony decided to teach me two famous dice games played in Hong Kong. I forgot what the first one was about because we didn't play it much, but after that game we played one called, Liar. It is played like poker, where you don't share the dice you rolled with anyone and state the matches of dice you have with your opposition. They have to say they have a better match and you go back and forth until you can't beat their match or think they are lying. Then you have to reveal your hand and the best set wins. You either have to have a higher number of matching numbers, or a higher numbered match of three or more. It seemed too simple at first, but then I realized there was a lot of room for low balling and bullshitting. I played one of them at a time and then watched them play. There was something missing for it to be a local game for me. I asked Inti how to say everything in Cantonese and she wrote it down for me on a piece of paper. Tony was impressed because he said that he doesn't even know how to represent the words needed in English. When I came back from the bathroom, I had my cheat sheet and started to play the game with them in their language.

This was my first real taste of the Cantonese language. Sure, I was a few drinks deep and buzzing, but I think my language learning skills are well oiled right now and I can think in a way to memorize a lot better than I would have been able to do in the US. I would roll my dice and check the sheet as quickly as I could. I had to state the number of the die and the amount of that number I had in combination with the opponent's. I also asked to learn how to say, "You lie", "I win", and "You lose". By the end of the night, I could count to a hundred by memory. I found Cantonese to feel less precise in pronunciation and in tone and it was thrilling for me that they understood me and we were able to continue playing in Cantonese. I never cared for Cantonese before, but now I think it's really cool. It's very loose and you can discern a lot of phrases and words to be of the same family decent as Mandarin.

We lasted the night and as the band was packing up, we finished our last drinks. I had a great time and I think they both enjoyed themselves too. They walked me back to my room and I asked Inti to stay with me. The trains weren't running any longer and a cab to her home would take 40 minutes. After all, she booked the room and I know we both had a long day. I can't imagine that she was going to be able to stay awake for the ride home. I think that she wanted me to force her to stay with me, but all I did was ask her to stay. Regrettably, she slowly left and before I could get my wits about to pay for her cab fare, I had fallen asleep.

It's true that I started to write this at 8:30, but I went back to sleep numerous times since then. I was in bed until about 4:30 PM today and felt a bit like Ken to wake up so late. I made noodles from the stuff I brought with me from the last hotel, showered, and went out to find a place to write my blog. I met up with Tony and we had some more Cantonese food together. This time, I had crispy goose with rice. Tony walked me to some stores to buy some smaller things that I can't buy in Shanghai, like a particular cologne, some deodorant spray, and other things. He walked me back to the harbor, where I am now, finishing my blog post in a Starbucks before trying to meet up with Inti again. Tony left to go do some more 007 secretive shit, and I am hoping to take the fairy across the river to meet up with Inti when she gets off from work in 15 minutes. I won't get my hopes up if she doesn't respond. I'm not sure what I will do tomorrow, but I will probably take the bus to the airport instead of the express train. Tony said it would be a better view. I can really look forward to visiting Hong Kong again in the future. What a great experience.

Even If It's All I Got

I packed up and went off to the other building to check out of my room in Hong Kong. Tony was too sleepy to meet for a bite to eat and Inti was on her way to work already, so I wasn't going to see my friends before I took off. I didn't feel like wandering the streets with my luggage, or leaving my bags in that small shoe of a lobby, so I decided to head to the airport. Tony tried to give me directions to the correct bus stop location over the phone. I broke my dollars at a currency exchange to have the right amount for the fare and when the bus came, I took a load off on the upper deck closer to the front window and just behind some older Chinese women.

The bus had WIFI, so I logged in to make some adjustments to my blog post. I hardly ever get the chance to read them after I post them and I wanted to get the picture Tony took of me looking at the Bruce Lee statue and place it in my previous post. As I logged in, my email notification told me Mike P just tried to call me on Skype. I logged in and called him back. It was great chatting with a close friend while winding around the city and watching it slowly open up to natural mountainscapes. I told him that I have been doing so well and enjoying myself so much. No-one likes to hear someone gloat, but Mike knows that I have been talking about moving to China since we first met over ten years ago and I am sure he was happy to hear me report back good news. I got off the bus at first terminal it came to.

My airline wouldn't let me check in early, so I walked around the place and followed signs to a place called "i-sports", which turned out to be an arcade. It was totally empty of customers. I was hoping that it was going to be a gym, but instead, it had a number of games that required physical activity. When I saw the virtual golf range, I knew I was going to drop some of my HK dollars hitting golf balls to pass the time. After a couple of rounds of smacking the shit out of some golf balls, I played the basketball shooting game, followed by a soccer shootout game, and finally a mountain biking game. I wasn't perspiring hard or anything, but it was nice to do something other than eat and shop at the airport. The clerks there were sleeping at their desk.

I remember I was supposed to call Micah and when I went to Skype him, a friend in Shanghai messaged me. She asked me to find a facial cleanser called "SK II" and she would pay me back right away if I brought it back for her. Micah must have fallen asleep, because he didn't answer his phone. I ordered Cantonese Duck at one of the restaurants for my last authentic Hong Kong duck while in Hong Kong and the manager went out of his way to make sure I was happy. Then I moseyed over to a Cantonese coffee café and had some Green Tea cake with Japanese coffee, while finishing fixing my blog. I used my Blue

Tooth keyboard to return some emails and then packed up to venture to another store. I visited three different makeup stores before finding one with SK II and I video conferenced my friend in Shanghai so she could check the products and pricing. The price ended up being the same as in Shanghai, so she passed. From that store I found an electronics store with a video game available for play, so I played that for a half hour until I could finally check in.

Security is reasonable in China. People treat with you with dignity and are courteous and friendly. I often feel like a criminal in America when going through security. The customs officers ask rude personal questions and stare you up and down. I don't miss that. It is funny though, because many non-Chinese citizens that are of the Chinese race will be standing in the foreigner lines with me. China only allows its citizens one citizenship. If you move to another country and become a citizen, you lose Chinese citizenship forever. On the other hand, there are many programs and special visas for people of Chinese decent. I have heard of some Chinese returning to China just to get a certification or a degree for next to nothing in cost. That includes Taiwanese. After getting through security, I found a gourmet sandwich shop and scarfed down a roll with Brea cheese and a Qingdao beer before my plane started boarding. It was nice walking down the ramp and into the plane directly, rather than being smooshed up against people in a bus and driven out onto the airfield like in Shanghai.

On the plane, I sat beside an older Chinese woman of

Holland citizenship that spoke in Danish to her daughter that sat beside her. It was beautiful listening to them switch between Danish and Mandarin. I read a China Daily newspaper and played chess on my iPhone until we landed. In the middle of the flight, I looked out and saw the dark blue night sky with the stars and bright shining moon. None of that exists in Shanghai, so I wanted to enjoy it while I could.

It was late when we arrived, so the express and subway trains weren't running any more. I figured out the right bus to take and when it pulled up, it was already jam packed. I thought it was hopeless getting on that bus, but was a bit worried that it might have been the last running bus of the night. I was surprised to see other people trying to cram on and someone put their luggage under the bus. The driver was yelling at them that he cannot fit any more bags, so I got on the bus carrying my suitcase. A bus driver assistant saw me and asked if I was going the full journey of the bus. I nodded, so she took me out of the bus and walked me around to the opposite side to show me where I could store my luggage. I was to stand on the steps beside the bus driver for an hour long bus ride back to my side of Shanghai.

Sure, it was awkward and uncomfortable, but what better metaphor is there for China? At one of the stops, a chair opened up and I grabbed it. I figured that the driver and the assistant only have to report the money charged for the seats. All of the standing people was money that they could pocket. The monitor on the driver's dashboard that should have showed a street-side blind spot, just showed a guy hanging onto to something for dear life. The TV on the bus played funny animal videos taken from America, often where someone or something got hurt. That was followed by a 15 minute news segment on the US ARMY and the US NAVY. It was showing long clips of the ARMY coming out of the ocean in those metal ships with the front drop hatch so troopers can invade from the beach. I started to feel really uncomfortable while the whole busload of Chinese stared in silence at the TV screen.

I suppose there has to be a dominating country in the world. I don't think it's humanly possible in this day and age to all share and hope for the best. It feels a little ironic, or by chance, that my home country is the one that is policing the world. I can understand how scary that feeling is when you are not a citizen of that country. The USA is the place that just about everyone shows mercy too. Not everyone, but almost everyone. I can understand how crazy it seems that the whole country allows gun ownership and the US has guns scattered about in households across America. On the surface, the US seems like an incredibly dangerous and wild country with a massively aggressive ARMY, NAVY, and Air Force, as well as having a country of well-armed citizens. Just as if you were visiting a friend's house that owned many weapons, as a foreigner nation, it must feel like walking on eggshells to deal with such an explosively dangerous country. The US will go to war at the drop of a hat. They are practicing for it day and night.

Finally, over an hour later, I was dropped off at a nearby

rail station and flagged a Taxi home. I had to be up the next day to go to work. I don't know if it is because I started going to work during the Chinese New Year's, or if it was especially busy, but the subway was crammed with people. I fear that this is normal and I was experiencing the light crowds before. This changes the game plan a lot. I didn't mind an hour train ride sitting, but sandwiched in between people like a concert crowd on a windy train ride is an awful way to have to start a daily routine. When I got to work, I found out that I would not be getting paid, because they would only be paying for the previous month and I only worked three days last month. Damn, already their end of the bargain isn't upheld. I don't like the sign of that, but Jeri said it will be fine. After work, I met with Heena and her friend Linda for dinner and tea. I played some instruments for them in a music shop and then went home.

Today is Saturday, so I didn't have the crazy crowds on the subway. That is one benefit of having to work the weekends. As BB King put it, the thrill is gone. I'll pretty much be out of money by the time work pays me. I still haven't filled my residency with the police or got my work Visa. I don't have a girlfriend waiting for me to come home to. I am not learning Chinese by speaking English all day long. I hardly have time to exercise and can't get a day off to take care of my body. My job has no vacation hours, so there is nothing to plan in the foreseeable future. It is about time to check up on my parents, their house, their yard, their dog, my friends, my friends' dogs, hang out with my good buddies, and take a trip out into surrounding Fairfax – but I can't. Instead, I must find a way to thrive on. I studied the maps and bus route for a long time. I don't see a way to avoid the subway commute. My stellar, number one apartment location, now doesn't seem so hot. The two hours added up over the week comes to a whole day in itself of being crammed up against people.

This is more the way I anticipated it being. Of course, two months of shopping and eating out with women in a big city is fantastic. Then I got the additional bonus of visiting HK and having friends there to welcome me. Now, I am getting back to ground zero. The students I have, I will devote my year to. I will work hard to understand the subject I am inspiring them to learn. I will change their life and push them closer to their dreams. My students will speak English on a level that I may only ever dream to obtain in Chinese. They will communicate to the ability that I wish I could in their language.

It was really nice getting out of the fishbowl and seeing over the rim for a while. Even if it's all I got, I got it. Now the story becomes anew and I can start to focus my long-term goals in new direction. I stand by my reply to a question someone once asked me in college, "What do you want to do when you are older?" I feel best about my life when I believe I am standing true to my reply, "The same thing, but on a higher level." Thanks for coming with me. I hope for the best, for me and for you. It's been a pleasure. Thank you.